Footprint Handbook

Recife &
Northeast Brazil

ALEX & GARDÊNIA ROBINSON

This is
Recife &
Northeast Brazil

Brazil's Northeast is one of South America's great secrets, right up there with the Peruvian Andes or the Brazilian Amazon for spectacular natural beauty. Thousands of miles of white-sand beaches are backed by swaying coconut groves, sweeping sand dune deserts or caramel-covered crumbling cliffs. Fishing villages turned low-key traveller towns – like Jericoacoara, Pipa or Canoa Quebrada – offer access and backpacker or boutique hotel beds. The coral sea is pocked with little islands like Fernando de Noronha fringed with turquoise bays and pristine reefs.

The *sertão* of the rugged interior is as wild and empty as the Australian outback with thorn bush and cactus broken by beehive-dome mountains and towering table-top escarpments daubed with prehistoric cave paintings. Winding rivers run between: the brilliant blue São Francisco in Alagoas and Sergipe, and the sprawling Parnaíba Delta in Piauí, whose filigree of river streams is interlaced with forest-covered islands.

And then there are the cities and towns, such as colonial Portuguese São Cristóvão and Olinda with sugar-cube cottages, the crumbling Afro-Brazilian São Luís on the edge of the arid Northeast and the sweltering Amazon, and Recife with its decaying baroque cathedrals and arty museums.

These and the towns of the interior play host to some of Brazil's liveliest cultural spectacles including the Recife and Olinda carnival, the biggest traditional Mardi Gras celebration in the world. The Junina festivals of Campina Grande and Caruaru are held in June, when millions congregate to dance *forró* from dusk till dawn, while the Bumba-Meu-Boi celebrations in São Luís involve a fusion of African music and dance and Portuguese and Amerindian lore.

Alex Robinson

Gardenia Robinson

Best of
Recife &
Northeast Brazil

top things to do and see

❶ Recife and Olinda

Spend a few days in the impossibly pretty Portuguese colonial town of Olinda, wandering the winding cobbled streets, marvelling at the brilliant baroque and rococo interiors and eating out in the streetside restaurants and café bars. And in the evening visit neighbouring Recife (a 20-minute cab ride away) for some of Brazil's hottest, hipster nightlife. Pages 28 and 43.

❷ Carnaval in Pernambuco

Carnival needn't mean Rio; Recife and its twin city Olinda host Brazil's biggest and best traditional street festival. Join the riot of dance and colour which takes over the streets in both cities for nearly a week around Mardi Gras. Unlike Rio or Salvador the party here is free as well as being frenetic and tremendous fun. Page 40.

❸ Fernando de Noronha

This tiny island sticking up from the inky depths of the Atlantic has some of the best snorkelling and diving in the region, as well as walks from craggy cliffs to coves of creamy sand, and championship-grade surfing. Hire a board and plunge into the glassy clear waves on Cacimba do Padre beach. Page 49.

❹ Ceará beaches

The state of Ceará has more than its fair share of gorgeous beaches. In Morro Branco they form canyons running to vast strands lapped by a gentle ocean. In Canoa Quebrada they're backed by toffee-coloured cliffs crumbling into pink, orange

and white sands, and in Jericoacoara they are blown into shimmering dunes pocked with aquamarine lakes, with world-class kite- and windsurfing. Pages 96, 97 and 101.

❺ Parque Nacional de Sete Cidades

Brazil's outback spreads for hundreds of kilometres behind the lush northeastern coast through arid, rocky escarpments, cactus and thorn scrub forests. In the Sete Cidades you can hike through some of the strangest landscape on Earth, past tortoiseshell-shaped domed hills cut by hundreds of hexagons, tubular rocks and narrow valleys hunted by puma and ocelot. Page 111.

❻ Alcântara

Sweltering on the edge of the Northeast and the frontier of the Amazon, this sugar boom town with decrepit Portuguese baroque buildings is a good base for exploring the little-visited beaches and islands of the Far Northeast, and to take in the Bumba-Meu-Boi festival in neighbouring São Luís. Page 122.

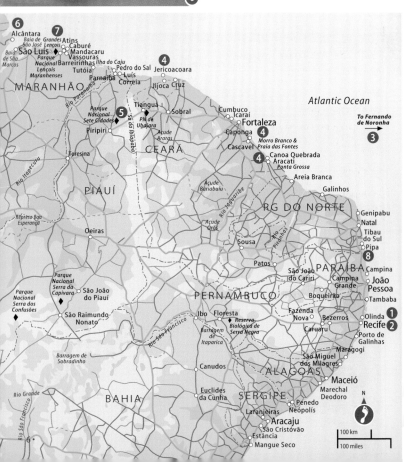

❼ Parque Nacional Lençóis Maranhenses

In the far north of the Northeast the prevailing winds have blown the huge empty beaches into a 100-km-deep white dune desert. Between May and September these are broken by hundreds of aquamarine and emerald lakes. Base yourself in the little beach village of Atins or the river town of Barreirinhas to explore them. Page 126.

❽ Pipa beach

The Northeast's most resolutely laid-back beach resort sits behind a string of bays and beaches, some shaded by coconut palms, others backed by craggy cliffs. Come to walk the sands and the strands of Atlantic coastal rainforest, surf the waves, sea-kayak with dolphins, sway in a hammock and sup by candlelight. Page 139.

Route planner

With more territory than South Africa, Brazil's Northeast offers enough attractions to last for months rather than weeks. Use the coastal cities and villages as a base, perhaps beginning in Recife and looping south in Alagoas and Sergipe via the beautiful beaches of the coast and old Portuguese towns, including Penedo on the São Francisco river and World Heritage-listed São Cristóvão. Consider flying from Aracajú to Fortaleza, and visiting southern Ceará from there, before heading north for the unforgettable overland route from Jericoacoara along the coast or through the outback to Maranhão and the dune deserts of the Lençóis Maranhenses. Fly back to Fortaleza (for the flight home) or a connection to somewhere else in Brazil.

One to two weeks

carnival, nightlife and dunes

Recife and its enchanting pastel-painted and cobbled twin town of Olinda lie at the heart of one of Brazil's most exciting and culturally vibrant states, Pernambuco. Come here for carnival and an unforgettable caper.

With one to two weeks you'll have to cherry pick locations from the itinerary and fly between locations. Allow at least a day to see the colonial buildings and sample the music and nightlife at a bar in Olinda or Old Recife. Two days will allow you to visit the Instituto Brennand to see Francisco Brennand's bizarre sculptures.

Fly from here to Fortaleza for a connection to Jericoacoara. Spend at least two days here, visiting the many lakes and dunes, relaxing on the beach and trying your hand at kitesurfing. If you can spare the time, spend two days travelling the coastal route to the Lençóis Maranhenses, then a day visiting the dunes from the little town of Barreirinhas.

From here it's an easy transfer to São Luís. Leave in the early morning then spend an afternoon exploring the old colonial centre before flying back to Fortaleza or Recife for the flight home.

A three- to four-week trip will give you plenty of time to explore the region in more depth. Take a week to see Recife and Olinda and around, going on two side trips, one to the arts and crafts town of Caruaru and another to spend a few days on Fernando de Noronha island, which has some of the best beaches and diving in South America.

You then have two choices. The first is to take the southern loop into Alagoas and Sergipe, to watch manatees and laze under the coconut palms on Praia do Patacho, and visit the old Portuguese towns of São Cristóvão and Penedo, then flying on to Fortaleza from Aracajú or Maceio. The second is to leave Recife for Natal – a morning's journey – and from there take a short trip south to Praia da Pipa where you can relax on the beach, visit the Atlantic coastal forest and sea-kayak with dolphins. From here you can continue north to Fortaleza through southern Ceará state, staying in an indigenous or fishing community for a few days, learning how to sail a *jangada* boat and sand-surfing on the dunes.

Fortaleza is a plane or bus change; stay overnight only if you have to before moving on to Jericoacoara for three to four days' kitesurfing. Take the overland jeep route to the Lençóis Maranhenses, stopping off along the way to explore the labyrinthine waterways of the Delta do Parnaíba. Look out for green iguana and howler monkeys in the trees, and four-eyed fish, with their eyes half in, half out of the water, in the shallow streams and brooks. Allow three days to see the Lençóis Maranhenses, visiting the dunes from Barreirinhas or the fishing community of Atins, set on a wild and windswept coast with endless beaches.

Take a morning bus to São Luís, then spend two or three days there, admiring the crumbling *azulejo*-fronted buildings of the old colonial centre, the sweltering sugar boom town of Alcântara and the city's long, white-sand beaches.

São Luís has regular flights to Fortaleza and Recife (on this route) as well as to Belém, Manaus, Rio and São Paulo.

When to go

… and when not to

Climate

Brazil's Northeast has warm temperatures all year round. There are strong perennial prevailing winds, creating dunes and perfect conditions for kite and wind-surfing (especially between July and December). The dune lakes of the Lençóis Maranhenses national park are only full between May and September, making this the best time to enjoy this route.

Humidity is relatively high in Brazil, particularly along the coast. The luminosity is also very high, and sunglasses are advisable.

Festivals

Carnaval dates depend on the ecclesiastical calendar and so vary from year to year. It's a movable feast, running for five riotous days from the Friday afternoon before Shrove Tuesday to the morning hangover of Ash Wednesday. Although this is its official ending, it unofficially finishes the following Sunday. For something authentic and traditional, head to Recife carnival.

Carnival dates
2017 23 February-1 March
2018 8-14 February
2019 28 February-6 March

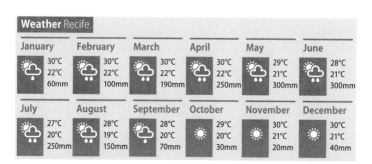

Weather Recife

January	February	March	April	May	June
30°C 22°C 60mm	30°C 22°C 100mm	30°C 22°C 190mm	30°C 22°C 250mm	29°C 21°C 300mm	28°C 21°C 300mm

July	August	September	October	November	December
27°C 20°C 250mm	28°C 19°C 150mm	28°C 20°C 70mm	29°C 20°C 30mm	30°C 21°C 20mm	30°C 21°C 40mm

February

Pré-Caju, a pre-carnival carnival in Aracajú, Sergipe 15 days before Salvador carnival and with a similar vibe, though on a far smaller scale.

June

Bumba-Meu-Boi, São Luís, Maranhão. Spectacular Afro-Portuguese-Amerindian festival in the old streets of colonial São Luís.
Festas Juninas (Festas do São João), Paraíba, Caruaru, Pernambuco and throughout Brazil. Brazil's major winter festival when everyone dresses up as a yokel, drinks hot spiced wine and dances *forró*.

July

Fortal, Brazil's largest out of season carnival in Fortaleza powered mostly by Bahian music. See www.fortal.com.br.

August

Festival de Inverno de Garanhuns, Pernambuco. One of the biggest quality music festivals in the Northeast, with a big programme of shows by names such as Alceu Valenca and Elba Ramalho. See www.fig.com.br.

What to do

Birdwatching

Almost a fifth of the world's bird species are Brazilian. The country is home to some 1750 species, of which 218 are endemic, the highest number of any country in the world. Many of these endemics live in the Atlantic coastal rainforests, stretches of which cling on in the Northeast in coastal Alagoas, around Praia do Pipa, in the sierras of Ceará and Pernambuco and in the Delta do Parnaiba.

Brazil also has the largest number of globally threatened birds: 120 of 1212 worldwide. This is accounted for partly by the numbers of critically threatened habitats that include the Atlantic coastal rainforest. Rare birds lost in the Northeast in recent years include the Alagoas curassow of the Atlantic coastal forests and Spix's macaw in the *caatinga* forests of the *sertão* interior.

Compared to Costa Rica or Ecuador, birding in Brazil is in its infancy, but awareness is increasing and there are some excellent birding guides in Brazil. It is no longer necessary to organize a birding trip through an international company (though many choose to do so; see page 157 for a list of international companies offering Brazilian birdwatching and wildlife tours). The best time for birding is September-October as it is quiet, relatively dry and flights are cheapest. **Ciró Albano** (www.nebrazilbirding.com) offers world-class guided birding trips in the Northeast. Two comprehensive websites are **www.worldtwitch.com** and **www.camacdonald.com**.

Cycling and mountain biking

Brazil is well suited to cycling, both on and off-road. On main roads, keep on the lookout for motor vehicles, as cyclists are very much treated as second-class citizens. Also note that when cycling on the northeastern coast you may encounter strong winds which will hamper your progress. There are endless roads and tracks suitable for mountain biking, and there are many clubs in major cities which organize group rides, activities and competitions.

Diving and snorkelling

The archipelago of Fernando de Noronha Marine National Park, some 350 km off the coast of Pernambuco in the Northeast, has coral gardens, drop-offs and wrecks which include a 50-m Brazilian navy destroyer with full armament. Visibility is up to 50 m, with both current-free and drift diving. Divers can expect to see at least two species of turtle, spinner dolphins, more than three species of shark, huge snapper and vast shoals of goatfish and jack.

Hang-gliding and paragliding

Hang-gliding and paragliding are possible in the Serras of Ceará state. There are state associations affiliated with **Associação Brasileira de Vôo Livre** (**ABVL**, T021-3322 0266, www.abvl.com.br), or **Brazilian Hang-gliding Association**, the national umbrella organization for hang-gliding and paragliding associations. A number of operators offer tandem flights for those without experience. *Rampas* (launch sites) are growing in number.

Guia 4 Ventos Brasil (www.guia4ventos. com.br) has a full list of launch sites (and much else besides).

Shopping tips

Arts and crafts

The Northeast is one of the best regions in Brazil for handicrafts. Good buys include: beautiful bead jewellery and bags made from rainforest seeds; clay figurines from Pernambuco; lace from Ceará; leatherwork, Buriti weavings in Maranhão (including attractive mats or *tapetes*); carvings in soapstone and in bone; *capim-dourado* gold-grass bags and jewellery from Tocantins which is sold widely in the Northeast; and African-type pottery, basketwork and *candomblé* artefacts in Recife and São Luís. Brazilian cigars are excellent for those who like mild flavours.

Cosmetics and herbal remedies

For those who know how to use them, medicinal herbs, barks and spices can be bought from markets – particularly the Mercado Central de Fortaleza. Coconut oil and local skin and haircare products (including fantastic conditioners and herbal hair dyes) are as good though far and cheaper than in Europe. Natura and O Boticário are excellent local brands, similar in quality to the Body Shop.

Fashion

Brazil has long eclipsed Argentina as the fashion capital of Latin America. Brazilian cuts, colours and contours are fresh and daring by US and European standards. Quality and variety is very high, from gorgeous bags and bikinis to designer dresses, shoes and denims. In the Northeast the best buys are in the boutique shops in the more modish beach villages, particularly Jericoacoara and Pipa (which are excellent for beach fashion), and in the big malls in Recife and Fortaleza.

Surfing

There are good conditions all along the coast. Brazilians love to surf and are well-represented in international competitions, which are frequently held on Fernando de Noronha island. There is also good surfing around Pipa in Natal and in parts of Sergipe and Alagoas. Tour companies in Pipa offer surf trips or lessons.

Wind and kitesurfing

There's no better place in the Americas for wind and kitesurfing than Brazil. The northeast coast receives an almost constant wind for pretty much 365 days of the year and, in the last five years, beach towns like Cumbuco and Jericoacoara in Ceará have turned from small resorts into world wind and kitesurf capitals. Agencies in these towns offer board rental and tuition.

Jewellery

Gold, diamonds and gemstones are good buys and there are innovative designs in jewellery. For something special and high quality, buy at reputable dealers such as **H Stern** or **Antonio Bernado**. Cheap, fun pieces can be bought from street traders. There are interesting furnishings made with gemstones and marble – some of them rather cheesy – and huge slabs of amethyst, quartz and crystal at a fraction of a New Age shop price. More interesting and unusual is the seed and bead jewellery, much of it made with uniquely Brazilian natural products, and based on original indigenous designs.

Music and instruments

Music is as ubiquitous as sunlight in Rio and browsing through a CD shop anywhere will be sure to result in at least one purchase. The best outlets in the Northeast are in Recife, Fortaleza and São Luís, all of which have their own musical styles, as well as lively music scenes.

Musical instruments are a good buy, particularly Brazilian percussion items. For example: the *berimbau*, a bow with a gourd sound-bell used in *candomblé*; the *cuica* friction drum, which produces the characteristic squeaks and chirrups heard in samba; assorted hand drums including the *surdo* (the big samba bass drum); and the *caixa*, *tambor*, *repinique* and *timbale* (drums that produce the characteristic Brazilian ra-ta-ta-ta-ta). The most Brazilian of hand drums is the tambourine, a misnomer for the *pandeiro* (which comes with bells), as opposed to the *tamborim* (which comes without). There are many unusual stringed instruments too: the *rabeca* (desert fiddle), the *cavaquinho* or *cavaco* (the Portuguese ancestor of ukulele), the *bandolim* (Brazilian mandolin), with its characteristic pear shape, and many excellent nylon-strung guitars.

Then there's Brazilian music itself. Only a fraction of the best CDs reach Europe or the USA.

Improve your travel photography

Taking pictures is a highlight for many travellers, yet too often the results turn out to be disappointing. Steve Davey, author of Footprint's *Travel Photography*, sets out his top rules for coming home with pictures you can be proud of.

Before you go

Don't waste precious travelling time and do your research before you leave. Find out what festivals or events might be happening or which day the weekly market takes place, and search online image sites such as Flickr to see whether places are best shot at the beginning or end of the day, and what vantage points you should consider.

Get up early

The quality of the light will be better in the few hours after sunrise and again before sunset – especially in the tropics when the sun will be harsh and unforgiving in the middle of the day. Sometimes seeing the sunrise is a part of the whole travel experience: sleep in and you will miss more than just photographs.

Stop and think

Don't just click away without any thought. Pause for a few seconds before raising the camera and ask yourself what you are trying to show with your photograph. Think about what things you need to include in the frame to convey this meaning. Be prepared to move around your subject to get the best angle. Knowing the point of your picture is the first step to making sure that the person looking at the picture will know it too.

Compose your picture

Avoid simply dumping your subject in the centre of the frame every time you take a picture. If you compose with it to one side, then your picture can look more balanced. This will also allow you to show a significant background and make the picture more meaningful. A good rule of thumb is to place your subject or any significant detail a third of the way into the frame; facing into the frame not out of it.

This rule also works for landscapes. Compose with the horizon two-thirds of the way up the frame if the fore-ground is the most interesting part of the picture; one-third of the way up if the sky is more striking.

Don't get hung up with this so-called Rule of Thirds, though. Exaggerate it by pushing your subject out to the edge of the frame if it makes a more interesting picture; or if the sky is dull in a landscape, try cropping with the horizon near the very top of the frame.

Fill the frame

If you are going to focus on a detail or even a person's face in a close-up portrait, then be bold and make sure that you fill the frame. This is often a case of physically getting in close. You can use a telephoto setting on a zoom lens but this can lead to pictures looking quite flat; moving in close is a lot more fun!

Interact with people

If you want to shoot evocative portraits then it is vital to approach people and seek permission in some way, even if it is just by smiling at someone. Spend a little time with them and they are likely to relax and look less stiff and formal. Action portraits where people are doing something, or environmental portraits, where they are set against a significant background, are a good way to achieve relaxed portraits. Interacting is a good way to find out more about people and their lives, creating memories as well as photographs.

Focus carefully

Your camera can focus quicker than you, but it doesn't know which part of the picture you want to be in focus. If your camera is using the centre focus sensor then move the camera so it is over the subject and half press the button, then, holding it down, recompose the picture. This will lock the focus. Take the now correctly focused picture when you are ready.

Another technique for accurate focusing is to move the active sensor over your subject. Some cameras with touch-sensitive screens allow you to do this by simply clicking on the subject.

Leave light in the sky

Most good night photography is actually taken at dusk when there is some light and colour left in the sky; any lit portions of the picture will balance with the sky and any ambient lighting. There is only a very small window when this will happen, so get into position early, be prepared and keep shooting and reviewing the results. You can take pictures after this time, but avoid shots of tall towers in an inky black sky; crop in close on lit areas to fill the frame.

Bring it home safely

Digital images are inherently ephemeral: they can be deleted or corrupted in a heartbeat. The good news though is they can be copied just as easily. Wherever you travel, you should have a backup strategy. Cloud backups are popular, but make sure that you will have access to fast enough Wi-Fi. If you use RAW format, then you will need some sort of physical back-up. If you don't travel with a laptop or tablet, then you can buy a backup drive that will copy directly from memory cards.

Recently updated and available in both digital and print formats, Footprint's Travel Photography by Steve Davey covers everything you need to know about travelling with a camera, including simple post-processing. More information is available at www.footprinttravelguides.com

Where to stay

There is a good range of accommodation options in Brazil. An *albergue* or hostel offers the cheapest option. These have dormitory beds and single and double rooms. Many are part of **Hostelling International (HI)** ⓘ *www.hihostels.com*; **Hostel World** ⓘ *www.hostelworld.com*, **Hostel Bookers** ⓘ *www.hostelbookers.com*, and **Hostel.com** ⓘ *www.hostel.com*, are all useful portals. **Hostel Trail Latin America** ⓘ *T0131-208 0007 (UK), www.hosteltrail.com*, managed from their hostel in Popayan, is an online network of hotels and tour companies in South America. A *pensão* is either a cheap guesthouse or a household that rents out some rooms.

Pousadas

A *pousada* is either a bed-and-breakfast, often small and family-run, or a sophisticated and often charming small hotel. A *hotel* is as it is anywhere else in the world, operating according to the international star system, although five-star hotels are not price controlled and hotels in any category are not always of the standard of their star equivalent in the USA, Canada or Europe. Many of the older hotels can be cheaper than hostels. Usually accommodation prices include a breakfast of rolls, ham, cheese, cakes and fruit with coffee and juice; there is no reduction if you don't eat it. Rooms vary too. Normally an *apartamento* is a room with separate living and sleeping areas and sometimes cooking facilities. A *quarto* is a standard room; *com banheiro* is en suite; and *sem banheiro* is with shared bathroom. Finally there are the *motels*. These should not be confused

---

Price codes

Where to stay	
$$$$	over US$150
$$$	US$66-150
$$	US$30-65
$	under US$30

Price of a double room in high season, including taxes.

Restaurants	
$$$	over US$12
$$	US$7-12
$	US$6 and under

Price for a two-course meal for one person, excluding drinks or service charge.

---

with their US counterpart: motels are used by guests not intending to sleep; there is no stigma attached and they usually offer good value (the rate for a full night is called the '*pernoite*'), however the decor can be a little garish.

Hidden Pousadas Brazil ⓘ *www.hidden pousadasbrazil.com*, offers a range of the best *pousadas*.

> **Tip...**
> It's essential to book accommodation at peak times.

Luxury accommodation

Much of the best private accommodation sector can be booked through operators. **Matuete**, www.matuete.com, has a range of luxurious properties and tours.

Camping

Those with an international camping card pay only half the rate of a non-member at **Camping Clube do Brasil** sites ⓘ *www.campingclube.com.br*. Membership of the club itself is expensive: US$70 for six months. It may be difficult to get into some Camping Clube campsites during high season (January to February). Private campsites charge about US$6-8 per person. For those on a very low budget and in isolated areas where there is no campsite available, it's usually possible to stay at service stations. They have shower facilities, watchmen and food; some have dormitories. There are also various municipal sites. Campsites tend to be some distance from public transport routes and are better suited to people with their own car. Wild camping is generally difficult and dangerous. Never camp at the side of a road; this is very risky.

Quality hotel associations

The better international hotel associations have members in Brazil. These include: **Small Luxury Hotels of the World** ⓘ *www.slh.com*; the **Leading Hotels of the World** ⓘ *www.lhw.com*; the **Leading Small Hotels of the World** ⓘ *www.leadingsmallhotelsoftheworld.com*; **Great Small Hotels** ⓘ *www.greatsmallhotels.com*; and the French group **Relais et Chateaux** ⓘ *www.relaischateaux.com*, which also includes restaurants.

The Brazilian equivalent of these associations are **Hidden Pousadas Brazil** ⓘ *www.hiddenpousadasbrazil.com*, and their associate, the **Roteiros de Charme** ⓘ *www.roteirosdecharme.com.br*. Membership of these groups pretty much guarantees quality, but it is by no means comprehensive.

Online travel agencies (OTAs)

Services like www.tripadvisor.com and OTAs associated with them, such as www.hotels.com, www.expedia.com and www.venere.com, are well worth using for both reviews and for booking ahead. Hotels booked through an OTA can be up to 50% cheaper than the rack rate. Similar sites operate for hostels (though discounts are far less considerable). They include the Hostelling International site, www.hihostels.com, www.hostelbookers.com, www.hostels.com and www.hostelworld.com.

Food
& drink

from a *chope* with *churrasco* to a *pinga* with *pesticos*

Food

While Brazil has some of the best fine dining restaurants in Latin America and cooking has greatly improved over the last decade, everyday Brazilian cuisine can be stolid. Mains are generally heavy, meaty and unspiced. Desserts are often very sweet. The Brazilian staple meal generally consists of a cut of fried or barbecued meat, chicken or fish accompanied by rice, black or South American broad beans and an unseasoned salad of lettuce, grated carrot, tomato and beetroot. Condiments consist of weak chilli sauce, olive oil, salt and pepper and vinegar.

The national dish – which is associated with Rio and not common in the Northeast – is a heavy campfire stew called *feijoada*, made by throwing jerked beef, smoked sausage, tongue and salt pork into a pot with lots of fat and beans and stewing it for hours. The resulting stew is sprinkled with fried *farofa* (manioc flour) and served with *couve* (kale) and slices of orange. The meal is washed down with *cachaça* (sugar cane rum). Most restaurants serve the *feijoada completa* for Saturday lunch (up until about 1630). Come with a very empty stomach.

Brazil's other national dish is mixed grilled meat or *churrasco*, served in vast portions off the spit by legions of rushing waiters, and accompanied by a buffet of salads, beans and mashed vegetables. *Churrascos* are served in *churrascarias* or *rodízios*. The meat is generally excellent, especially in the best *churascarias*, and the portions are unlimited, offering good value for camel-stomached carnivores able to eat one meal a day.

In remembrance of Portugal, but bizarrely for a tropical country replete with fish, Brazil is also the world's largest consumer of cod, pulled from the cold north Atlantic, salted and served in watery slabs or little balls as *bacalhau* (an appetizer/bar snack) or *petisco*. Other national *petiscos* include *kibe* (a deep-fried or baked mince with onion, mint and flour), *coxinha* (deep-fried chicken or meat in dough), *empadas* (baked puff-pastry patties with prawns, chicken, heart of palm or meat), and *tortas* (little pies with the same ingredients). When served in bakeries, *padarias* or snack bars these are collectively referred to as *salgadinhos* (savouries).

There are myriad unusual, delicious fruits in Brazil, many with unique flavours. They include the pungent, sweet cupuaçu, which makes delicious cakes, the tart *camu-camu*, a large glass of which holds a gram of vitamin C, and açai – a dark and highly nutritious berry from a *várzea* (seasonally flooded forest) palm tree, common in the Amazon. Açai berries are often served as a frozen paste, garnished with *xarope* (syrup) and sprinkled with *guaraná* (a ground seed, also from the Amazon, which has stimulant effects similar to caffeine). Brazil also produces some of the world's best mangoes, papayas, bananas and custard apples, all of which come in a variety of flavours and sizes.

The Northeast also has its own regional cuisine – which is strong on seafood and dried meat. In Ceará, Pernabuco and Paraiba this is called *carne do sol* – dried beef or goat jerky, cooked in a flavour-bursting stew. Along the coast look out for sea food dishes like *bobó do camarão*, a thick prawn and seafood broth served with rice. Tapioca pancakes – dished up with savoury butter, cheese or meat, or served sweet with condensed milk or honey are widely available as a snack or as an option at breakfast.

Eating cheaply

The cheapest dish is the *prato feito* or *sortido*, an excellent-value set menu usually comprising meat/chicken/fish, beans, rice, chips and salad. The *prato comercial* is similar but rather better and a bit more expensive. Portions are usually large enough for two and come with two plates. If you are on your own, you could ask for an *embalagem* (doggy bag) or a *marmita* (takeaway) and offer it to a person with no food (many Brazilians do). Many restaurants serve *comida por kilo* buffets where you serve yourself and pay for the weight of food on your plate. This is generally good value and is a good option for vegetarians. *Lanchonetes* and *padarias* (diners and bakeries) are good for cheap eats, usually serving *prato feitos*, *salgadinhos*, excellent juices and other snacks.

The main meal is usually taken in the middle of the day; cheap restaurants tend not to be open in the evening.

Drink

The national liquor is *cachaça* (also known as *pinga*), which is made from sugar cane, and ranging from cheap supermarket and service-station firewater, to boutique distillery and connoisseur labels. Mixed with fruit juice, sugar and crushed ice, *cachaça* becomes the principal element in a *batida*, a refreshing but deceptively powerful drink. Served with pulped lime or other fruit, mountains of sugar and smashed ice it becomes the world's favourite party cocktail, caipirinha. A less potent caipirinha made with vodka is called a *caipiroska* and with sake a *saikirinha* or *caipisake*.

Some genuine Scotch whisky brands are bottled in Brazil. They are far cheaper even than duty free; Teacher's is the best. Locally made and cheap gin, vermouth and Campari are pretty much as good as their US and European counterparts.

Wine is becoming increasingly popular and Brazil is the third most important wine producer in South America. The wine industry is mainly concentrated in the south of the country. Reasonable national table wines include Château d'Argent, Château Duvalier, Almadén, Dreher, Preciosa and more respectable Bernard Taillan, Marjolet from Cabernet grapes, and the Moselle-type white Zahringer. There are some interesting sparkling wines in the Italian spumante style (the best is Casa Valduga Brut Premium Sparkling Wine), and Brazil produces still wines using many international and imported varieties. The best bottle of red is probably the Boscato Reserva Cabernet Sauvignon, but it's expensive (at around US\$20 a bottle); you'll get far higher quality and better value buying Portuguese, Argentine or Chilean wines in Brazil.

Brazilian beer is generally lager, served ice-cold. Draught beer is called *chope* or *chopp* (after the German Schoppen, and pronounced 'shoppi'). There are various national brands of bottled beers, which include Brahma, Skol, Cerpa, Antarctica and the best Itaipava and Bohemia. There are black beers too, notably Xingu. They tend to be sweet. The best beer is from the German breweries in Rio Grande do Sul and is available only there.

Brazil's fruits are used to make fruit juices or *sucos*, which come in a delicious variety, unrivalled anywhere in the world. *Açai acerola*, *caju* (cashew), *pitanga*, *goiaba* (guava), *genipapo*, *graviola* (*chirimoya*), *maracujá* (passion fruit), *sapoti*, and *tamarindo* are a few of the best. Fruits associated particularly with the Northeast inclue *umbu,* mangaba and seriguela all of which are tangy and deeply refreshing. *Vitaminas* are thick fruit or vegetable drinks with milk. *Caldo de cana* is sugar-cane juice, sometimes mixed with ice. *Água de côco* or *côco verde* is coconut water served straight from a chilled, fresh, green coconut. The best known of many local soft drinks is *guaraná*, which is a very popular carbonated fruit drink, completely unrelated to the Amazon nut. The best variety is *guaraná Antarctica*. Coffee is ubiquitous and good tea entirely absent.

Menu reader

A
água de côco coconut water
arroz doce rice pudding

B
bacalhau salt cod
bauru sandwich made with melted cheese, roast beef and tomatoes

C
cachaça sugar cane rum
caipirinha cocktail of crushed fruit (usually limes), *cachaça* and lots of sugar and ice
caju cashew
caldo de cana sugar cane juice
caldo de feijão bean soup
chope/chopp draught beer
churrasco mixed grilled meat
churrasqueira restaurant serving all-you-can-eat barbecued meat
côco verde coconut water served from a chilled, fresh, green coconut
comida por kilo pay-by-weight food
coxinha shredded chicken or other meat covered in dough and breadcrumbs and deep fried
curau custard flan-type dessert made with maize

E
empadas or **empadinhas** puff-pastries with prawns, meat or palm hearts

F
farofa fried cassava flour
feijoada hearty stew of black beans, sausages and pork
frango churrasco grilled chicken

K
kibe a petisco deep-fried or baked mince with onion, mint and flour

M
mandioca frita fried manioc root
maracujá passion fruit
misto quente toasted ham and cheese sandwich
moqueca seafood stew cooked with coconut and palm oil

P/Q
padaria bakery
palmito palm heart
pamonha paste of milk and corn boiled in a corn husk
pão de queijo a roll made with cheese
pastéis deep-fried pastries filled with cheese, minced beef, or palm heart
peixe fish
petisco a tapas-style snack
picanha rump, a popular cut of beef
pinga sugar cane rum
prato feito/prato comercial set meal
queijo cheese

R
requeijão ricotta-like cream cheese
roupa velha literally meaning 'old clothes', a dish of shredded dried meat served with rice *mandiocas*

S
salgadinhos savoury snacks such as *empadas* and *tortas*
sortido inexpensive set meal
suco fruit juice

T
tortas small pies filled with prawns, chicken, palm hearts or meat

V
vatapá fish and prawn stew cooked in a creamy peanut sauce
vitaminas fruit or veg drinks with milk

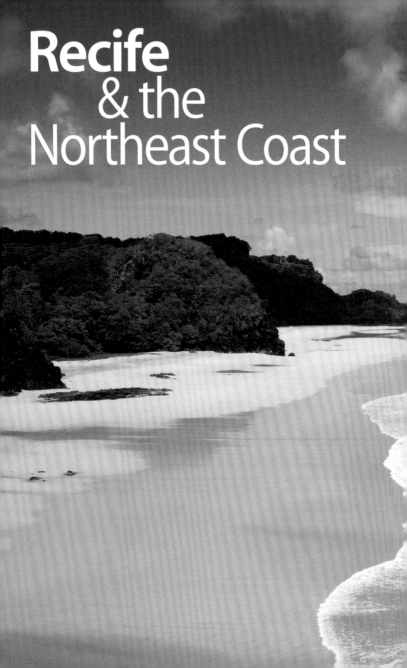

Recife
& the
Northeast Coast

The four states that comprise this region – Sergipe, Alagoas, Pernambuco and Paraíba – are often overlooked by visitors. Most whizz through, perhaps stopping at the beach at Porto de Galinhas or Fernando de Noronha, or in colourful, colonial Olinda. But those who spend time here, sampling the arts scene in Recife or the great festivals in the Sertão, find it one of the most diverse and least spoilt parts of Brazil.

In the first centuries of its colonial history, the region grew rich through sugar. Pernambuco retains many magnificent buildings from that period, while convents in Olinda and Igarassu are fine examples of Iberian baroque.

After the decline in the sugar trade, the proud intellectual tradition continued, with notables such as Marechal Deodoro, the founder of the Brazilian republic, and Gilberto Freyre, who helped forge Brazil's identity.

The region has never been more culturally exciting than today. Artists flourish in Olinda, while numerous festivals showcase the country's most innovative film-making. Carnaval in Recife or Olinda is the best and most traditional in the country.

Recife
& around

Recife is one of the most attractive large cities in Brazil, with many fine colonial buildings from the sugar boom huddled under the customary skyscraper blocks of flats, watching over little shady squares or sitting on the edge of the filigree of canals and waterways that divide up the city. The colonial heart, Recife Antigo, was a no-go area until 20 years ago, but it's now the centre of the city's booming music and alternative culture scene. To the south of the centre are a string of urban beach suburbs – Pina, Boa Viagem and Piedade – which, although frequented by bull sharks, are among the cleanest urban beaches in the country (apart from on busy weekends when locals leave rubbish on the sand). Most of Recife's hotels lie here.

Neighbouring Olinda, which has now been absorbed into the Recife conurbation, is a delightful little colonial town of hilly cobbled streets and brightly coloured houses. It preserves some of the most beautiful baroque churches in the Northeast and its low-key, relaxed atmosphere and wealth of *pousadas* make it a better place to stay than Recife itself.

Many of Brazil's most famous contemporary avant-garde musicians are from Pernambuco, and Recife-Olinda is considered to be one of Brazil's musical capitals. Carnaval here is one of the best in the country, with three days of African-Brazilian cultural processions and relentless partying.

Essential Recife

Finding your feet

International and domestic flights arrive at **Gilberto Freyre Airport** at Guararapes, 12 km from the city centre, near the hotel district of Boa Viagem. You can travel to the centre via metro, regular buses or by taxi. Long-distance buses arrive at the **Terminal Integrado dos Passageiros (TIP)**, 20 km from Recife city centre and 26 km from Olinda in the satellite municipality of Jaboatão dos Guararapes. A metro runs from here to central Recife and Boa Viagem. See Transport, page 41.

Getting around

Street names can be hard to see, especially at night, so look out for landmarks. The *metrô* (which is an overground light rail) leaves from the Central station on two lines: the Linha Centro (which connects to the *rodoviária*), and the Linha Sul, which runs to Shopping Recife, Tancredo Neves and the airport, all of which are close to Boa Viagem.

Orientation

The old colonial city centre consists of three sections sitting on islands formed by the rivers Capibaribe, Beberibe and Pina: **Recife Antigo** (aka Bairro do Recife), **Santo Antônio** and **São José**. These areas preserve the city's principal historic buildings. The inner city neighbourhoods of **Boa Vista**

and **Santo Amaro** lie immediately to the east and have few sights of tourist interest.

The centre is always very busy by day; the crowds and narrow streets, especially in the Santo Antônio district, can make it a confusing city to walk around. But this adds to its charm. **Armazens do Porto waterside port complex**, with restaurants, bars and shops, occupies the renovated warehouses of Old Recife.

Beyond here are the beach neighbourhoods: **Brasília Teimosa** (where the sea is dirty) and then **Boa Viagem**, **Setúbal** and **Piedade**. These are reached by bridge across a small bay called the Bacia do Pina. **Olinda**, the old capital, is 7 km to the north (see page 43).

Safety

Although the streets are generally too full to present danger it is wise to be vigilant when the streets are quiet. Always take a taxi after dark if you are walking alone or in a pair.

Opportunistic theft is, unfortunately, a regular occurrence in the streets of Recife and Olinda (especially on the streets up to Alto da Sé). Keep a good hold on bags and cameras, and do not wear a watch. Prostitution is reportedly common in Boa Viagem, so choose nightclubs with care. If you experience any problems, contact the Delegacia do Turista (tourist police), at the international airport, T081-3184 3437.

1 Recife orientation

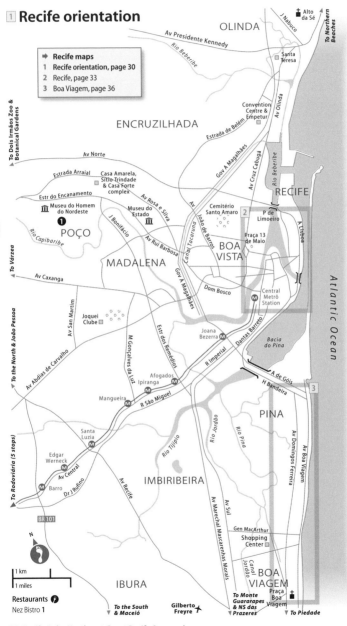

Recife maps
1 Recife orientation, page 30
2 Recife, page 33
3 Boa Viagem, page 36

OLINDA

Av Presidente Kennedy

Rio Beberibe

J Nabuco

Alto da Sé

Santa Teresa

To Northern Beaches

ENCRUZILHADA

Estrada de Belém

Convention Centre & Empetur

Av Olinda

Gov A Magalhães

Av Cruz Cabugá

Rio Beberibe

RECIFE

To Dois Irmãos Zoo & Botanical Gardens

Av Norte

Estrada Arraial

Casa Amarela, Sítio Trindade & Casa Forte complex

Museu do Homem do Nordeste

Estr do Encanamento

Av Rosa e Silva

Museu do Estado

Av

Canal Tacaruna

Cemitério Santo Amaro

P de Limoeiro

A Lisboa

2

POÇO

Rio Capibaribe

J Bonifácio

Av Rui Barbosa

J Pessoa

Av João de Barros

Praça 13 de Maio

MADALENA

Gov A Magalhães

BOA VISTA

To Várzea

Av Caxanga

Dom Bosco

Central Metrô Station

Atlantic Ocean

Joquei Clube

Av San Martim

Estr dos Remédios

Joana Bezerra

Dantas Barreto

Bacia do Pina

To the North & João Pessoa

Av Abdias de Carvalho

M Gonçalves da Luz

R Imperial

A de Góis

3

Afogados

Ipiranga

H Bandeira

Mangueira

R São Miguel

Rio Jordão

Rio Jordão

Rio Pina

PINA

Av Domingos Ferreira

Av Boa Viagem

Santa Luzia

Rio Tijipio

Edgar Werneck

To Rodoviária (5 stops)

Barro

Av Central

Dr J Rufino

Av Recife

IMBIRIBEIRA

Av Sul

Av Marechal Mascarenhas Morais

BR 101

N

1 km
1 miles

IBURA

Gen MacArthur

Shopping Center

Canal Jordão

BOA VIAGEM

Praça Boa Viagem

Restaurants
Nez Bistro 1

To the South & Maceió

Gilberto Freyre

To Monte Guararapes & NS das Prazeres

To Piedade

Recife's architecture is far less celebrated than its pretty neighbour, the former Portuguese capital of Olinda, but it retains some of the most important baroque architecture in Latin America, albeit in a dreadful state of disrepair. Rua da Aurora, which watches over the Capibaribe River, is lined with stately Palladian and neoclassical buildings. The islands to the south, over the filigree of bridges, are dotted with imposing churches and surprisingly lavish civic structures, especially around the Praça da República.

The city began with the Dutch at the twin forts: the **Forte do Brum**, on the island of **Recife Antigo** (Old Recife), which faces the open ocean; and the **Forte das Cinco Pontas**, on the neighbouring island of Santo Antônio. Both were built by the Dutch in 1630, seven years before Maurice of Nassau sacked and burned Olinda. The two forts controlled access to the Dutch port of **Mauritsstadt**, as Recife was first known, at the northern and southern entrances respectively.

Recife Antigo

This 2-km-long island, facing the open ocean on one side and the Rio Beberibe on the other, lies at the heart of old Recife. Until the 1990s its cobbled streets of handsome colonial buildings were a no-go area, frequented only by drug users and prostitutes. However, the area has been almost completely rehabilitated and Recife Antigo is now the spiritual heart of the city. The **Marco Zero** point, in the Praça Rio Branco, is the official centre of the city and the locus of activity for Recife's vibrant carnival. The best Pernambucan bands play on the stage here until dawn during carnival week and the streets nearby are busy with bars and little makeshift restaurants most evenings and especially at weekends. The liveliest street is Rua da Moeda.

The well-preserved whitewashed and terracotta-roofed **Forte do Brum** ① *Praça Comunidade Luso Brasileira s/n, T081-3224 7559, Tue-Fri 0900-1630, Sat and Sun 1400-1700, US$0.70, (1629),* is now an army museum, with huge Dutch and Portuguese canons on its bulwarks, exhibition rooms with photographs and memorabilia from Brazil's Second Word War campaign in Italy, and a dusty collection of colonial documents, including some early Dutch maps of Brazil. At the other end of Recife Antigo is the **Kahal Zur Israel Synagogue**, now a **museum** ① *R do Bom Jesus 197, T081-3224 2128, www.kahalzurisrael. com in English, www.arquivojudaicope.org.br in Portuguese, Tue-Fri 0900-1700, last entry 1630, Sun 1400-1800 last entry 1730, US$3,* an exact replica of the first synagogue to be built in the Americas, dating to 1637. Under the Dutch, the 'New Christians' (Jews and Muslims forced to convert under the Inquisition), were given freedom to worship. After the city was re-conquered by the Portuguese the synagogue was destroyed and the Jews either fled or were expelled. Many went north to the Dutch colony of Suriname, which retains a large Jewish population to this day.

There are two other sights worth seeing in this area. One of the city's first churches, the elegant, sky-blue **Igreja de Nossa Senhora do Pilar** ① *R de São Jorge s/n,* dating from 1680 underwent four years extensive refurbishment after being badly looted and lying decrepit for decades roofless. The crumbling church situated in one of the poorer communities of Recife once had magnificent ceiling paintings which have now been painted over. The restored chapel's ceiling is covered with Portuguese *azulejo* tiling. The **Torre de Malakoff**

ON THE ROAD
Naná Vasconcelos

Brazilian music without Recife's master percussionist Naná Vasconcelos would be like jazz without Charles Mingus. Bossa nova had been introduced into the USA by Stan Getz. But it was Naná and Paranense Airto Moreira who placed Brazilian percussion in the upper echelons of the serious jazz world. Naná was introduced to the US jazz scene by Miles Davis who went to one of the percussionist's concerts in the 1970s. And during a 25-year sojourn in New York he added his trademark *berimbau* and percussion to scores of records by artists like the CODONA trio (which he led with Don Cherry and Colin Walcott), Jan Garbarek, Pat Metheny, Gato Barbieri and numerous others. His most remarkable work, though, is purely Brazilian. Together with Egberto Gismonti and on albums like *Dança das Cabeças* (ECM), he created a new musical genre which fused jazz, classical and Brazilian styles. And his *Fragmentos* (Nucleo Contemporaneo/Tzadik) and *Storytelling* (EMI) albums are complex, mesmerizing tapestries of percussion and vocals that beautifully evoke Brazilian landscapes and local people.

ⓘ *Praça do Arsenal da Marinha, T081-3184 3182, Tue-Fri 1000-1800, Sat 1500-1800, Sun 1500-1900 free*, the venue works as a cultural centre hosting occasional art exhibitions, music performances and theatre plays. It is a 19th-century mock-Mudejar tower with a small **observatory** ⓘ *Sun 1600-2000, free*, on its upper floor. It's worth visiting if only for the sweeping view over the city.

Santo Antônio and São José

The bulk of Recife's historical monuments lie in the twin neighbourhoods of Santo Antônio and São José on the island immediately to the south of Recife Antigo (linked by the Buarque de Macedo and Mauricio de Nassau bridges). These neighbourhoods are interesting to wander around (during the day only) and are replete with magnificent baroque churches. Most impressive of all is the **Capela Dourada da Ordem Terceira do São Francisco** ⓘ *R do Imperador Dom Pedro II, Santo Antônio, T081-3224 0530, www. capeladourada.com.br, Mon-Fri 0800-1130 and 1400-1700, Sat 0800-1100, US$1.40*, (1695-1710 and 19th century), in the church of Santo Antônio of the Convento do São Francisco. This is one of the finest baroque buildings in Northeast Brazil and is a National Monument.

The lavish façade conceals a gorgeous gilt-painted interior with ceiling panels by Recife's Mestre Athayde, Manuel de Jesus Pinto. It is his finest work. Pinto was born a slave and bought his freedom after working on a series of Recife's magnificent churches, including the Concatedral de São Pedro dos Clérigos (see below). The chapel was designed and paid for in 1695 by a wealthy Franciscan lay brotherhood, the Ordem Terceira de São Francisco de Assis.

The adjacent **Igreja São Francisco** is said to be the oldest church in the city. It sits immediately south of the **Praça da República**, one of the city's stateliest civic squares, graced by a fountain, shaded by palms and overlooked by a number of handsome sugar-boom buildings. These include the **Palácio do Campo das Princesas** ⓘ *Praça da República s/n, Thu-Fri 0900-1100 and 1400-1600, Sun 1000-1200, free, miniskirts,*

Tip...
If you're interested in architecture the Capela Dourada da Ordem Terceira do São Francisco should not be missed.

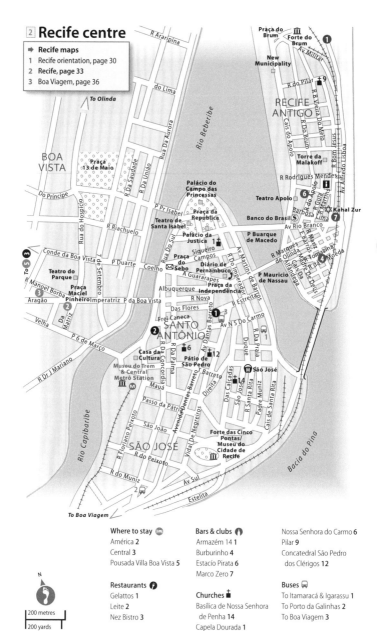

2 Recife centre

➡ **Recife maps**
1 Recife orientation, page 30
2 Recife, page 33
3 Boa Viagem, page 36

Where to stay 🛏
América **2**
Central **3**
Pousada Villa Boa Vista **5**

Restaurants 🍴
Gelattos **1**
Leite **2**
Nez Bistro **3**

Bars & clubs 🎵
Armazém 14 **1**
Burburinho **4**
Estacío Pirata **6**
Marco Zero **7**

Churches ✝
Basílica de Nossa Senhora
de Penha **14**
Capela Dourada **1**

Nossa Senhora do Carmo **6**
Pilar **9**
Concatedral São Pedro
dos Clérigos **12**

Buses 🚌
To Itamaracá & Igarassu **1**
To Porto da Galinhas **2**
To Boa Viagem **3**

shorts, long shorts and flip-flops only allowed on Sun, a neoclassical pile with a handsome interior garden by Roberto Burle Marx, which was formerly the governor's palace; the pink **Teatro de Santa Isabel** ① *Praça da República s/n, T081-3355 3323, www.teatrosantaisabel. com.br, free guided visits Sun 1400 and 1700 in English, and almost nightly performances*, (1851), which has a lavish auditorium; and the imposing mock-French **Palácio da Justiça**, topped with a French Renaissance cupola.

Colonial Recife's other great church is the **Concatedral de São Pedro dos Clérigos** ① *Pátio de São Pedro, R Barão da Vitória at Av Dantas Barreto, T081-3224 2954, Mon-Fri 0800-1200 and 1400-1700*, which overlooks one of the city's best-preserved colonial squares. It's a towering baroque building with a beautiful painted and carved octagonal interior with a trompe l'oeuil ceiling (by Manuel de Jesus Pinto (see Capela Dourada, above). The surrounding area has many little shops, restaurants and bars. There are sporadic music and poetry shows Wednesday to Sunday evenings. Also worth visiting is the 18th-century **Basílica e Convento de Nossa Senhora do Carmo** ① *Av Dantas Barreto, Santo Antônio, T081-3224 3341, Mon-Fri 0900-1700, Sat 0800-1200, free*, named after the city's patron saint, which has a magnificent painted ceiling and high altar.

One of the best places in Northeast Brazil to buy arts and crafts is a stroll to the south, next to the Ponte 6 de Março. The **Casa da Cultura** ① *R Floriano Peixoto s/n, Santo Antônio, T081-3224 0557, www.casadaculturape.com.br, Mon-Fri 0900-1900, Sat 0900-1800, Sun 0900-1400*, in the former state penitentiary building, is now a gallery of hundreds of shops and stalls selling clay figurines, leatherwork, lace and ceramics from all over Pernambuco, including the famous arts and crafts town of Caruaru (see page 53). Immediately west of the Casa da Cultura is Recife's other Dutch fort, the **Forte das Cinco Pontas**. This is now home to the **Museu da Cidade do Recife** ① *T081-3355 3107, www.recife.pe.gov.br/ cultura/museucidade.php, Tue-Fri 0900-1700, Sat and Sun 1300-1700, free*, which shows a cartographic history of the settlement of Recife.

The **Basílica de Nossa Senhora de Penha** ① *Praça Dom Vital, São José, T081-3424 8500, Mon 0800-1600, Tue-Fri 0800-1700*, is an Italianate church a few streets north of the fort, which holds a traditional 'blessing of São Felix' on Fridays, attended by hundreds of sick Pernambucans in search of miracles. It reopened in 2015 after an extensive refurbishment.

The **Museu de Arte Moderna Aloisio Magalhães** ① *R da Aurora, 265, Boa Vista, T081-3355 6871, https://blogmamam.wordpress.com, Tue-Fri 1200-1800, Sat and Sun 1300-1700, free*, shows modern Brazilian and contemporary art (much of it from Recife and the Northeast), in a series of galleries set in a beautiful 19th-century townhouse overlooking the Capibaribe River.

Suburban Recife

The **Oficina Brennand** ① *Propriedade Santos Cosme e Damião s/n, Várzea, T081-3271 2466, www.brennand.com.br, Mon-Thu 0800-1700, Fri 0800-1600, Sat-Sun 1000-1600, US$3.80, no public transport, taxi from Olinda/Boa Viagem US$14 one way, or take the metrô to Camaragibe and get a taxi from there (US$4.50 one way)*, is a Dali-esque fantasy garden and museum preserving hundreds of monumental ceramic sculptures by Latin America's most celebrated ceramic artist, Francisco Brennand. Enormous snake penises in hobnailed boots are set in verdant lawns; surrealist egret heads look out over a Burle Marx garden from 10-m-high tiled walls; haunting chess-piece figures in top hats gaze at tinkling fountains. The museum has a very good air-conditioned restaurant and gift shop.

The Brennands are one of the wealthiest old-money families in Brazil. Ricardo Brennand – not to be outdone by his cousin – has his own museum 10 minutes' taxi ride away. The **Instituto Ricardo Brennand** ⓘ *Alameda Antônio Brennand, Várzea, T081-2121 0352, www.institutoricardobrennand.org.br, Tue-Sun 1300-1700 (last entry 1630), US$5*, has a priceless collection of European and Brazilian art (including the largest conglomeration of Dutch-Brazilian landscapes in the world), books, manuscripts and medieval weapons housed in a fake Norman castle with its own moat and giant swimming pool.

Boa Viagem

Recife's principal beach neighbourhood (and the site of most of the better hotels), lies around 6 km south of town in the neighbourhood of Boa Viagem. The 8-km promenade, lined with high-rise buildings, commands a striking view of the limpid green Atlantic. Sadly the sea here is plagued by bull sharks (*Carcharhinus leucas*) which were forced out of their natural mangrove habitat to the south, after a spate of ill-considered coastal developments, which include the Porto do Suape. You can go fishing on *jangadas* at Boa Viagem at low tide. The main *praça* has a small but decent food and crafts market at weekends.

Essential Boa Viagem

Access

To get there from the centre, take any bus marked 'Boa Viagem'; from Nossa Senhora do Carmo, take buses marked 'Piedade', 'Candeias' or 'Aeroporto', which run along Avenida Domingos Ferreira, two blocks parallel to the beach, all the way to Praça Boa Viagem (at Avenida Boa Viagem 500). To get to the centre, take the bus marked 'CDU' or 'Setubal' from Avenida Domingos Ferreira. The PE-15 Boa Viagem to Olinda bus runs along the Avenida Boa Viagem and stops at the Praça Boa Viagem. It is fast and frequent.

Listings Recife and around *maps p30, p33 and p36*

Tourist information

Recife and Boa Viagem

Seturel
Centro de Convenções, Complexo Rodoviário de Salgadinho, Av Professor Andrade Bezerra s/n, Salgadinho, Olinda, T081-3182 8300, www2.recife.pe.gov.br/servicos/turista.
The main office for the Pernambuco tourist board is between Recife and Olinda. There are other branches in Praça de Boa Viagem (T081-3463 3621), at the *rodoviária* (TIP), and at the airport (T081-3224 2361, open 24 hrs). They cannot book hotels, but the helpful staff speak English and can offer leaflets and decent maps.

Where to stay

Recife

The standard of hotels is poor by international standards; knock at least 2 stars off any rating compared to hotels in Asia or Europe. There are very few decent hotels in Recife's city centre; even business travellers seem to prefer Boa Viagem and the beach. If you chose the centre, the best place to stay is **Boa Vista**. Be careful walking back to hotels after dark. During **Carnaval** and for longer stays, many individuals rent private rooms and houses in Recife and Olinda; listings can be found in the classified ads of *Diário de Pernambuco* or on http://pe.olx.com.br/grande-recife/imoveis/temporada.

$$$ Pousada Villa Boa Vista
R Miguel Couto 81, Boa Vista, T081-3223 0666, www.pousadavillaboavista.com.br.
The only modern hotel in town, with plain, comfortable a/c rooms (all en suites have modern bathrooms and powerful showers), around a courtyard. Quiet, safe and a 5-min taxi ride from the centre.

Boa Viagem detail

➡ **Recife maps**
1 Recife orientation, page 30
2 Recife, page 33
3 Boa Viagem, page 36

Atlantic Ocean

200 metres
200 yards

Where to stay 🛏
Aconchego 1
Coqueiral 2
Cosmopolitan Hostel 9
Grand Mercure
   Atlante Plaza 8
Hostel Boa Viagem 11
Hotel Pousada Casuarinas 3
Piratas da Praia 4
Pousada da Julieta 5
Pousada da Praia 6
Recife Monte 7
Transamerica Prestige
   Beach Class
   International 10

Restaurants 🍴
Chica Pitanga 2
Ilha da Kosta 5
La Capannina 6
La Maison 7
Parraxaxa 8
Picanha Tio Dadá 14

Bars & clubs 🍸
Haus Lajetop
   & Beergarden 9

$$ Central
Av Manoel Borba 209, Boa Vista, T081-3222 2353, hotelcentralrecife@hotmail.com.
A splendid 1920s listed building with original French-style open-lifts and plain, but freshly painted rooms, enormous old iron bathtubs, upper floors have wonderful views.

$ América
Praça Maciel Pinheiro 48, Boa Vista, T081-3221 1300, www.hotelamericarecife.com.br.
Frayed, very simple rooms with low, foamy beds, lino floors and tiny en suites. The best rooms are on the upper floors with views out over the city.

Boa Viagem
Boa Viagem is the main tourist district with plenty of hotels many of them overlooking the beach. The main beachfront road is Av Boa Viagem; hotels here are mostly tower blocks and tend to be more expensive.

$$$$ Transamerica Prestige Beach Class International
Av Boa Viagem 420, T0800-012 4400, www.transamericagroup.com.br.
The newest of the city's huge skyscraper beach hotels near the best restaurants and on a broad section of the beach, with modern, spacious rooms (the best with views), a tiny gym and a slightly scruffy pool area.

$$$$-$$$ Grand Mercure Atlante Plaza
Av Boa Viagem 5426, T081-3302 3333, http://grandmercure.com.br/2015/hotel/grand-mercure-atlante.
This glittering beachfront skyscraper is in a superb location right on the beach. Front-facing rooms (and the panoramic lift) offer wonderful views, but they are in need of renovation and service. It's the best place to stay in Boa Viagem, but a long way from the 5-star it claims to be.

$$$ Aconchego
Félix de Brito e Melo 382, T081-3464 2960, www.hotelaconchego.com.br.
Motel-style rooms around a pleasant pool area, with a/c, sitting room, Wi-Fi, restaurant

and bar. The English-speaking owner will collect from the airport. Also has a sister hotel in Porto de Galinhas.

$$$-$$ Coqueiral
R Petrolina 43, T081-3326 5881, www.hotelcoqueiral.com.
Dutch-owned with small, homely a/c rooms and a pretty breakfast room. Recommended.

$$ Cosmopolitan Hostel
R Paulo Setubal 53, T081-3204 0321, www.cosmopolitanhostel.com.
Simple mixed and sex-segregated dorms, doubles and singles in a decent location near the beach.

$$ Hostel Boa Viagem
R Aviador Severiano Lins 455, T081-3326 9572, www.hostelboaviagem.com.br.
Doubles and singles with a/c and dormitories in a well-located HI hostel. A 10-min walk from the beach, pool, owners are from Caruaru so can arrange trips. Dorms with en suites, some without window or extractor fan. In need of renovation.

$$ Hotel Pousada Casuarinas
R Antonio Pedro Figueiredo 151, T081-3325 4708, www.pousadacasuarinas.com.br.
Quirky and charming *pousada* decorated with arts and crafts from Pernambuco state. Lush communal area shaded by mango and banana trees. Owners speak English. Good location.

$$ Pousada da Julieta
R Prof Jose Brandão 135, T081-3327 2958, www.hoteljulieta.com.br.
Very good value for the location, 1 block from the beach, though the furnishings and decor are very worn.

$$ Pousada da Praia
Alcides Carneiro Leal 66, T081-3326 7085, www.hotelpousadadapraia.com.br.
Very simple tiled rooms – some pocket-sized and with little more than a spongy bed, others are larger suites with space for up to 6. All are a/c and come with a TV, safe and Wi-Fi and there is a rooftop breakfast and lounge area.

$$ Recife Monte
On the corner of R Petrolina and R dos
Navegantes 363, T081-2121 0909,
www.recifemontehotel.com.br.
A big tower with 150 rooms and a string
of smarter duplex suites watching over
a gloomy atrium with a small shaded
pool. Rooms are good value for the
category and the crowd are
predominantly business travellers.

$ Piratas da Praia
Av Conselheiro Aguiar 2034, 3rd floor, T081-
3326 1281, www.piratasdapraia.com.br/en.
A/c rooms and dorms are colourful and fun,
bright public areas (no a/c) include a living
area with TV and sofa, a room for reading
and a well-appointed kitchen. Close to
restaurants and bars.

Restaurants

Recife
The best Recife restaurants are in Boa
Viagem (see below) and adjacent Pina.
Be careful of eating the local crabs, known
as *guaiamum*; they live in the mangrove
swamps which take the drainage from
Recife's *mocambos* (favelas).
    There are many cheap *lanchonetes*
catering to office workers but these are
closed in evening.

$$$ Leite
Praça Joaquim Nabuco 147/53, near the Casa
de Cultura, Santo Antônio, T081-3224 7977,
www.restauranteleite.com.br.
This formal Portuguese-Brazilian fusion
restaurant, with black-tie waiters and a
pianist, is one of the oldest in the country
and has been serving Portuguese standards
like *bacalhau* (smoked salted cod) for
120 years. More modern options on the
menu (which has more than 50 dishes)
include king prawns fried in garlic butter
and served with cream cheese sauce and
Brazil nut rice. It is frequently voted the best
in the city.

$$$ Nez Bistro
Praça de Casa Forte, 314, T081-3441 7873,
www.nezbistro.com.br. Mon-Sat dinner,
plus Fri-Sun lunch.
Dishes with French and Italian influences,
Good wine selection.

$ Gelattos
Av Dantas Barreto, 230 T081-3224 6072.
Great juices (*sucos*); try the delicious *guaraná*
do amazonas with nuts. Snacks include
hamburgers and sandwiches.

Boa Viagem
Restaurants on the main beach road of
Av Boa Viagem are pricier than in the centre.
Venture a block or 2 inland for cheaper
deals. There are many a/c cheapies in the
Shopping Center (Recife, T081-3464 6000,
www.shoppingrecife.com.br). Many of the
better restaurants are closed on Mon.

$$$ La Maison
R Capitão Rebelinho 106, T081-3325 1158.
This fondue restaurant in a low-lit basement
has an illicit dive bar feel and cheesy 1970s
decor, but it's good fun, attracts a lively
crowd and has stodgy desserts like peach
melba on the menu.

$$ Chica Pitanga
R Petrolina 19, T081-3465 2224,
www.chicapitanga.com.br.
Upmarket, excellent food by weight.
Be prepared to queue. Recommended.

$$ Ilha da Kosta
R Pe Bernardino Pessoa 50, T081-
3466 2222, www.grupoilha.com.br.
One of half a dozen good-value restaurants
serving everything from steaks and Bahian
stews to sushi and roast chicken. These sit
alongside a variety of *petisco* snacks.

$$ La Capannina
Av Cons Aguiar 538, T081-3465 9420.
Italian pizzas, salad, pasta and sweet
and savoury crêpes. Recommended.

$$ Parraxaxá
Av Fernando Simões Barbosa 1200, T081-3463 7874, www.parraxaxa.com.br.
Rustic-style, award-winning buffet of northeastern cuisine, with tapioca breakfasts and a generous spread of dishes at lunch and dinner time. Staff are dressed in mock-*sertanejo* clothing.

$$ Picanha Tio Dadá
R Baltazar Pereira 100, T081-3465 0986.
Lively *churrascaria* and traditional northeastern Brazilian restaurant with lunchtime buffets.

$$ Sushimi
Recife Shopping, T081-3216 9867, www.sushimi.com.br.
Classic, Japanese fast-food in sterile surroundings. One of a range of options in **Shopping Center Recife** (T081-3464 6000, open 1000-2200).

Bars and clubs

Recife
Recife is renowned for its lively nightlife. There is frequent live music both in public spaces and in Recife's numerous theatres. The websites www.abrilprorock.info, and www.pernambuco.com/divirtase/capadivirtase have details of what's on.

Recife Antigo is the best place in the city for weekend nightlife. Many exciting bands and DJs play in the bars and clubs around R Tomazino (R do Burburinho) and the Marco Zero (the epicentre of Recife carnival); and there is always a lively crowd. The area is not safe to walk to so take a taxi.

Armazém 14
Av Alfredo Lisboa s/n, Cais do Porto, Recife Antigo.
One of the top live music venues for the alternative scene. Big names like Mundo Livre and Mombojo play here.

Burburinho
R Tomazina 106, T081-3224 5854, www.barburburinho.com.br. Mon, Wed and Thu.
A legendary live music and comedy club in Recife Antigo. A range of sounds from Beatles tributes to psychedelic *forró* funk to *frevo* rock and all things mixed. Live comedy on Thu nights. Other bars lie nearby; start here and wander.

Estelita
Av Saturnino de Brito 385, Cabanga, T081-3127 4143, wwww.facebook.com/estelitarecife.
Live concert venue and bar that serves snacks and sandwiches. Good live bands, look out for Otto who plays here.

Boa Viagem

Haus Lajetop e Beergarden
Av Herculano Bandeira, 513, Galeria Joana Darc, Pina, north Boa Viagem, T081-3039 6304, www.facebook.com/GaleriaJDArc.
Rooftop bar and restaurant with a modish contemporary industrial look, serving gourmet Brazilian snacks and meals. Weekly free DJ. Alternative and gay crowd.

Festivals

Recife
For **Carnaval**, see box, page 40.
1 Jan Universal Brotherhood.
12-15 Mar Parades to mark the city's foundation.
Mid-Apr Pro-Rock Festival, a week-long celebration of rock, hip-hop and *mangue beat SP* at Centro de Convenções, Complexo de Salgadinho and other venues. Check *Diário de Pernambuco* or *Jornal de Comércio* for details.
Jun Festas Juninas, see box, page 64.
11-16 Jul Nossa Senhora do Carmo, patron saint of the city.
Aug Mes do Folclore.
1-8 Dec Festival of Iemanjá, with typical foods and drinks, celebrations and offerings to the orixá.
8 Dec Nossa Senhora da Conceição.

FESTIVALS
Carnaval in Pernambuco

The most traditional and least touristy big carnival in Brazil takes place in Recife, its twin city Olinda, and the little towns nearby. Whilst there are few international tourists, Brazilian visitor numbers are as high as those in Bahia. The music is the most exciting in Brazil, and it is Pernambuco's own. Whilst Salvador pounds to *afoxé* and *axé*, and Rio to samba, Recife and Olinda reverberate to pounding *maracatú*, up-tempo, brassy *frevo* and alternative raucous *mangue* beat. The dancing is some of the best and most acrobatic in the country, with frevo dancers leaping, falling into the splits, twirling and throwing tiny, sparkly miniature umbrellas.

Pernambuco carnival is held in the street – unlike Rio and like Salvador. The difference is that, whilst you have to pay in Salvadoro, in Pernambuco, the celebrations here are almost all free. The crowds are big but only oppressive at the opening parade. Recife's carnival takes place in the old city centre, which is dotted with gorgeous Portuguese baroque churches and crumbling mansions, while sitting on two islands between the Beberibe and Capibare and the Atlantic. On the Friday, in the streets around the **Pátio de São Pedro** (Marco Zero) in Recife Antigo, there are big, spectacular maracatú parades with troupes of up to 100 drummers and blocos dressed in colourful costumes and swirling white dresses. This square forms the focus of Recife carnival for the following week, with a big sound stage hosting wonderful live acts. Carnival officially opens with the huge **Galo da Madrugada** (Cock of the Dawn parade), which is said by locals to be the largest street gathering in the world. Despite its name the parade usually begins at around 1000 on Carnival Saturday. Floats with many of the most famous stars – such as **Lenine**, **Alceu Valença** and **Eddie** – pass through the teeming crowds under a baking tropical sun. Try and get a place in one of the shaded bandstands at the side of the street as the heat can be oppressive. These can be booked up to a fortnight in advance at the central post office on Avenida Guararapes in Recife. Carnival shows continue until dawn on stages dotted around old Recife for the next five nights. In neighbouring Olinda the party is on the steep cobbled streets, between pretty 18th-century houses and opulent churches and overlooking the shimmering Atlantic. Troupes of *frevo* dancers wander through the throng playing and dancing with effortless gymnastic dexterity.

There are parties in other areas throughout both cities. These include the parade of the **Virgens do Bairro Novo** (Bairro Novo Virgins) in Olinda, led by outrageously camp drag queens, and the **Noite dos Tambores Silenciosos** (the Night of the Silent Drums), held in a pretty colonial church square in one of the poorest inner-city neighbourhoods. It's one of the most spectacular percussion events in Latin America, with a strongly African, sacred, ritualistic feel.

The most spectacular of the Carnival celebrations near Recife are held at **Nazaré da Mata**, where there are traditional parades and music.

Shopping

Recife
Arts and crafts
Casa da Cultura, *R Floriano Peixoto, Santo Antônio, T081-3224 0557, www. casadaculturape.com.br.* Some 150 arts and crafts shops selling contemporary and antique figurines, prints and art work. Prices for ceramic figurines are lower than Caruaru.
Centro do Artesanato de Pernambuco, *Av Alfredo Lisboa, Armazém 11, Recife Antigo, T081-3181 3151, www. artesanatodepernambuco.pe.gov.br.* A big complex of small shops and stalls selling typical Pernambuco art, including ceramic figurines, knitwear and clothing.

Markets
Cais de Alfândega, *Recife Barrio.* With local artisans work, 1st weekend of the month.
Domingo na Rua, *in Recife Barrio.* Sun market stalls of local *artesanato* and performances.
Feira do Recife Antigo, *Altura do Centro Judaico, every Sun 1400-2000.* Arts and crafts, foodstuffs (including Recife's famous *bolo de rolo*) and miscellany.
Fruit and veg market, *Feira Agroecológica, Praça de Casa Forte. Sat 0500-1000.* Organic market that supports small producers, good for pictures and an early breakfast after a late night out.
Hippy fair, *Feira de Casa Forte, Praça de Casa Forte, every 2nd and 4th Sat, 1300-2100.*
Mercado São José (1875), *Praça Dom Vital s/n, São José. Mon-Sat 0600-1700 and Sun 0600-1200.* Not a touristy place, be cautious. Great for local products and handicrafts.
Sítio Trindade, *Estrada do Arraial 3259, Casa Amarela, https://pt-br.facebook.com/ sitio.trindade.* Sat craft fair during the feast days of 12-29 Jun, fireworks, music, dancing, local food. On 23 Apr, here and in the Pátio de São Pedro, one can see the *xangô* dance. Herbal remedies, barks and spices at Afogados market.

Shopping malls
Shopping Recife, *R Padre Carapuceiro 777, between Boa Viagem and the airport, T081-3464 6000, www.shoppingrecife.com.br.* One of the largest in the Northeast, with plenty of Brazilian and international fashion chains, bookshops and a huge food court.
Shopping Tacaruna, *Av Agamenon Magalhães 153, T081-3412 6000, www. shoppingtacaruna.com.br.* The largest shopping centre in the northwest of the city.

Boa Viagem
Hippy fair, Feira de Boa Viagem, *Praça Boa Viagem, seafront. Daily Mon-Fri 1400-2200 and Sat-Sun 1000-2200.* Life-sized wooden statues of saints.

What to do

Recife
Diving
Offshore are some 20 wrecks, including the remains of Portuguese galleons; the fauna is very rich.
Aquáticos, *Cais das Cinco Pontas, s/n, São José, T081-3424-5470, www.aquaticos.com.* Good facilities, book departures and night dives in advance.

Transport

Recife
Air
Gilherto Freyre Airport, T081-3322 4180, www.aeroportorecife.com, is considered to be the best airport in Brazil. It's modern and spacious, with a tourist office, banks, shops, post office, car rental (see Car hire, below) and tour agencies, and tourist police.

Airport taxis cost US$3.30 to the seafront (about 3 km) on *bandeira* 1 and US$15.40 to Olinda (about 22 km). The Aeroporto *metrô* station (on R Dez de Junho, in front of Praça Ministro Salgado Filho, just outside the airport terminal) connects to **Shopping Recife** and **Recife Central** station in the city centre via the blue Linha Sul line (US$0.60).

You can change for a *metrô* to the *rodoviária* (on the Camaragibe branch of the Linha Centro, US$1) at Joana Bezerra or Central. The a/c bus No 42 runs (Mon-Fri 0530-1920, Sat 0615-1850, no bus on Sun, US$1) from the airport to **Shopping Recife**, then along the entire length of Boa Viagem (along Av Conselheiro Aguiar and Av Domingos Ferreira, which are parallel to the seafront), then continuing to **Recife Antigo** and returning to the airport through **Boa Vista**. The non-a/c bus No 33 runs along a similar route (daily 0400-2310, US$1.40). There is no direct bus from the airport to **Olinda**; instead take bus Nos 42 or 33 to **Boa Viagem** and change, catching bus No 910 (daily 0330-2225, US$1.30) which runs from both Praça Nossa Senhora da Boa Viagem and Av Boa Viagem to Praça do Varadouro in Olinda (the closest bus stop to the colonial centre; no buses are allowed to circulate within this small area). Bus No 370 (TIP/TI Aeroporto, US$1, daily 0400-2250) connects the **airport** and the *rodoviária*.

Flights to **Lisbon, Frankfurt, Miami, Panama City, Buenos Aires** and **Sal** (**Cape Verde**). There are domestic flights to 32 destinations including **Brasília, Curitiba, Campina Grande, Fernando de Noronha, Fortaleza, Ilheus, João Pessoa, Juazeiro do Norte, Maceió, Manaus, Natal, Porto Alegre, Rio de Janeiro, Salvador, Santarem** and **São Paulo**.

Bus

Local City buses cost US$1; they are clearly marked and run frequently until about 2230. Many central bus stops have boards showing routes; also see www.granderecife.pe.gov.br.

The new bus system, Corredor Norte-Sul (known as BRT) covers the outer suburbs of Recife to the city centre, via a fast bus lane.

Buses stop at **Sitio Historico, Praça da República, Forte do Brum**, the **airport**, **Olinda**, among other places. Buses run daily 0430-2230, US$0.60.

Buses to the nearby destinations of **Igarassu** (every 15 mins) and **Itamaracá** (every 30 mins) leave from Av Martins de Barros, in front of **Grande Hotel**.

Long-distance The *rodoviaria*, T081-3207-1088, has 3 floors. All the bus platforms, left luggage, restaurants and the tourist information booth (helpful for maps and transport information) are on the 1st floor. The 3rd floor has shops and a cinema. The 2nd floor provides access to Recife's small *metrô*, outside which there are numerous vans and *colectivos* that run to Greater Recife and Pernambuco (including Caruaru and Porto de Galinhas).

To get to **Recife city centre** from the *rodoviária*, take the *metrô* to Central station (30 mins). If going to **Boa Viagem**, get off the *metrô* at Central or Joanna Bezerra station and change to the Linha Sul for Boa Viagem. To reach **Olinda** from the *rodoviária* take the *metrô* to Recife Central and then bus No 983 (Rio Doce/Princesa Isabel, daily 0400-2250, US$1.00) to the Largo do Varadouro.

To **Cabo** (every 20 mins) and beaches south of Recife buses run from Cais de Santa Rita. To **Caruaru**, numerous daily, 2 hrs, US$8.80. To **Salvador**, 4 daily, 12 hrs, US$45.50 (fastest at night). To **Fortaleza**, 5 daily, 13 hrs, US$57.50. To **João Pessoa**, numerous daily, 2 hrs, US$7. To **Natal**, 9 daily, 4-5 hrs, US$21. To **Rio**, 2 daily, 44 hrs, US$140. To **São Paulo**, 2 daily 1630, 50 hrs, US$125. To **São Luís**, 2 daily, 25 hrs, US$77. To **Maceió**, 12 daily, US$14, 5 hrs.

Car hire

There are several car hire booths in Guararapes Airport at the arrivals floor, T081-3322 4180, **Localiza** T081-3341 2082, **Avis** T081-3322 4016, **Movida** T081-3322 4895, **Da Vinci** T081-3341 2441.

About 7 km north of Recife is the old capital, Olinda (population 350,000), which is a UNESCO World Heritage Site, founded in 1537. The compact network of cobbled streets is steeped in history and very inviting for a wander. A programme of restoration was initiated to comply with the title of National Monument, but while some of the churches and magnificent buildings have been renovated, much is still in need of repair.

Sights

Whilst Olinda city has an ornate church on almost every corner, there are two which rank among the finest in South America: the Igreja e Convento Franciscano de Nossa Senhora das Neves (Brazil's first Franciscan convent) and the Basilica e Mosteiro de São Bento. The **Igreja e Convento Franciscano de Nossa Senhora das Neves** ① *Ladeira de São Francisco 280, T081-3429 0517, Mon-Sat 0900-1230 and 1400-1730, US$1.25, children free, Mass Tue at 1900, Sat at 1700, Sun at 0800*, (1585), is one of the oldest religious complexes in South America. It has a modest, weather-beaten exterior, but the interior preserves one of the country's most splendid displays of woodcarving, ecclesiastical paintings and gilded stucco. The Franciscans began work on the buildings – which comprise the convent, the church of Nossa Senhora das Neves and the chapels of São Roque and St Anne – in 1585. Even if you are in a rush, be sure to visit the cloisters, the main church and the São Roque chapel, which has a glorious painted ceiling. The entire complex is covered in beautiful Portuguese *azulejo* tiles depecting scenes from the life of St Francis and from Lisbon before the 1755 earthquake.

The **Basilica e Mosteiro de São Bento** ① *R São Bento, T081-3429 3288, daily 0900-1145, 1400-1700, Mass daily at 0630, Sun at 1000, with Gregorian chant; monastery closed except with written permission, free*, is another very early Brazilian church. Founded in 1582 by Benedictine monks, it was burnt by the Dutch in 1631 and restored in 1761. It is the site of Brazil's first law school and was the first place in Brazil to abolish slavery. The vast, cavernous nave is fronted by a towering tropical cedar altarpiece covered in gilt. It is one of the finest pieces of baroque carving in the Americas. There are intricate carvings and paintings throughout the chapels.

It's worth making the short, but very steep, climb up the **Alto da Sé** to the simple **Igreja da Sé** ⓘ *daily 0900-1700*, (1537), for the much-photographed views out over Olinda, the palm tree-fringed beaches and the distant skyscrapers of Recife. The church was the first to be built in Olinda and has been the city's cathedral since 1677. In the late afternoon and especially at weekends, there are often *repentista* street troubadours playing in the little cathedral square and women selling *tapioca* snacks. The **Igreja da Misericórdia** ⓘ *R Bispo Coutinho, daily 1145-1230, 1800-1830*, (1540), a short stroll downhill from the cathedral, has some beautiful *azulejo* tiling and gold work but seemingly random opening hours. The **Igreja do Carmo** (1581), on a small hill overlooking Praça do Carmo, is similarly impressive. Olinda has many handsome civic buildings too, including streets of 17th-century houses with latticed balconies, heavy doors and brightly painted stucco walls.

There's a thriving arts and crafts community in Olinda and this is a good place to stock up on regional souvenirs. Look out for terracotta figurines and woodcarvings. The figurines are often by named artisans (look for their autograph imprinted in the clay on

Olinda

Olinda Hostel **3**
Pousada Baoba **5**
Pousada Luar de Olinda **8**
Pousada do Amparo **6**
Pousada d'Olinda **4**
Pousada dos Quatro
  Cantos **7**

Pousada São Francisco **9**
São Pedro **10**

Restaurants 🍴
Creperia **1**
Maison do Bonfim **2**
Oficina do Sabor **5**

Bars & clubs 🍸
Bodega do Veio **7**
Cantinho da Sé **4**
Marola **3**
Preto Velho **8**

Where to stay 🛏
7 Colinas **1**
Casa de Chica **2**

the base) and are becoming collectors' items. You'll find many shops selling arts and crafts around the cathedral and in the handicraft shops at the **Mercado da Ribeira** ⓘ *R Bernardo Vieira de Melo*, and the **Mercado Eufrásio Barbosa** ⓘ *Av Segismundo Gonçalves at Santos Dumont, Varadouro*, currently undergoing renovation which is due to finish in June 2016. Every Friday at 2200 there are serenades in Olinda, with a troupe of musicians leaving the Praça João Alfredo (aka Praça da Abolição) and walking throughout the old centre.

The beaches close to Olinda are polluted, but those further north, beyond Casa Caiada, at **Janga**, and **Pau Amarelo**, are beautiful, palm-fringed and seldom crowded (although the latter can be dirty at low tide). There are many simple cafés where you can eat *sururu* (clam stew in coconut sauce), *agulha frita* (fried needle-fish), *miúdo de galinha* (chicken giblets in gravy), *casquinha de carangueijo* (seasoned crabmeat) and *farinha de dendê* (served in crab shells).

To get to the beaches, take either a 'Janga' or 'Pau Amarela' bus; to return to Recife, take a bus marked 'Varodouro'.

> **Tip...**
> Visit the Dutch fort on Pau Amarelo beach where there is a small craft fair on Saturday nights.

Listings Olinda *map p44*

Tourist information

The Secretaria de Turismo
Av Liberdade 68, Carmo, T081-3493 3770, www.facebook.com/olindaturismo. Daily 0900-2100.
Provides a complete list of all historic sites and a useful map, *Sítio Histórico*.

Where to stay

Travellers tend to use Olinda as a base rather than Recife as it is safer, prettier and its sights, restaurants and bars are concentrated in a relatively small area. Transport to and from Recife is straightforward (see page 41). Prices at least triple during Carnaval when 5-night packages are sold. Rooms at regular prices can often be found in Boa Viagem during this time. In the historic centre, accommodation is mostly in converted mansions, which are full of character. If you can afford it, staying in one of these *pousadas* is the ideal way to absorb Olinda's colonial charm. All *pousadas*, and most of the cheaper hotels outside the old city, have a pool.

$$$ 7 Colinas
Ladeira de Sao Francisco 307, T081-3493 7766, www.hotel7colinas.com.br.
Spacious, fully renovated 1960s hotel with all mod cons, set in beautiful private, gated gardens and with a large swimming pool. Rooms are spacious and set in delightful Niemeyeresque annexes. All have huge glass windows letting in ample light. Decent (if overpriced) bar and restaurant. Helpful and courteous staff.

$$$ Pousada Baobá
R do Sol 147, Carmo, T081-3429 0459, www.pousadabaobadeolinda.com.br.
On a busy Olinda street, this place has modestly sized and simply decorated a/c rooms with fitted shelves, big mirrors and tiny bedside tables, with or without en suite bathroom. Public areas are bright and colourful, staff attentive and the hotel has a small pool.

$$$ Pousada do Amparo
R do Amparo 199, T081-3429 6889, www.pousadadoamparo.com.br.
Olinda's best hotel is a gorgeous 18th-century house, full of antiques and atmosphere.

Rooms have 4-poster beds and each is decorated differently.

$$ Casa de Chica
R 27 Janeiro 43, T081-9963 3337,
www.casadechica.com.br.
Boxy but well-kept white-tile and whitewash rooms in a bright little *pousada* next to São Pedro church. Attractive public areas.

$$ Olinda Hostel
R do Sol 233, T081-3429 1592,
www.alberguedeolinda.com.br.
HI youth hostel with doubles or fan-cooled 8-bed dorms with shared en suite bathroom. The hostel has a tropical garden, TV room, and a shady area with hammocks next to a pool.

$$ Pousada d'Olinda
P João Alfredo 178, T081-3494 2559,
www.pousadadolinda.com.br.
Great location. Basic dorms and doubles around a pool, garden and communal breakfast area. English, French, German Arabic and Spanish spoken.

$$ Pousada dos Quatro Cantos
R Prudente de Morais 441, T081-3429 0220,
www.pousada4cantos.com.br.
A large converted townhouse with a little walled garden and terraces. The maze of bright rooms and suites are decorated with Pernambuco arts and crafts and furnished mostly with antiques. Warm, welcoming and full of character.

$$ Pousada Luar de Olinda
R do Amparo, 183, T081-3439 1162,
www.pousadaluardeolinda.com.br.
Well located at the heart of the historical centre. Basic but with good views and friendly service. A/c rooms.

$$ Pousada São Francisco
R do Sol 127, T081-3429 2109,
www.pousadasaofrancisco.com.br.
Outside the historic centre on a busy road but within walking distance. Well-kept and airy a/c rooms with little terraces, slate floors and pokey bathrooms housed in a

modern 2-storey hotel overlooking a pool and bar area.

$$ São Pedro
R 27 Janeiro 95, T081-3439 9546,
www.pousadapedro.com.
Quiet little *pousada* with a walled garden, a small pool shaded by frangipani and bamboo. Has a delightful breakfast area and lobby decorated with art and antiques. The rustic rooms are tiny especially on the lower floors.

Restaurants

In the evening stalls around the cathedral serve *tapioca* (a manioc pancake stuffed with cheese, fruit or syrup) and cheap and very tasty *acarajé* (similar to falafel, stuffed with prawn paste). The traditional Olinda drinks, *pau do índio* (with 32 herbs) and *retetel* are manufactured on R do Amparo.

There are a number of *lanchonetes* and fast-food options along the seafront, including **Mama Luise** and **Gibi** (Av Min Marcos Freire), and **Leque Moleque** (Av Sigismundo Gonçalves 537).

$$$ Oficina do Sabor
R do Amparo 355, T081-3429 3331,
www.oficinadosabor.com.
Traditional Lusitanian dishes like Portuguese *bacalhau* (salted codfish) and *surubim* (catfish) in passion fruit soubise with sautéed sweet potato and rice. There are plenty of vegetarian options.

$$ Creperia
R Prudente de Morais 168, T081-3429 2935.
Savoury and sweep crêpes, pizzas and *petiscos* (bar snacks) served to a middle-class crowd in an open-plan dining area.

$$ Maison do Bonfim
R do Bonfim 115, T081-3429 1674.
English-trained chef Jeff Colas serves a choice of European dishes like mini vol-au-vent de roquefort and *carpaccio com rúcula e tomate seco e mostarda francesa* (carpaccio with rocket and sun-dried tomato with

French mustard) in this attractive Portuguese townhouse on the most elegant colonial street in the city.

Bars and clubs

Like Recife, Olinda is known for its vibrant nightlife. Beginning at dusk, but best after 2100, the Alto da Sé becomes the scene of a small street fair, with arts, crafts, makeshift bars, barbecue stands, and impromptu traditional music. Every Fri night band musicians walk the streets serenading passers-by. Each Sun from 1 Jan to **Carnaval** there is a mini carnival in the streets of the city, with live music and dancing.

Bodega do Véio
R do Amparo 212, T081-3429 0185, www.casadeolinda.com.
An Olinda institution run by Edival Hermínio with live music Thu-Sun. Sat nights are generally devoted to *pe na serra forró*. Great *petiscos* (especially the *prato frio*) and caipirinhas, and always a vibrant crowd.

Cantinho da Sé
Ladeira da Sé 305, www.facebook.com/ Cantinho-da-Sé.
Lively, good view of Recife, crêpes and *petiscos* and often with live music at weekends.

Marola
Tr Av Dantas Barreto 66, T081-3429 2499, www.marolabar.blogspot.co.uk.
Funky wooden *barraca* on the rocky shoreline, specializing in seafood. Great *caiprifrutas* (frozen fruit drink with vodka). Can get crowded. Recommended.

Preto Velho
Alto da Sé, Live samba at weekends.
Especially lively on Sat.

Festivals

Feb Carnaval. Thousands of people dance through the narrow streets of the old city to the sound of the *frevo*, the brash energetic music that normally accompanies a lively dance performed with umbrellas. The local people decorate them with streamers and straw dolls, and form themselves into costumed groups (*blocos*), which you can join as they pass (don't take valuables). Among the best-known *blocos*, which carry life-size dolls, are **O homem da meianoite** (Midnight Man), **A Corda** (a pun on 'the rope' and 'acorda' – wake up!), which parades in the early hours, **Pitombeira** and **Elefantes**. Olinda's carnival continues on Ash Wed, but is much more low-key, *a quarta-feira do batata* (Potato Wednesday, named after a waiter who claimed his right to celebrate Carnaval after being on duty during the official celebrations). The streets are very crowded with people dancing and drinking non-stop. The local cocktail, *capeta* (guaraná powder, sweet skimmed milk and vodka) is designed to keep you going.
12-15 Mar Foundation Day, 3 days of music and dancing, night-time only.

What to do

Local guides with ID cards wait in Praça do Carmo; some are former street children and half the fee (about US$15 for a full 1- to 3-hr tour of the city in English, French, Spanish, Italian and German) goes to the charity **ACNO** (the association of native guides of Olinda). Gerinaldo, an ACNO senior guide, takes bookings for all guides, T081-9879 92828.
Cariri Ecotours, *based in Natal but operates throughout the region, T081-9660 1818, www.caririecotours.com.br.* Trips throughout Pernambuco and the Northeast. Excellent service and itineraries, including tailor-made options.

Some 60 km south of Recife, Porto de Galinhas (meaning 'port of chickens' because slaves were smuggled here in chicken crates) was one of the first of a string of low-key beach resorts discovered in the 1990s. Back then it was little more than a beach and two sandy streets. The myth of its tranquil charm endures, but it is only a myth. Today Porto de Galinhas is well on its way to becoming a full-scale resort comparable those near Porto Seguro in Bahia. The sandy streets are now paved and lined with shops and restaurants, while the beaches are backed with *pousadas* and resort hotels for several kilometres north and south of the town. But it has sandy beaches and natural pools in the reef close to the shore, where you can swim at high tide.

Listings Porto de Galinhas

Tourist information

Centro de Informacões Turisticas
R da Beijupirá s/n, T081-3552 1461.
The tourist centre has maps, and information on transport, hotels and tour operators.

Where to stay

There are plenty of cheap *pousadas* and hotels in town along R da Esperança and its continuation R Manoel Uchôa; also along R Beijapurá, which runs off R da Esperança.

$$$$ Village Porto de Galinhas
7 km from town, T081-3552 2945,
www.villageportodegalinhas.com.br.
All-inclusive family beach resort right on the ocean and with a large pool, restaurant, a/c rooms.

$$ HI Liras da Poesia
Praça 18, T081-3552 2332, www.
hostelportodegalinhas.com.br.
Very clean, well-kept, a/c rooms and several dorms. To get there take the right turn

(away from the sea) off R Beijupira opposite R Carauna and walk inland for 400 m. The *hostel* is in a little *praça* 150 m before the Estrada Maracaipe.

What to do

Diving
AICA Diving, *Nossa Senhora do Ó, T081-3552 1895, www.aicadiving.com.br.* Run by Mida and Miguel. For diving and canoeing trips, as well as excursions to Santo Aleixo Island.

Transport

There is no *rodoviária;* buses stop and depart from the entrance to town. Buses and minivans run to **Recife**, at least hourly. Some hotels offer transfers, about U$40 per car, for up to 4 people in a taxi sent by the hotel, and will have your name on a placard. The journey now takes about 40 mins from the airport since the inauguration of the expressway Rota do Atlântico in 2014.

Fernando de Noronha island rises from the deep, on the eastern edge of the mid-Atlantic ridge 350 km off the coast. It is blessed with exceptional natural beauty: rugged like the west of Ireland, covered in *maquis* like Corsica and fringed by some of the cleanest and most beautiful beaches in the Atlantic. Many of the beaches are exposed to the full force of the ocean and pummelled by powerful bottle-green surf that has earned the island the nickname 'the Hawaii of the Atlantic'. Surf championships are held on Cacimba do Padre Beach. However, there are numerous coves where the sea is kinder and the broad beaches are dotted with deep clear-water rock pools busy with juvenile reef fish. The water changes through shades of aquamarine to deep indigo and is as limpid as any on earth. Diving here rivals Mexico's Cozumel and the Turks and Caicos.

Despite the fact that two-thirds of the island is settled, Noronha is an important nesting ground for turtles and marine birds: both the island itself and the seas around it are a marine park, protected by Instituto Chico Mendes de Conservação da Biodiversidade (ICMBio). All that is needed to make it a sanctuary of international standing is to remove the non-native feral monitor lizards (brought here in the 20th century to kill rats), the goats and the abundant cats and dogs. Tourism, however, is controlled and only limited numbers can visit the island at any time. Book well in advance.

Essential Fernando de Noronha

Access

Flights to the island from Recife and Natal are run by **TRIP** (www.voetrip.com.br) or from Recife by **GOL** (www.voegol.com.br). **CVC** (www.cruisevacationcenter.com) operates a small cruise liner, which sails from Recife to Noronha and then back to Recife via Fortaleza and Natal. See Transport, page 52.

Getting around

Buggy hire, motorbike hire and jeep tours are available in town.

Tip...
Bring repellent, although there are far fewer mosquitos here than on the coast.

When to go

The 'rainy' season is April to July. The vegetation turns brown in the dry season (August to March), but the sun shines all year round.

Time

Noronha is one hour later than Brazilian Standard Time.

Entry fee

Entry to the island is limited and there is a tax of US$15 per day for the first week of your stay. In the second week the tax increases each day.

Money

Take sufficient reais as it's difficult to change money.

Sights

The island is in reality an archipelago comprising one principal land mass and dozens of stony rocky outcrops. Some of the best beaches lie immediately south of the town, clustered around an imposing granite pinnacle of **Morro do Pico**. The most beautiful are **Conceição**, **Boldró**, **Americano**, **Baía do Sancho**, **Cacimba do Padre** and the turquoise cove at **Baía dos Porcos**, which sits on the edge of the beginning of the marine park. Beyond is the **Baía dos Golfinhos**, with a lookout point for watching the spinner dolphins in the bay. On the south, or windward side, there are fewer beaches, higher cliffs and the whole coastline and offshore islands are part of the marine park. As with dive sites, Instituto Chico Mendes de Conservação da Biodiversidade (ICMBio) restricts bathing in low-tide pools and other sensitive areas to protect the environment.

There are good opportunities for hiking, horse riding and mountain biking. A guide will take you to the marine park and to beaches such as **Atalaia**, which has the best snorkelling.

Wildlife and conservation

The island is a UNESCO World Heritage Site. It may look like an ecological paradise but it has been the victim of much degradation. Almost all of the native vegetation was chopped down in the 19th century, when the island was used as a prison, to prevent prisoners from hiding or making rafts. A giant native rodent, recorded by Amerigo Vespucci, was wiped out and linseed, feral cats, dogs, goats, rats, mice, tegu (*teju* in Portuguese) lizards and cavies were introduced in the 16th century. These continue to damage bird- and turtle-nesting sites and native vegetation.

Nonetheless, the island remains an important sanctuary for sea bird species. Ruddy turnstone (*Arenaria interpres*), black and brown noddy (*Anous minutus and stolidus*), sooty tern (*Onychoprion fuscatus*), white tern (*Gygis alba*), red-billed and white-tailed

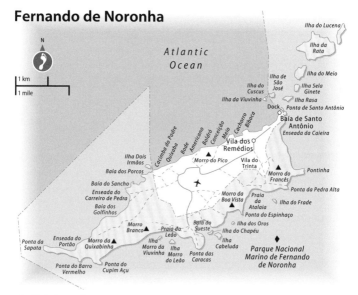

Fernando de Noronha

Atlantic Ocean

N

1 km
1 mile

Ilha do Lucena
Ilha da Rata
Ilha do Meio
Ilha de São José
Ilha do Cuscus
Ilha Sela Ginete
Ilha da Viuvinha
Ilha Rasa
Dock
Ponta de Santo Antônio
Baía de Santo Antônio
Enseada da Caieira
Cacimba do Padre
Quixaba
Bode
Americano
Boldró
Conceição
Meio
Cachorro
Biboca
Vila dos Remédios
Morro do Pico
Vila do Trinta
Ilha Dois Irmãos
Baía dos Porcos
Morro do Francês
Pontinha
Baía do Sancho
Ponta da Pedra Alta
Enseada do Carreiro de Pedra
Morro da Boa Vista
Praia da Atalaia
Ilha do Frade
Baía dos Golfinhos
Ponta do Espinhaço
Morro Branco
Praia do Leão
Ilha dos Oros
Baía do Sueste
Ilha do Chapéu
Ponta da Sapata
Enseada do Portão
Morro da Quixabinha
Ilha Morro da Viuvinha
Ilha Morro do Leão
Ponta das Caracas
Ilha Cabeluda
Parque Nacional Marino de Fernando de Noronha
Ponta do Barro Vermelho
Ponta do Cupim Açu

BACKGROUND
Fernando de Noronha

The island was discovered in 1503 by Amerigo Vespucci and was for a time a pirate lair. In 1738 the Portuguese built a charming little baroque church, Nossa Senhora dos Remedios, some attractive administrative buildings and a fort, O Forte dos Remédios, which was used as a prison for political dissidents by the military dictatorship in the late 20th century. The most famous was the communist leader Luis Carlos Prestes, who led the famous long march, the Prestes Column, in 1925-1927. Many people were tortured and murdered here.

The islands were occupied by the USA during the Second World War and used as a naval base. US guns sit outside the *prefeitura* in the centre of the main town, Vila dos Remédios, which overlooks the coast on the eastern shore.

tropicbird (*Phaethon aethereus* and *Phaethon lepturus*), masked, red-footed and brown booby (*Sula dactylatram*, *Sula sula* and *Sula leucogaster*) and magnificent frigatebird (*Fregata magnificens*) all nest here. Some endemic bird species still survive: the Noronha vireo (*Vireo gracilirostris*); a tyrant flycatcher, the Noronha elaenia or cucuruta (*Elaenia spectabilis reidleyana*); and the Noronha eared dove or arribaçá (*Zenaida auriculata noronha*). There is an endemic lizard (*Mabuya maculate*) and at least 5% of the fish species are unique to the archipelago. The most spectacular animals are the nesting hawksbill (*Eretmochelys imbricata*) and green turtles (*Chelonia mydas*), and the spinner dolphins (*Stenella longirostris*). Good terrestrial wildlife guides are non-existent on Noronha. There are a number of reasonable dive shops; though ichthyological knowledge is minimal.

Listings Fernando de Noronha *map p50*

Tourist information

For information see www.noronha.pe. gov.br or www.ilhadenoronha.com.br.

Instituto Chico Mendes de Conservação da Biodiversidade (ICMBio) has imposed rigorous rules to prevent damage to the nature reserve and everything, from development to cultivation of food crops to fishing, is strictly administered. Many locals are now dependent on tourism and most food is brought from the mainland.

Where to stay

Some of the most luxurious hotels on the island are built on illegally occupied land and are not listed here.

$$$$ Solar dos Ventos
Near the airstrip, T081-3619 1347,
www.pousadasolardosventos.com.br.
Well-appointed wood, brick and tile bungalows with a spectacular bay view. Friendly owners.

$$$$ Zé Maria
R Nice Cordeirol, Floresta Velha, T081-3619 1258, www.pousadazemaria.com.br.
Spacious bungalows with cream tile floors, hardwood ceilings and generous beds. Verandas and hammocks have views out to the Morro do Pico. The highlight is the delicious, but small deep-blue half-moon pool.

$$$ Pousada do Vale
300 m from Vila dos Remedios town centre, T081-3619 1293, www.pousadadovale.com.

Friendly, well-run *pousada* with comfortable en suite rooms decorated with mosaics. The best are the duplex wooden bungalows.

$$$ Pousada Recanto dos Corais
Conj Residencial Floresta Nova, T081-3619 1147, www.pousadacorais.com.br.
10 simple a/c rooms, small pool.

Restaurants

$$$ Mergulhão
Porto Santo Antonio, T081-3619 0215, www.mergulhaonoronha.com.br.
Modern Bahian food served outdoors, best time is late afternoon, when the sun is lower. Lovely sunset view. At lunchtime bring a hat to shield yourself from the hot sun. Busy, especially in high season. When making a reservation ask for a table with a view.

$ Açai e Raizes
BR-363, Floresta Velha.
Roadside sandwich bar with snacks, puddings and delicious cream of *cupuaçu* and *açai*.

Bars and clubs

Vila dos Remédios town, which is the size of a postage stamp, has several bars with lively weekend *forró* from 2200 on weekends, and a bar with live reggae nightly in high season.

What to do

It is possible to see hatching turtles in season; for details, contact **Fundação Pró-Tamar**, Alameda Boldró s/n, Caixa Postal 50, CEP 53990-000, Fernando de Noronha, T081-3619 1171, www.tamar.org.br/base.php?cod=20.

Diving
The main dive shops in Noronha all offer the same dive locations, as well as dive 'baptism' for complete beginners. Diving costs US$65-140 for 2 tanks and is by far the best in Brazil aside from Atol das Rocas (2 days off Bahia); if you are on a tight budget shop around. Some companies also run longer live-aboard trips. The principal operators are: **Atlantis Divers** (T081-3619 1371, www.atlantisdivers.com.br); **Águas Claras** (T081-3619 1225, www.aguasclaras-fn.com.br); and **Noronha Divers** (T081-3619 1112, www.noronhadivers.com.br). **Trip Noronha**, *T019-3808 5265, www.tripnoronha.com.br.* Offer tours around the island, attractive *pousada* packages and dive trips.

Transport

Air   Daily flights to **Recife** with TRIP (1 hr 20 mins, from US$200 return). To **Natal** with **TRIP** (1 hr, US$200 return). Daily flights to **Recife** with GOL (1 hr to Recife, from US$200). **GOL** also offers daily flights to **São Paulo** with a stopover in Recife.

West of Recife

centres for arts and crafts, and famous festivals

Bezerros
The town of Bezerros (population 52,000), 15 km west of Recife on the BR-232, is set next to the Rio Ipojuca. It has some old houses, fine *praças* and churches. Some, like the **Igreja de Nossa Senhora dos Homens Pretos**, São José and the **Capela de Nossa Senhora**, date from the 19th century. The former railway station has been converted into the **Estação da Cultura**, with shows and other cultural performances. The city's best-known artist and poet is José Borges (born 1935), whose work has been exhibited internationally, however, the main attraction is handicrafts, which are found in the district of **Encruzilhada de São João** and in shops dotted around the centre. Most typical are the Papangu masks, made of painted papier mâché, and used during Carnaval. Wooden toys are also popular, as well as items made from leather and clay. About 10 km from the centre of Bezerros, near the

village of Serra Negra, a small ecotourism park, **Serra Negra Ecological Tourism Trail**, has been set up. Trails lead to caves and springs; the flora is typical of the *agreste*.

Carnaval in Bezerros is famed throughout Brazil and is known as **Folia do Papangu** (see Festivals, below).

Caruaru

Situated 134 km west of Recife, the small town of Caruaru (population 254,000, altitude 554 m) in the *sertão* is famous for its huge **Festas Juninas**, held throughout June (see page 64), and its little clay figures (*figurinhas* or *bonecas de barro*) originated by Mestre Vitalino (1909-1963) which are very typical of Northeast Brazil. Most of the potters live at **Alto da Moura**, 6 km away, where you can visit the **Casa Museu Mestre Vitalino** ⓘ *buses from Caruaru, a bumpy 30-min ride, US$1.80*, once owned by Vitalino and containing personal objects and photographs, but no examples of his work. UNESCO has recognized the area as the largest centre of figurative art in the Americas. It is also possible to buy the arts and crafts in Caruaru itself. The town hosts a number of markets, which were originally devoted to foodstuffs but which now also sell arts and crafts. The most famous is the **Feira da Sulanca**, held in the city centre on Tuesdays, with some 10,000 stalls and 40,000 visitors.

The *rodoviária* is 4 km west of town; buses from Recife stop in the town centre. Alight here and look for the Livraria Estudantil (bookshop), at Rua Duque de Caxias as a continuation of Rua Vigário Freire on the corner of Avenida Rio Branco; this is a useful landmark. Follow the pedestrianized lane downhill from the bookshop, turn right on Rua 15 de Novembro to the first junction, 13 de Maio; turn left, and finally cross the river to the Feira do Artesanato (arts and crafts market).

During the **Festas Juninas**, it's possible to take a tourist train, **Trem do Forró**, from Recife, which is a very spirited affair with bars, and bands playing in the carriages. The train has been running every June for over 25 years, U$27. See www.facebook.com/TremDoForro and www.caruaru.pe.gov.br for information.

Fazenda Nova and Nova Jerusalém

During Easter Week each year, various agencies run package tours to the little country town of **Fazenda Nova**, 23 km from Caruaru. Just outside the town is **Nova Jerusalém**. Every day from the day before Palm Sunday up to Easter Saturday, an annual Passion play is enacted here on an open-air site about one third the size of the historic quarter of Jerusalem. Nine stages are used to depict scenes from the Passion of Christ, which is presented using 50 actors and 500 extras to re-enact the story with the audience following in their footsteps. *TV Globo* stars often play the starring roles and the sound and lighting effects are state of the art. Performances begin at 1800 and last for about three hours.

There is little accommodation in Nova Jerusalém/Fazenda Nova and it is usually full during the Passion. **Empetur** in Recife/Olinda has details of agencies that offer trips. During the Easter period there are direct bus services from Recife (and from Caruaru at other times).

Listings West of Recife

Tourist information

Bezerros

Associação dos Artesãos de Bezerros
R Luiz de Souza 11 T081-9969 0151.
The artisans' association.

Secretaria de Turismo
R 15 de Novembro s/n, Centro,
T081-3728 6706.

Where to stay

Caruaru
A large number of cheap *hospedarias* can be found around the central square, Praça Getúlio Vargas.

$$$ Grande Hotel São Vicente de Paulo
Av Rio Branco 365, T081-3721 5011, www.grandehotelcaruaru.com.br.
A reasonable, centrally located hotel with a/c, laundry, garage, bar, restaurant, pool and TV. It also houses the local cinema.

$$ Center Plaza
7 de Setembro 84, T081-3722 4011.
Rooms and more expensive suites. The breakfast is good and there's a pool. As the hotel is in the town centre it can be noisy, but otherwise recommended.

$$ Central
R Vigario Freire 71, T081-3721 5880, http://citihoteis.com.br.
Suites or rooms, all with a/c, TV, good breakfast, in the centre. Recommended.

Festivals

Bezerros
Feb Carnaval celebrations are famous throughout Brazil and known as **Folia do Papangu**. Papangu characters wear masks that resemble a cross between a bear and a devil and are covered from head to foot in a costume like a bear skin (or an all-covering white tunic).
Jun São João.

Caruaru
Mar/Apr Semana Santa, Holy Week, with lots of folklore and handicraft events.
18-22 May The **city anniversary**.
13 Jun Santo Antônio.
24 Jun São João, a particularly huge *forró* festival, part of Caruaru's **Festas Juninas**.

The whole town lights up with dancing, traditional foods, parties like the **Sapadrilha**, when the women dress as men, and the **Gaydrilha**, where the men dress as women, and there is even a *Trem do Forró*, which runs from Recife to Caruaru, rocking the whole way to the rhythms.
Sep Micaru, a street carnival. Also in Sep is **Vaquejada**, a Brazilian cross between rodeo and bullfighting; biggest in the Northeast.

Shopping

Bezerros
The city's main attraction is handicrafts, which are found in the district of **Encruzilhada de São João**; items in leather, clay, wood, papier mâché and much more.

Caruaru
Caruaru is most famous for its markets which, combined, are responsible for about 70% of the city's income. The **Feira da Sulanca** is basically a clothes market supplied mostly by local manufacture, but also on sale are jewellery, souvenirs, food, flowers and anything else that can go for a good price. The most important day is Mon. There is also the **Feira Livre** or **do Troca-Troca** (free, or barter market). On the same site, Parque 18 de Maio, is the **Feira do Artesanato**, leather goods, ceramics, hammocks, basketware and all the popular crafts of the region; it is tourist orientated but it is on a grand scale and is open daily 0800-1800.

Transport

Caruaru
Bus Buses from the centre, at the same place the Recife buses stop, to the *rodoviária*, US$1.40. Many buses to **Recife**, 2 hrs express, US$12.50. Bus to **Fazenda Nova** at 1030, 1 hr, US$7.50, returns to Caruaru at 1330.

Paraíba

Travellers used to bypass Paraíba, but they are beginning to discover that there are many reasons to stop. The beaches are some of Brazil's best and least spoilt. Some of the most important archaeological sites in the Americas are tucked away in the haunting, rugged landscapes of its interior and the state capital, João Pessoa, is an attractive colonial city with a lively nightlife. Each year in June, Campina Grande, on the edge of the *sertão*, hosts one of the country's biggest festivals, the Festa do São João, with live music and up to a million people dancing *forró* into the small hours.

The dense tropical forest that once covered the entire coastal strip now survives only in patches, one of which is within the city of João Pessoa; forming one of the largest urban wilderness areas in the world. The seaboard is marked for much of its length by offshore reefs. Inland from the coastal plain the Zona da Mata is an abrupt line of hills and plateaux, a transitional region between the humid coast and the much drier interior. Most people live in this zone, especially in and around the state capital and a couple of other industrial centres.

João Pessoa and around

state capital with a small town atmosphere and colonial architecture

João Pessoa (population 598,000) is set on the Rio Paraíba amid tropical forest. The atmosphere is restful and laid-back, yet there are plenty of bars and restaurants along the beachfront, which are particularly popular at weekends. The main beach, Tambaú, is pleasant but rather built up. From Recife, it is a two-hour bus ride (126 km), on a good road through sugar plantations, to João Pessoa.

Essential João Pessoa

Finding your feet

Presidente Castro Pinto Airport is 11 km south of the centre. A taxi from the airport to centre costs US$11, to Tambaú US$32. The *rodoviária* (Terminal Rodoviário Severino Camelo) is 10 minutes west of the centre. A taxi from the bus station to the centre costs US$3.50, to Tambaú US$7.40.

Sights

The well-preserved Centro Histórico has several churches and monasteries that are worth seeing. The **Centro Cultural São Francisco** ① *Praça São Francisco 221, T083-3218 4505 www.igrejadesaofranciscopb.org, Mon-Fri 0830-1700 and Sat-Sun 0900-1400, US$1.20*, one of the most important baroque structures in Brazil, includes the beautiful 16th-century church of São Francisco and the Convento de Santo Antônio, which houses the **Museu Sacro e de Arte Popular**, with a magnificent collection of colonial artefacts. This is the best point to see the sunset over the forest.

① João Pessoa orientation

→ **João Pessoa maps**
1 João Pessoa orientation, page 56
2 Tambaú & Manaíra, page 58

BACKGROUND
João Pessoa

The Portuguese did not gain a foothold on this part of the coast until the end of the 16th century. Their fort became the city of Filipéia, which grew to become the third largest in Brazil. This was later re-named Parahyba and then João Pessoa, in honour of the once state governor who refused to form alliances with other powerful politicians during the 1930s run for the vice-presidency. This led to his assassination, an event that swept his running mate, the fascist Getúlio Vargas, to power. Pessoa's *nego* ('I refuse') is written on the state's flag.

Other tourist points include the **Casa da Pólvora**, an old gunpowder store which has become the city museum, and **Museu Fotográfico Walfredo Rodrígues** ⓘ *Ladeira de São Francisco, Mon-Fri 0800-1200 and 1330-1700*. The **Teatro Santa Rosa** ⓘ *Praça Pedro Américo, Varadouro, T083-3218 4382, Mon-Fri 0800-1200 and 1330-1800*, was built in 1886 with a wooden ceiling and walls. The **Espaço Cultural José Lins de Rego** ⓘ *R Abdias Gomes de Almeida 800, Tambauzinho, T083-3243 0707, Mon-Fri 0900-1800*, a cultural centre named after the novelist, includes an art gallery, history and science museums, several theatres, cinema and a planetarium. The **Fundação Casa de José Américo** ⓘ *Av Cabo Branco 3336, T083-3214 8523*, should be visited by those interested in modern literature and politics; it is in the former house of the novelist and sociologist.

João Pessoa prides itself in being a green city and is called 'Cidade Verde'. Its parks include the 17-ha **Parque Arruda Câmara**, also known as Bica, located north of the centre in the neighbourhood of Roger; it has walking trails, an 18th-century fountain, an aviary and a small zoo. **Parque Solon de Lucena** or **Lagoa** is a lake surrounded by impressive palms in the centre of town, the city's main avenues and bus lines go around it. **Mata** or **Manancial do Bouraquinho** is a 471-ha nature reserve of native Mata Atlântica, one of the largest urban forest reserves in the world. It is located south of the centre and administered by Instituto Chico Mendes de Conservação da Biodiversidade (ICMBio) ⓘ *T083-3244 2725, 3244 4100*, which organizes guided walks; access is otherwise restricted.

Urban beaches

João Pessoa's urban beachfront stretches for some 30 km from **Ponta do Seixas** (south) to **Cabedelo** (north); the ocean is turquoise green and there is a backdrop of lush coastal vegetation. By the more populated urban areas the water is polluted, but away from town the beaches are reasonably clean; some spots are calm and suitable for swimming while others are best for surfing.

The beach of **Tambaú** lies right in the centre of this 30-km-long strip and is, for all intents and purposes, the centre of the João Pessoa. It has many hotels, restaurants, the state tourism centre and clean sand. It is about 7 km from the old colonial city centre along Avenida Presidente Epitáceo Pessoa. The pier by **Hotel Tambaú** has pleasant views (take bus No 510 'Tambaú' from outside the *rodoviária* or the city centre, alight at Hotel Tropical Tambaú). South of Tambaú are **Praia de Cabo Branco** and **Praia do Seixas** and, to the north, are the beaches

Tip...
Praia Ponta do Seixas, as well as the adjacent, more urbanized, Praia do Cabo Branco to the north and Praia do Penha to the south are much better for swimming than Tambaú.

of **Manaíra**, **Bessa**, **Intermares**, **Poço** and **Camboinha**, before reaching the port of Cabedelo (see below).

② Tambaú & Manaíra

➡ **João Pessoa maps**
1 João Pessoa orientation, page 56
2 Tambaú & Manaíra, page 58

Nobile Inn Royal Praia **5**
Pousada Verde Mar **10**
Solar Filipéia **9**
Tropical Tambaú **3**
Xênius **4**

Where to stay 🛏
Hostel Manaíra **2**
Littoral **1**
Littoral Tambaú Flat **6**

Restaurants 🍴
Adega do Alfredo **1**
Mangai **3**

Around João Pessoa

About 14 km south of the centre, down the coast, is the **Cabo Branco** lighthouse at the little forested cape of **Ponta do Seixas**, the 'Cape of the Rising Sun', the most easterly point of continental Brazil and South America (34° 46' 36" W), and thus the first place in the Americas where the sun rises. There is a panoramic view from the cliff top and the beautiful beach below, **Praia Ponta do Seixas**; coming here to watch sunrise is one of João Pessoa's most traditional romantic experiences.

Penha has a 19th-century church where devotees petition the saints for succour, leaving notes all over the building and crawling up the steps to the nave in obeisance. Take bus No 507 'Cabo Branco' from outside the *rodoviária* to the end of the line and hike up to the lighthouse from there. Or at low tide you can walk from Tambaú to Ponta do Seixas in about two hours.

The port of **Cabedelo**, on a peninsula between the Rio Paraíba and the Atlantic Ocean, is 18 km north by road or rail. Here, Km 0 marks the beginning of the **Transamazônica Highway**. At the tip of the peninsula are the impressive but run-down walls of the 17th-century fortress of **Santa Catarina**, in the middle of the commercial port. The **Mercado de Artesanato** is at Praça Getúlio Vergas in the centre.

The estuary of the Rio Paraíba has several islands; there is a regular boat service between Cabedelo and the fishing villages of **Costinha** and **Forte Velho** on the north bank; Costinha had a whaling station until the early 1980s.

The beaches between João Pessoa and Cabedelo have many bars and restaurants and are very popular with the locals on summer weekends (**Bar do Sumé**, Rua Beira Mar 171, Praia Ponta do Mato, Cabedelo, has good fish and seafood). Take a bus marked 'Cabedelo–Poço' for the beach as most 'Cabedelo' buses go inland along the Transamazônica. A taxi from Tambaú to Cabedelo costs US$17.50.

At Km 3 of the Transamazônica, about 12 km from João Pessoa, is the access to **Jacaré**, a pleasant beach on the Rio Paraíba (take the 'Cabedelo' bus and walk 1.5 km or take the train and walk 1 km, taxi from Tambaú US$7). There are several bars along the riverfront where people congregate to watch the lovely sunset to the sounds of Ravel's *Bolero*. Here you can hire a boat along the river to visit the mangroves or ride in an ultralight aircraft. See What to do, page 61.

From Tambaú tour boats leave for **Picãozinho**, a group of coral reefs about 700 m from the coast, which at low tide turn into pools of crystalline water, suitable for snorkelling (US$14 per person). Further north, boats leave from Praia de Camboinha to **Areia Vermelha**, a large sandbank surrounded by corals. This becomes exposed at low tide, around the full and new moon, and is a popular bathing spot (US$14 per person tour, US$3.50 per person transport in a *jangada*). Floating bars are set up at both locations, travel agencies arrange trips.

Listings João Pessoa *maps p56 and p58*

Tourist information

João Pessoa

PBTUR
Centro Turístico Almte Tamandaré 100, Tambaú, T083-3214 8185. Open 0800-1800; other branches at the rodoviária, *and airport.*
Provides useful information, pamphlets and maps. Some staff speak good English, and some French.

Where to stay

João Pessoa
The town's main attractions are its beaches, where most tourists stay. Hotels in the centre are poorer and tend to cater for business clients. The centre is very quiet after dark and it is difficult to find a restaurant. Cheaper hotels can be found near the *rodoviária*; look carefully as some are sleazy. The most convenient beach and the focus of nightlife and restaurants is Tambaú. There are good restaurants and a few hotels in Manaíra, north of Tambaú. There are also a few in the southern beach suburb of Cabo Branco, but this is quieter and has fewer eating options.

$$ Guarany Hotel
R Almeida Barreto 181 and 13 de Maio, T083-2106 8787, www.hotelguarani.com.br.
A pleasant, safe, good-value establishment with a self-service restaurant. Cheaper in low season, or without a/c and TV.

$$ Hotel JR
R João Ramalho de Andrade, T083-2106 8700, www.hoteljr.com.br.
Business hotel with basic facilities and a restaurant. The largest and most comfortable in the centre.

Urban beaches
Accommodation can also be found in the outer beaches such as **Camboinha** and **Seixas**, and in **Cabedelo**.

$$$ Littoral Hotel
Av Cabo Branco 2172, T083-2106 1100, www.hotellittoral.com.br.
An unprepossessing block in a great seafront location. With a pleasant swimming pool set in leafy gardens and modern, simply appointed rooms with small balconies. There are often discounts for online advanced bookings.

$$$ Littoral Tambaú Flat
Av Epitacio Pessoa 5000, T083-2107 8800,
www.littoral.com.br.
Furnished apartments with a pool and sauna.
Cheaper in low season.

$$$ Nobile Inn Royal Praia
R Coração de Jesus s/n, T083-2106 3000.
Comfortable a/c rooms with fridges, pool.

$$$ Tropical Tambaú
Av Alm Tamandaré 229, T083-2107 1900,
www.tropicalhotel.com.br.
An enormous round building on the
seafront which looks like a rocket-launching
station and has comfortable motel-style
rooms around its perimeter. Good service.
Recommended.

$$$ Xênius
Av Cabo Branco 1262, T083-3015 3535,
-www.xeniushotel.com.br.
Popular standard 4-star hotel with a pool,
good restaurant. Well-kept but standard a/c
rooms, low-season reductions.

$$ Pousada Verde Mar
Av João Maurício 293, T083-3576 1718.
Oceanfront hotel with clean and well-kept
en suite rooms with TV and a/c. Basic but
good breakfast. Bathroom is separated from
the room by an opaque glass door. Rooms
close to reception are noisy.

$$ Solar Filipéia
R Isidro Gomes 44, Tambaú, T083-3219 3744,
www.hotelfilipeia.com.br.
Great location, large, bright rooms with
bathrooms in tile and black marble and good
service. Good value. In need of renovation.

$ Hostel Manaíra
R Major Ciraulo 380, Manaíra, T083-
3247 1962, www.manairahostel.com.br.
Friendly hostel close to the beach, with
a pool, internet, barbecue, cable TV and
breakfast. A real bargain.

Restaurants

João Pessoa
There are few eating options in the city
centre. Locals used to eat at the stalls in
Parque Solon de Lucena next to the lake,
but now the park is going through a massive
redevelopment scheduled to finish in
summer 2016. New restaurants inside the
park are part of the project.

$ Recanto do Picuí
R Feliciano Dourado 198.
Regional food, many branches in town.

Urban beaches
Every evening on the beachfront, stalls sell
all kinds of snacks and barbecued meats. At
Cabo Branco there are many straw huts on
the beach serving cheap eats and seafood.

$$$ Adega do Alfredo
R Coração de Jesus s/n, T083-3226 3354.
Very popular traditional Portuguese
restaurant in the heart of the club and
bar area.

$$ Mangaí
Av General Édson Ramalho 696, Manaíra,
T083-3226 1615.
This is one of the best restaurants in the
Northeast to sample the region's cooking.
There are almost 100 different hot dishes to
choose from, sitting in copper tureens over a
traditional wood-fired stove some 20 m long.

Festivals

João Pessoa
Feb Pre-carnival celebrations in João
Pessoa are renowned: the *bloco* **Acorde
Miramar** opens the celebrations the Tue
before Carnaval. On Wed, known as **Quarta
Feira de Fogo**, thousands join the **Muriçocas
de Miramar**, forming a *bloco* second only to
Recife's **Galo da Madrugada** with as many as
300,000 people taking part.
5 Aug The street celebrations for the
patroness of the city, **Nossa Senhora das
Neves**, last for 10 days to the rhythm of *frevo*.

What to do

João Pessoa
Cliotur, *Av Alm Tamandaré 361, loja 04, T083-3247 4460, www.facebook.com/cliotur*. Trips to the *sertão*. Also offers light adventure activities.
Roge Turismo, Av manoel Morais 435, Manaíra, T083-2106 6900, www.rogetur.com.br. A large agency with a range of regional and city tours.

Transport

João Pessoa
Air The **airport**, T083-3041 4200, has flights to 12 cities including **Brasília**, **Fortaleza**, **Maceió**, **Recife** and **Salvador**. Avianca, **GOL** and **TAM** fly to **São Paulo** or **Rio**. Alternatively, the airline **GOL** flies from São Paulo or Rio to **Recife**, then provides free bus transport to João Pessoa.

Bus From the *rodoviária*, R Francisco Londres, Varadouro, 10 mins west of the centre, T083-3222 6567, or Lagoa (Parque Solon de Lucena), take bus No 510 for **Tambaú**, No 507 for **Cabo Branco**. All city buses stop at the *rodoviária* and most go via the Lagoa (Parque Solon de Lucena). The *rodoviária* has a luggage store and helpful **PBTUR** information booth.

Buses to **Recife** every 30 mins, US$7, 2½ hrs. To **Natal** with **Nordeste**, every 2 hrs, US$10-14 2½ hrs. To **Fortaleza**, 2 daily, 10 hrs, US$35. To **Campina Grande** with **Real**, every 30 mins, US$7, 2 hrs. To **Juazeiro do Norte**, 5 daily, US$35, 10 hrs. To **Salvador** 1 daily, US$50, 16 hrs.

Car hire All the principal Brazilian companies operate in João Pessoa, see www.aluguetdecarro.com.br.

Train The *ferroviária*, Av Sanhauá, Varadouro, T083-3221 4257, has train connections to **Bayeux** and **Santa Rita** in the west, and **Cabedelo** to the north.

Paraíba coast

some of the least developed beaches of the Northeast

The Paraíba coastline has 117 km of beautiful beaches and coves, surrounded by cliffs and coconut groves.

Tambaba
The best-known beach of the state is Tambaba, the only official nudist beach of the Northeast and one of only two in Brazil. It is located 49 km south of João Pessoa in a lovely setting: the green ocean, warm water, natural pools for swimming formed by the rocks, cliffs up to 20 m high full of caves, palms and lush vegetation. Two coves make up this famous beach: in the first beachwear is optional, while the second one is only for nudists. Strict rules of conduct are enforced: unaccompanied men are not allowed in this area and anyone behaving inappropriately will be asked to leave. The only infrastructure is one bar, where meals are available.

Access is from **Jacumã**, via the BR-101, 20 km south from João Pessoa to where the PB-018 goes 3 km east to Conde and continues 11 km to the beach of Jacumã; from here a dirt road goes 12 km south to Tambaba. Buses run hourly to Jacumã from the João Pessoa *rodoviária*. In summer, dune buggies can be hired at Jacumã to go to Tambaba. A buggy from João Pessoa to Tambaba costs US$21 per person (leaves 0930, returns 1730). A day-trip by taxi costs US$52.

Between Jacumã and Tambaba are several good beaches such as **Tabatinga**, which has many summer homes built on the cliffs, and **Coqueirinho**, which is surrounded by pleasant vegetation, and is good for bathing, surfing and exploring caves. There are plenty of cheap and mid-range *pousadas* at both and a very good seafood restaurant, Canyon de Coqueirinho, on the beach at Coqueirinho. Near the border with Pernambuco is the 10-km-long beach of **Pitimbu**.

Campina and around

The best beaches of northern Paraíba are in the vicinity of the fishing village of **Campina**; although there is little infrastructure in this area, the shore is worth a visit. Access is via a turn-off to the east at Km 73.5 of the BR-101, 42 km north of João Pessoa. It is 28 km along a dirt road (PB-025) to Praia Campina, with a wide stretch of fine sand, palms and hills in the background. Nearly 3 km south is **Praia do Oiteiro**, in which the white sand stands out in contrast with the multi-coloured cliffs and calm blue ocean. About 2 km north of Campina is **Barra do Mamanguape**, where **Instituto Chico Mendes de Conservação da Biodiversidade (ICMBio)** runs a preservation centre for the marine manatee.

Some 85 km from João Pessoa is **Baia da Traição**, a fishing village and access point for a number of beaches. Its name means 'Bay of Betrayal' and refers to the massacre of 500 residents of a sugar plantation in the 16th century. There is a reserve near the town where wood and string crafts are made by the local indigenous people, and an annual festival, **Festa do Toré**, takes place on 19 April. Fisherman offer boat tours to the area's less accessible beaches (US$14 per person). **Barra de Camaratuba**, 17 km north of Baia da Traição, is a popular surfing beach.

Listings Paraíba coast

Where to stay

Tambaba

$$ Jacuma's Lodge
Av Beira Mar, Praia de Jacumã, T083-3290 1977, www.jacuma.tur.br.
Very simple tiled a/c rooms decorated with lacy rugs, curtains and counterpanes sitting in a small hotel right on the beach. There's a pleasant shady pool area with tables, sun loungers and a paddling pool for children.

$$ Pousada Corais de Carapibus
Av Beira Mar, Carapebus, T083-3290 1179, www.coraisdecarapibus.com.br.

A few kilometres south of Jacumã. With bath, pool, restaurant and a nice breeze since it is located on a cliff across from the ocean.

Transport

Tambaba
Bus From Tambaba a dirt road leads 12 km north to the beach of **Jacumã**, from where the PB-018 goes 11 km west to **Conde** and continues 3 km to the BR-101, which runs 20 km north to **João Pessoa**. There are hourly buses from Jacumã to **João Pessoa** 0530-1900.

The Sertão

dry interior with ancient rock paintings and fossilized dinosaur footprints

The semi-arid region of thorn and bush that makes up the hinterland of the Northeast is known as the *sertão*. The Transamazônica runs right through the heart of the region, due west of João Pessoa as the BR-230, and along the axis of the state of Paraíba.

Campina Grande

Set in the Serra da Borborema, 551 m above sea level and 130 km west of João Pessoa, the second city in Paraíba has a very pleasant climate. It's worth a visit for its famous São João celebrations in June (see box, page 64), the largest of its kind in Brazil, although the town has little to keep you at other times.

Known as the 'porta do sertão' (door of the sertão), Campina Grande (population 340,500) is an important centre for light industry and an outlet for goods from most of Northeast Brazil. In the 1920s it was one of the most important cotton producing areas in the world; a decline in this industry brought a decrease in prosperity in the 1940s and 1950s and the diversification of industry to areas such as sisal and leather.

The city's two universities have been instrumental in technological development and reactivation of the local economy and today Campina Grande has the honour of making every single pair of Brazil's famous fashion flip-flops, Havaianas, which are sold all over the world.

Sights Avenida Floriano Peixoto is the main street running east–west through the entire city, with Praça da Bandeira at its centre. The **Museu Histórico de Campina Grande** ① Av Floriano Peixoto 825, Centro, T083-3310 6182, Tue-Sat 0800-1200, 1300-1700, is the city museum housed in a 19th-century building, with a very well-displayed photo and artefact collection reflecting the cycles of prosperity and poverty in the region. The **Museu do Algodão** ① R Benjamin Constant s/n, Estação Ferroviária, T083-8875 9854, Tue-Sat 0800-1200 and 1300-1700, free, has machines and related equipment used in the cotton industry in the 16th and 17th centuries. **Sitio São João** ① R Luiza Bezerra Mota, T083-9981 6529, daily 1000-2300, the new museum of 500 sq m, is a small village celebrating the culture of Northeast Brazil with local houses, food and music.

The **Teatro Municipal Severino Cabral** ① Av Floriano Peixoto, www.teatroseverinocabral. art.br, is a modern theatre where there are regular performances. The main parks in town are: the **Parque do Açude Novo** (Evaldo Cruz), a green area with playgrounds, fountains and restaurants; the nearby **Parque do Povo** with its forródromo where the main festivities of the city take place; and the **Açude Velho**, a park around a dam south of the centre. The **Mercado Central**, where a large roof has been built over several blocks of old buildings, sells regional crafts and produce and is worth a visit.

The new multimedia museum **Museu de Arte Popular da Paraíba (MAP)** ① R Dr Severino Cruz, T083-3310 9738, was designed by Oscar Niemeyer and is nicknamed três pandeiros (three tambourines), after the three circular structures that form the building, representing music, literature (de Cordel) and arts and crafts. The prominent Brazilian musicians Sivuca, Jackson do Pandeiro and Luiz Gonzaga are celebrated here.

Around Campina Grande

About 10 km north from Campina Grande is **Lagoa Seca**, where figures in wood and sacking are made, and there is a **Museu do Índio** ① Convento Ipuarana, T083-3366 1204, Mon-Fri 0700-1200, US$0.50. There is also a pousada with a pool, **Magia do Verde** (T083-99106 2761, www. magiadoverde.com.br).

Essential Campina Grande

Finding your feet

João Suassuna Airport is 7 km south of centre on the road to Caruaru. A taxi from the airport to the centre costs US$14. A city bus runs to Praça Clementino Procópio, behind Cine Capitólio. The rodoviária is a 20-minute bus ride from the centre.

FESTIVALS

Festas Juninas – the world's greatest barn dance

Carnaval is essentially an urban, black Brazilian celebration. The Festas Juninas, which take place throughout Brazil during June, are a rural celebration. While carnival pounds to samba, the Juninhas pulsate to the triangle and accordion of *forró*. Rather than wearing feathers and sequins, Juninas revellers dress up as *caipiras* (yokels) in tartan shirts and reed hats; and they eat *canjica* (maize porridge) and drink *quentão* (a Brazilian version of mulled wine). And they do it in enormous numbers. During the most important weekend of the festivals – the eve of St John's Day on 23 June – over one million mock-*caipiras* descend on the little backland towns of Campina Grande in Paraíba and Caruaru in Pernambuco. Both towns are entirely taken over by *forró* bands, cowboys, stalls selling *doce de leite* and other country produce, and the percussion of fireworks and bangers. Foreign visitors are still a rare curiosity.

Some 35 km east of Campina Grande, off the road to João Pessoa, is **Ingá**, site of the **Pedra de Itacoatiara Archaeological Centre**, where inscriptions dating back to 10,000 years old were found on a boulder 25 m long and 3 m high. A small museum at the site contains fossils of a giant sloth and a Tyrannosaurus rex. During the June festivities there is a train service to Itacoatiara.

At the **Boqueirão** dam on the Rio Paraíba, 70 km southeast of town, there is a hotel-*fazenda* **Chique-Chique** (T083-3391 1469, hfchique@hotmail.com).

Cariri

The *sertão* proper begins near São João do Cariri an hour or so from Campina Grande. This is an area of fascinating rock formations, with giant weather-worn boulders sitting on top of gently curved expanses of rock that look out over a plain of low bushes and stunted trees. Although the vegetation is quite different to the landscape itself; the arid conditions and the size of the trees recalls the Australian outback (the rocks themselves have been compared to the Devil's Marbles).

The most spectacular of all the formations sit in the private grounds of **Fazenda Pai Mateus** (www.paimateus.com.br). Like various other sites in Paraíba and Rio Grande do Norte, boulders here are covered in important pre-Columbian rock art, some of which have been controversially dated as pre-Clovis (making it older than the accepted datings) from the first waves of American population coming from over the Bering Strait. A famous local holy man lived inside one of the giant hollowed-out stones and the views from his former home at sunset are particularly spellbinding.

The *fazenda* itself is a very pleasant place to stay and there is rich, though depleted wildlife in the area and good birdwatching. Tours can be organized with **Cariri Ecotours** (see page 47); guides provide fascinating information about the archaeological sites but have little knowledge of the fauna in the region. The *fazenda*'s guides are informative about life in the *sertão* and the use of medicinal plants, but again as ever in Brazil, knowledge of birds and animals is poor.

North of Cariri, 46 km from Campina Grande, is **Areial**, the main town of the Brejo Paraibano, a scenic region of green hills and valleys, with a pleasant climate, where colonial sugar *fazendas* have been transformed into hotels.

Patos

West of Campina Grande the landscape turns to vast, flat expanses, flanked by rolling hills and interesting rock formations; very scenic when green, but a sad sight during the prolonged *sertão* droughts. Situated 174 km from Campina Grande is Patos (population 84,500), the centre of a cattle-ranching and cotton-growing area. It's also an access point for the **Serra do Teixeira**, 28 km away, which includes **Pico do Jabre**, the highest point in the state, at 1130 m above sea level. There are various hotels and restaurants in Patos.

Sousa

About 130 km northwest of Patos, the pleasant *sertão* town of Sousa (population 59,000), has high temperatures year-round and is gaining fame for the nearby dinosaur tracks and prehistoric rock carvings (see below). Within the town, the **Igreja do Rosário**, on Praça Matriz, has paintings dating to the Dutch occupation of the area. It currently functions as a school.

About 3 km from the centre, atop a hill, is a **statue of Frei Damião**, an important religious leader of the Northeast who died in 1997. Frei Damião was an Italian friar who came to Brazil in the 1930s and stayed to become an inspiration for the faith of its most recent generation of dispossessed. He is seen as belonging to the same tradition as O Conselheiro and Padre Cícero.

The *rodoviária* is 1 km from the centre, there are no city buses but it's possible to walk (hot) or take a moto-taxi (US$0.70) or taxi (US$53.50).

Vale dos Dinossauros Fossilized dinosaur prints of up to 90 different species, which inhabited the area between 110 and 80 million years ago, have been found in a number of sites in the Sousa region. These were extensively studied by the Italian palaeontologist Giussepe Leonardi in the 1970s and 1980s. The Vale dos Dinossauros, on the sedimentary riverbed of the Rio do Peixe, is one of the closest sites to Sousa; it has some impressive Iguanodontus prints.

Access is 4 km from town along the road north to Uiraúna; the best time to visit is the dry season, July to October. The area has no infrastructure and is best visited with a guide. Tours can be organized through **Cariri Ecotours** in Natal (see page 47) and can be combined with visits to Cariri.

Listings The Sertão

Tourist information

Campina Grande

Codemtur
T083-3310 6100, www.facebook.com/codemturpmcg.

PBTUR
T156.

Sousa

Secretaria de Turismo
R Vereador José Vieira de Figueiredo 84, T083-8167 2070.

Where to stay

Campina Grande
There are many hotels around Praça da Bandeira.

$$$ Garden
R Engenheiro José Bezerra 400,
Mirante Km 5, T083-3310 4000,
www.gardenhotelcampina.com.
The vast hotel complex is Campina Grande's best hotel, sitting on a hill 5 km from the centre, with views out over the city.

$$ Mahatma Gandhi
R Floriano Peixoto 338, T083-3321 5275.
Rooms with bath, a/c and fridge. Good location but needs renovation.

$$ Souto Maior
Floriano Peixoto 289, T083-3321 8043.
Rooms include bath, a/c and fridge.

$$ Village
R Octacílio Nepomuceno 1285, Catole, 4 km from the rodoviária nova, T083-3310 8000, www.hoteisvillage.com.br.
This business hotel is in a good location near the shopping centre mall and is equipped with tennis courts swimming pools, hot tubs and a spa. Recommended.

$$-$ Campina Hostel
R Irineu Joffily 115, Centro, T083-3321 1100, www.campinahihostel.com.br.
Great location, walking distance to Parque do Povo. Good, safe hostel but could be cheaper, especially at high season.

$ Verona
R 13 de Maio 232, T083-3341 1926.
With bath, fan, good value, friendly service.

Cariri
A visit to **Fazenda Pai Mateus** (www. paimateus.com.br), can be organized through **Cariri Ecotours**, see page 47.

Festivals

Campina Grande
Apr Micarande, the out-of-season Salvador-style carnival.
Jun-Jul Campina Grande has the largest **São João** celebrations in Brazil; from the beginning of Jun into the 1st week of Jul the city attracts many visitors; there are bonfires and *quadrilhas* (square dance groups) in every neighbourhood; *forró* and invited artists at the Parque do Povo; *quentão*, *pomonha* and *canjica* are consumed everywhere.
Aug The annual **Congresso de Violeiros**, which gathers singers and guitarists from all across the Northeast.

Transport

Campina Grande
Air There are daily flights to **Recife** with **Nordeste**. A taxi to the **airport**, T083-3332 9023, costs US$7. The City bus **Distrito Industrial** runs from Praça Clementino Procópio, behind Cine Capitólio. For transport to the airport, see box, page 63.

Bus The *rodoviária*, Av Argemiro de Figueredo, T083-3337 329, 3337 3001, is a 20-min bus ride from the centre. To **João Pessoa**, with **Real**, every 30 mins, US$7, 2 hrs. To **Souza** with **Transparaíba**, 6 daily, US$12.50, 6 hrs. To **Juazeiro do Norte** with **Transparaíba**, 2 daily, US$40, 9 hrs. To **Natal** with **Nordeste**, daily at 0800, US$50, 18 hrs.

Car hire See www.alugueldecarro.com.br for car hire companies.

Souza
Bus To **Campina Grande**, 6 daily, US$9, 6 hrs. To **João Pessoa**, 6 daily, US$28, 8 hrs. To **Juazeiro do Norte**, 4 daily, US$7, 3½ hrs.

Sergipe
& Alagoas

Few tourists stop off in these two tiny states between Bahia and Pernambuco, and herein lies their charm. Both have fine beaches, easily accessible from the state capitals: Aracaju and Maceió. And both have a series of very pretty Portuguese towns where even Brazilian visitors are still a novelty. The most impressive are Penedo (on the banks of Brazil's 'other' great river, the São Francisco, which forms the border between the two states), Marechal Deodoro (the birthplace of the founder of the Brazilian Republic) and the Portuguese capital of Sergipe, São Cristóvão (which is Brazil's fourth oldest town). Of the capitals, Maceió is the more salubrious, with some good beaches and lively nightlife.

Aracaju

sleepy northeastern capital, gateway to São Cristóvão

Founded in 1855, the state capital of Aracaju (population 462,600) stands on the south bank of the Rio Sergipe, about 10 km from its mouth and 327 km north of Salvador. The town is the best base for visiting the UNESCO World Heritage Site of São Cristóvão and the colonial village of Laraneiras. Most visitors stay at Praia Atalaia (see below), a 10-minute taxi (US$16) or 20-minute bus ride south of town. Here, the beaches are long, broad and lined with numerous little *pousadas*, restaurants and beach bars and which brim over with vibrant nightlife at weekends.

In Aracaju the river itself is pleasant enough and lined with handsome buildings, but the city centre is tawdry and unpleasant, especially at night, and there is very little to see.

Overlooked by most international visitors, Aracaju has a lively off-season carnival immediately prior to the one in Salvador, with the same music and floats. The commercial area is on Rua Itabaianinha and Rua João Pessoa, leading up to Rua Divina Pastora and Praça General Valadão.

Aracaju beaches

Praia Atalaia is the nearest beach to Aracaju and a much better place to stay. Although it can't compete with Bahia or Alagoas, there is a long stretch of fine white sand, lined with *forró* clubs, restaurants and bars. The beach is lively with families and smooching couples who wander along the esplanade at sunset and the entire area feels as safe and old fashioned as a British Butlins seaside resort. There's even an artificial lake in a tiny theme park where you can hire pedal boats.

Continuing south along the Rodovia Presidente José Sarney is a long stretch of sand between the mouths of the Rio Sergipe and Rio Vaza Barris; the further you go from the Sergipe, the clearer the water. One of the best beaches is the 30-km-long **Nova Atalaia**, on Ilha de Santa Luzia across the river. It is easily reached by ferry from the **Espaço Zé Peixe** ① *Av Ivo do Prado 25, near Praça General Valadão.*

A new cultural centre, opened in 2015, was built on the site of the old Terminal Hidroviário. Aracaju's main pier eventually closed down after the construction of the Aracaju–Barra dos Coqueiros bridge. It was turned into a memorial to celebrate the legendary José Martins Ribeiro Nunes (1927-1912), better known as Zé Peixe who was for many years the helmsman of the vessels crossing the river. There are good views and a restaurant.

Essential Aracaju

Finding your feet

Santa Maria Airport is 12 km from the centre. Interstate buses arrive at the new *rodoviária* 4 km west of the centre, which is linked to the local bus system from the adjacent terminal (buy a ticket before going on to the platform). Bus No 004 'Santa Maria/Mercado' goes to the centre, US$0.80. A taxi from the *rodoviária* to Atalalaia costs US$14, to the centre US$10. Buses from Laranjeiras and São Cristóvão (45 minutes) arrive at the **old bus station** at Praça João XXIII. Look for routes written on the side of buses and at bus stations in town. See Transport, page 69.

Listings Aracaju

Tourist information

Bureau de Informaçães Turísticas de Sergipe
Centro de Turismo, Praça Olímpio Campos s/n, Centro T079-3179 1947. Daily 0800-2000.
The principal tourist office has town maps and staff speak some English.

Emsetur
Trav Baltazar Goís 86, Edif Estado de Sergipe, 11th-13th floors, T079-3179 7553. Mon-Fri 0700-1300.

Tourist booth
Arcos da Orla de Atalaia 243, between R Maynard and Rotary, www.visitearacaju. com.br. Daily 1000-2100.

On the seafront on Praia Atalaia, but staff do not speak English and information is limited. There are other branches at the airport (0600-2400) and the *rodoviária* (0800-2230).

Where to stay

The city centre is unpleasant and seedy at night and pretty much all the hotels are scruffy and home to more than just humans. Staying here is not recommended. Atalaia Beach is only 10 mins by taxi and is far more salubrious with a bigger choice of services.

Atalaia Beach
Hotels are invariably blocky affairs but there are plenty of them, along the main

thoroughfare, Av Santos Dumont, next to the beach.

$$$$ Celi Praia
Av Oceânica 500, T079-2107 8000, www.celihotel.com.br.
This big beige block looks like a set of offices, which is appropriate as it caters principally to business clientele. Rooms are plain but large, modern and comfortable. All have balconies.

$$ Raio de Sol
R François Hoald 89, T079-3212 8600, www.pousadaraiodesol.com.br.
Well-kept, bright a/c rooms in a block 50 m back from the beach. Quieter than on the sea front. Courteous, efficient staff.

$$ San Manuel
R Niceu Dantas 75, Atalaia, T079-3218 5200, www.sanmanuelpraiahotel.com.br.
Pleasant, modern, well-appointed rooms decorated in tile and cream walls with Wi-Fi, international TV and business facilities (including conference rooms). The best views have sea views and terraces.

$ Pousada Relicário
Av Santos Dumont 622, Atalaia, T079-3243 1584.
A mock-Chinese *pousada* with simple plain a/c and fan-cooled rooms right next to one of the main beach nightlife areas.

Restaurants

$$$ Cantina d'Italia
Av Santos Dumont s/n, T079-3243 3184, www.facebook.com/cantinaditaliaracaju.
The chicest and priciest option on the beachfront serving pizza and pasta to the city's middle classes. The best tables are on the upper deck.

$ Cariri
Av Santos Dumont 243, T079-3243 1379, www.cariri-se.com.br.
Northeastern cooking including *frango caipira* (chicken cooked in a tomato and onion sauce) and *carne do sol* (beef jerky).

Live *forró* music Tue-Sat. One of several similar lively clubs on this part of the beach.

Festivals

1 Jan **Bom de Jesus dos Navegantes**, procession on the river.
1st weekend in Jan **Santos Reis** (Three Kings/Wise Men).
Feb/Mar Pre-carnival Carnaval.
Jun **Festas Juninas**.
8 Dec Both Catholic (**Nossa Senhora da Conceição**) and *umbanda* (*Iemenjá*) festivals.

Shopping

The *artesanato* is interesting, with pottery figures and lace a speciality. A fair is held in **Praça Tobias Barreto** every Sun afternoon. The **municipal market** is a block north of the Espaço Zé Peixe.

What to do

Tours
Private tour operators offer trips around the city, including rafting on the Rio São Francisco and the river delta. Look out for pamphlets in the hotels or enquire at the tourist office.
There are no tours available to São Cristóvão. You will have to hire a taxi (around US$35 for a round trip to Aracaju) or take local buses (see Transport, below).

Transport

Air The **airport**, Av Senador Júlio César Leite, Atalaia, T079-3212 8501, is 12 km from the centre. Flights to **Brasília**, **Maceió**, **Rio de Janeiro**, **Salvador**, **São Paulo** and **Recife**, as well as other destinations, with **Avianca**, www.avianca.com.br, **Azul**, www.voeazul.com.br, **GOL**, www.voegol.com.br, and **TAM**, www.tam.com.br.

Bus Long-distance buses run from the new *rodoviária*, 4 km from the centre. For transport from the *rodoviária*, see box, page 68. Buses from the city centre to the *rodoviária* and to Atalaia Beach run from Praça João XXIII, the terminal near the Espaço Zé Peixe and from Capela at the top of Praça Olímpio Campos. To **Salvador**, at least 10 a day, 6-7 hrs, US$20. To **Maceió**, 8 daily, US$15. To **Penedo**, 1 daily, 7 hrs, US$6 (best to go via Neópolis (125 km from Aracaju) with a smaller **Coopetaju** bus, www.coopetaju.

com.br, US$9, 3-4 hrs, and then take a ferry across the river to Penedo (20 mins). To **Recife**, 4 daily, US$28, 7 hrs (fastest at night). To **Estância**, US$3, 2 hrs, many buses. Buses run from both the new *rodoviária* and the old bus station at Praça João XXIII to **Laranjeiras** and **São Cristóvão** (45 mins, US$2.50).

Around Aracaju

pretty, crumbling colonial towns

São Cristóvão

The old Sergipe capital lies 23 km southwest of Aracaju on the road to Salvador, sitting pretty on a little hill and on the shores of a briny lake. Founded by Cristóvão de Barros in 1590, it is Brazil's fourth oldest town. The colonial centre focuses on Praça São Francisco, which was inscribed on the World Heritage list in 2010. It is surrounded on all sides by unspoilt Portuguese buildings.

The **Igreja e Convento de São Francisco** ① *Praça São Francisco, Tue-Fri 0900-1700, Sat and Sun 1300-1700, US$1.80*, has a beautiful, simple, baroque façade with a scrolled pediment, and an interior covered with lavish paintings. It also houses a sacred art museum, the **Museu de Arte Sacra e Histórico de Sergipe**, which has more than 500 priceless 18th- and 19th-century ecclesiastical objects. Other buildings on the square include the **Museu de Sergipe** (same opening hours), in the stately former **Palácio do Governo**, and the churches of **Misericórdia** (1627) and the **Orfanato Imaculada Conceição** (1646, permission to visit required from the sisters).

The streets surrounding Praça São Francisco are equally unspoilt, with whitewashed mansions, townhouses and churches offset by the oil-paint yellows and blues, green slat-shutters and woodwork. As tourists are few and far between, São Cristóvão is far less commercialized than the colonial cities of Minas or Bahia.

There are other squares in town. The Praça Senhor dos Passos is lined by more Portuguese buildings and churches, including **Igreja Senhor dos Passos** and **Terceira Ordem do Carmo** (both built 1739), while on the Praça Getúlio Vargas (formerly Praça Matriz) is the 17th-century **Igreja Matriz Nossa Senhora da Vitória** ① *all are open Tue-Fri 0900-1700, Sat and Sun 1500-1700*. Also worth seeing is the old **Assembléia Legislativa** ① *R Coronel Erundino Prado*.

The town is lively only during both the Sergipe pre-Carnaval celebrations, **Carnaval** itself and Easter, when the streets are strewn with mosaics created with hundreds of thousands of flower petals.

Laranjeiras

This tiny, sleepy colonial town lies some 23 km northwest of Aracaju at a bend in the sluggish Cotinguiba River. The town was originally founded in 1605 and has several churches dating back to the imperial period, when it was an important producer of sugar. The 19th-century **Capela de Sant'Aninha** has a wooden altar inlaid with gold. There's a lively market on Saturday mornings. It is reached by taking the São Pedro bus from the old *rodoviária* in the centre of Aracaju (45 minutes).

Estância

Estância (57,000), some 70 km south of Aracaju on the BR-101, is one of the oldest towns in Brazil. Its colonial buildings are decorated with Portuguese tiles (none are open to the public). The town's heyday was at the turn of the 20th century and it was one of the first places in Brazil to get electricity and a telephone system. Estância is also called 'Cidade Jardim' (Garden city) because of its parks. The month-long festival of São João in June is a major event and there are some superb, little-visited beaches nearby, including the **Praia do Saco** sitting in a forest-backed half-moon bay.

Rio São Francisco

Other than the colonial towns, by far the most interesting excursion from Aracaju is to the canyons and beaches of the Rio São Francisco. The blue waters course their way through the hills of Minas Gerais and the desert backlands of Bahia before cutting through a series of dramatic gorges near the **Xingó** dam, and subsequently through fields of windswept dunes before washing out into the deep green Atlantic in northern Sergipe. A number of Atalaia-based tour operators run day-trips to the river mouth stopping at deserted beaches along the way; US$35-42 per person, depending on numbers.

Listings Around Aracaju

Where to stay

Sao Cristóvão and Larajeiras
Only Laranjeiras has anything in the way of accommodation, with a couple of very simple *pousadas*. There is no accommodation in Sao Cristóvão and both towns are best visited as day trips.

Estância
There are a number of cheap, very simple hotels around the Praça Barão do Rio Branco.

$$ Jardim
R Joaquim Calazans 202, Estância, T079-3522 1656, www.hoteljardim-se.com.br.
A modern home in what looks like a converted townhouse. There's a range of tile and whitewash a/c rooms and a huge buffet breakfast.

$ Turismo Estanciano
Praça Barão do Rio Branco 176, T079-3522 1404, www.hotelestanciano.com.br.
Very simple en suites with little more than a bed, fridge and a table in a delightful tumble-down hotel.

Restaurants

São Cristóvão and Laranjeiras
There are very simple and basic restaurants ($) in the old centre.

Festivals

São Cristóvão
Mar **Senhor dos Passos**, held 15 days after Carnaval.
8 Sep **Nossa Senhora de Vitória**, the patron saint's day.
Oct/Nov **Festival de Arte** (moveable).

Laranjeiras
Jan The main festival in Laranjeiras is **São Benedito** in the 1st week of the month.

Estância
Jun The month-long festival of **São João** is a major event.

Shopping

São Cristóvão
Nivaldo Artesania, *Praça Senhor dos Passos 37, Centro (in front of the Igreja do Senhor dos Passos), http://arteerestauracaonivaldooliveira.*

blogspot.co.uk. Beautiful hand-block prints, paintings, little knick-knacks (including fridge magnets) and crafts. The owner Nivaldo runs an educational arts project for local children. Well worth a visit.

Transport

São Cristóvão and Laranjeiras
Bus São Pedro buses run between both towns both the old and the new *rodoviárias*

in **Aracaju** (45 mins, US$2). Taxis from Aracaju charge US$38-45 for a round trip. Negotiate to include Laranjeiras.

Estância
Bus Many buses stop at the *rodoviária*, on the main road. To **Salvador**, 4 hrs, US$8-10.

Maceió

one of coastal Brazil's most attractive and safest cities

The capital of Alagoas, Maceió (population 780,000) has a small, pretty colonial centre and a relaxed feel, with a string of beautiful white-sand beaches nearby. There are also a handful of low-key beach resorts a short bus ride away; the best is at Praia do Frances, near the old Portuguese capital of Marechal Deodoro. The city has a lively street carnival and traditional Festas Juninas.

Maceió beaches
The sea in Maceió is an impossibly brilliant shade of misty greens and blues and it washes onto some of the finest white-sand beaches in urban Brazil. **Trapiche**, **Sobral** and **Avenida**, immediately in front of the city, look appetizing and are pounded by impressive surf but they are far too filthy for anything but brown trout. The best beaches for bathing (and the best places to stay in Maceió) are **Pajuçara**, **Ponta Verde** and **Jatiúca**, becoming increasingly plush the further they are from the centre.

Pajuçara has the bulk of the budget accommodation and a nightly crafts market. At weekends there are wandering musicians and entertainers here, and patrols by the cavalry on magnificent Manga Larga Marchador horses. Periodically, especially on *candomblé* anniversaries, there are rituals to the *orixá* of the sea, Yemanjá. There is a natural swimming pool 2 km off the beach, **Piscina Natural de Pajuçara**, and low tide leaves lots of natural pools to explore in the exposed reef. Check the tides; there is no point going at high tide. *Jangadas* (simple platforms with sails) cost US$14 per person per day (or about US$26 to have a *jangada* to yourself). On Sunday or local holidays in high season the beach gets overcrowded. At weekends lots of *jangadas* anchor at the reef, selling food and drink.

The next beach is **Ponta Verde**, which is quieter and forms the cape separating Pajuçara from the best of the urban beaches, **Jatiúca**. The better hotels are here and the beach is fronted by a pretty esplanade, lined with cafés and smart restaurants. It is tastefully lit at night. The principal restaurant area in Maceió lies just inland of northern Jatiúca.

After Jatiúca the beaches are: **Cruz das Almas**, **Jacarecica** (9 km from the centre), **Guaxuma** (12 km), **Garça Torta** (14 km), **Riacho Doce** (16 km), **Pratagi** (17 km) and **Ipioca** (23 km). Cruz das Almas and Jacarecica have good surf. Bathing is best three days before and after a full or new moon because tides are higher and the water is more spectacular.

Essential Maceió

Finding your feet

Flights arrive at **Zumbi dos Palmares Airport** 25 km from the city centre and beaches. A **Transporte Tropical** bus runs from the airport to the most popular city beach, Ponta Verde/Pajuçara (every 30 minutes 0630-2100, US$0.80, allow 45 minutes); look for name of the beach on the front of the bus. Taxis charge a flat rate of around US$17. Interstate buses arrive at the *rodoviária* 5 km from the centre, situated on a hill, with good views. Take bus Nos 711 or 715 to Ponta Verde/Pajuçara or buses marked 'Ouro Preto/centro'; these run every few minutes. A taxi from the bus station to Pajuçara costs around US$7. See Transport, page 76.

Getting around

Ponta Verde, Pajuçara and adjacent Praia de Jaticúa are easy to walk around as is the commercial centre. You will need to take public transport between them. Local buses connect Ponta Verde and Pajuçara with the tiny historic city centre every few minutes, leaving from the beachside road Avenida Robert Kennedy/Alvaro Otacilio and stopping at various points including the cathedral. Bus stops are little blue elongated concrete stands. *Combis* for the nearby beaches like Praia do Frances and Marechal Deodoro leave from in front of the Hospital Santa Casa.

Sights

The centre of Maceió can easily be wandered around in less than an hour. It is pretty, with a handful of handsome Portuguese buildings and some half-decent art deco. On Praça dos Martírios (Floriano Peixoto) is the **Palácio do Governo**. Inside are the **Fundação Pierre Chalita**, with Alagoan painting and religious art, and the church of **Bom Jesus dos Mártires** (1870), covered in handsome *azulejo* tiles. These are two of the oldest buildings in the city and well worth visiting. The **cathedral**, Nossa Senhora dos Prazeres (1840) is on Praça Dom Pedro II. The **Instituto Histórico e Geográfico** ① *R João Pessoa 382, T082-3223 7797*, has a small but good collection of indigenous and Afro-Brazilian artefacts.

Unfortunately polluted, the entrance to **Lagoa do Mundaú** is 2 km south at **Pontal da Barra**, and limits the city to the south and west. Shrimp and fish are sold at the lagoon's small restaurants and handicraft stalls but it's best to avoid eating here. The local government has plans to clean the lagoon in the near future. It's a pleasant place for a drink at sundown. Boats make trips in the lagoon's channels.

Listings Maceió *map p74*

Tourist information

Sedetur
Av da Paz 1108, Centro, T082-3315 1713, www.turismoalagoas.com.
The state tourism authority also has branches at the airport and *rodoviária*. The website has a comprehensive list of public services, hotels, restaurants, bars and other contacts. Far more convenient is the **tourist information post** (on Pajuçara Beach, next to the Sete Coqueiros artisan centre).

Semptur
Av da Paz 1422, Centro, T082-3336 4409, www.maceioturismo.com.br.
Offers information on the city and environs, including maps.

Where to stay

There are many hotels on Pajuçara mostly along Av Dr Antônio Gouveia and R Jangadeiros Alagoanos but many of the cheapest are not to be trusted with your belongings. The best rooms are on the beaches Ponta Verde and Jatiúca. It can be hard to find a room during the Dec-Mar holiday season, when prices go up.

$$$$ Ponta Verde Praia
Av Álvaro Otacílio 2933, Ponta Verde, T082-2121 0040, www.hotelpontaverde.com.br.

Range of a/c rooms are all well-appointed. The best on the upper floors have wonderful sweeping views out over the sea.

$$ Coqueiros Express
R Desportista Humberto Guimarães 830, Ponta Verde, T082-4009 4700, www.coqueirosexpress.com.br.
The best rooms in this spruce, well-run hotel are on the upper floors and have partial sea views. All are well appointed and decorated in tile and light green and hanging with faux-modernist minimalist *jangada* prints.

Maceió

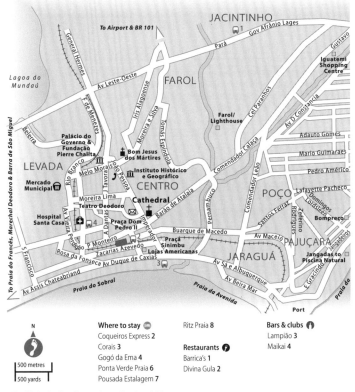

Where to stay 🛏
Coqueiros Express **2**
Corais **3**
Gogó da Ema **4**
Ponta Verde Praia **6**
Pousada Estalagem **7**

Ritz Praia **8**

Restaurants 🍴
Barrica's **1**
Divina Gula **2**

Bars & clubs 🍸
Lampião **3**
Maikai **4**

$$ Pousada Estalagem
R Engenheiro Demócrito Sarmento Barroca 70, T082-3327 0088, www.pousadaestalagem.com.br.
Flats with little cookers in a quiet backstreet above a photo shop. Some have space for up to 6 in one room, making this in the $ category for groups.

$$ Ritz Praia
R Eng Mário de Gusmão 1300 Laranjeiras, Ponta Verde, T082-2121 4600, www.ritzpraia.com.br.
This is a hotel of 2 halves. The rooms on the upper 4 floors are bright and airy and have

views. Those yet to be refurbished are rather gloomy but well-maintained have frowsty en suites with marble fittings.

$ Corais
R Desportista Humberto Guimarães 80, Pajuçara, T082-3231 9096, www.hotel pousadadoscorais.com.br.
Very basic, musty rooms in corridors around a little garden courtyard. All are frayed, fancooled and en suites. Perfect if you plan to spend as little time as possible asleep and as much time as possible on the beach, which is only a few hundred metres away.

$ Gogó da Ema
R Laranjeiras 97, T082-3327 0329, www.hotelgogodaema.com.br.
Very simple tile and lime green rooms dominated by large double beds with decent mattresses.

Restaurants

The best restaurants, bars and clubs are on and around R Engenheiro Paulo B Nogueira on Jatiúca Beach. There are many other bars and restaurants in Pajuçara and along Av Antônio Gouveia.

For 5 km from the beginning of Pajuçara, through Ponta Verde and Jatiuca in the north, the beaches are lined with *barracas* (thatched bars) with music, snacks and meals until 2400 (later at weekends). Vendors on the beach sell beer and food during the day; clean and safe.

There are many other bars and *barracas* at Ponto da Barra, on the lagoon side of the city and a string of cheap but highquality stalls next to the **Lampião club** in Jatiúca in front of the **Maceió Atlantic** suites hotel. Local specialities include oysters, *pitu*, a crayfish (now scarce), and *sururu*, a type of cockle. The local ice cream, 'Shups', is recommended.

$$$ Divina Gula
R Engenheiro Paulo B Nogueira 85, T082-3235 1016, www.divinagula.com.br. Closed Mon.

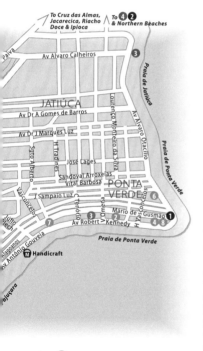

Buses 🚌
Rodoviária 1
To Marechal Deodoro
  & Praia do Francês 2
To Riacho Doce 3
To Praia Francês 4

The best restaurant in the city, with a lively atmosphere and busy crowd. The large menu includes many heavily cheesed Italian options, pizzas, seafood and northeastern meat dishes. Portions are large enough for 2.

$$-$ Barrica's
Av Álvaro Otacílio 39, Ponta Verde, T082-3227 0909.
One of the liveliest of the waterfront bars in Maceió with live music every night, a buzzing crowd and a range of dishes from pasta to grilled or fried meat or fish, the inevitable pizzas and a handful of veggie options.

Bars and clubs

The bars here are relaxed and varied and there are nightclubs to suit most tastes.

Lampião
Praia de Jatiúca s/n, diagonally opposite the Maceió Atlantic suites hotel.
A very lively beachside *forró* bar with live bands every night playing live music to an eager crowd. The house band dress up as Lampião himself – in straw hats and with yokely shirts and leather jerkins – and they are fronted by a bottle-blonde in a sparkly cap, who has everyone up and dancing. Packed on Fri and Sat. Food available.

Maikai
R Empresário Carlos Da Silva Nogueira, T082-3305 4400, www.maikaimaceio.com.br.
Restaurant and adjacent club with space for thousands and a range of northeastern acts, playing music from *forró* to *axé*. Currently the busiest and most popular club in town.

Festivals

27 Aug **Nossa Senhora dos Prazeres**.
16 Sep **Freedom of Alagoas**.
8 Dec **Nossa Senhora da Conceição**.
15 Dec **Maceiofest**, a great street party with *trios elêctricos*.
24 Dec **Christmas Eve**.
31 Dec **New Year's Eve**, half-day.

What to do

José dos Santos Filho (Del), *T082-3241 4966 or T082-8859 3407 (mob), jalbino.filho@ hotmail.com.* Bespoke tourist guide offering entertaining city tours or trips to Marechal Deodoro, Praia do Francês and beyond, including visits to Nelson da Rebeca's house in Marechal Deodoro. Very friendly, knowledgeable guide with a comfortable a/c car and reasonable English.

Transport

Air The **airport** is on Rodovia BR-104, Km 91, T082-3036 5200, www.infraero.gov.br. There are flights to **Aracaju**, **Brasília**, **Florianópolis**, **Rio de Janeiro**, **Salvador**, **São Paulo**, **Recife**, **Belo Horizonte** and **Porto Alegre** with Azul, www.voeazul.com.br, **GOL**, www.voegol. com.br and **TAM**, www.tam.com.br.

Bus Taxis from town go to all the northern beaches (eg 30 mins to **Riacho Doce**), but buses run as far as **Ipioca**. The **Jangadeiras** bus marked 'Jacarecica-Center, via Praias' runs past all the beaches as far as **Jacarecica**. From there you can change to 'Riacho Doce–Trapiche', 'Ipioca' or 'Mirante' buses for **Riacho Doce** and **Ipioca**. These last 3 buses can also be caught in the centre on the seafront avenue below the Praça Sinimbu (US$0.80 to Riacho Doce). To return take any of these options, or take a bus marked 'Shopping Center' and change there for 'Jardim Vaticana' bus, which goes through Pajuçara. *Combis* to **Marechal Deodoro**, **Praia do Francês** and **Barra de São Miguel** leave from opposite the Hospital Santa Casa in front of the Texaco service station. A *combi* to Marechal Deodoro costs US$1.40, 30 mins, calling at Praia do Francês in each direction. The last bus back from Praia do Francês to Maceió is at 1800.

 Long-distance The 'Ponte Verde/ Jacintinho' bus runs via Pajuçara from the centre to the *rodoviária*, also take 'Circular' bus (25 mins Pajuçara to *rodoviária*). To

Recife, 10 a day, 3½ hrs express (more scenic coastal route, 5 hrs), US$10. To **Aracaju**, US$14, 5 hrs (potholed road). To **Salvador**, 4 a day, 10 hrs, US$35 (*rápido* costs more). Luggage store is available.

To **Penedo**, 4 buses a day and *combis* from outside the *rodoviária*. There is a left luggage facility at the *rodoviária*.

Car hire Localiza, and others have offices at the airport and in hotels.

Marechal Deodoro

attractive laid-back colonial town unspoilt by tourism

The former capital of Alagoas is 22 km south of Maceió across the impressive brackish lakes that give the state its name, and just behind one of the best resort beaches in the Northeast, Praia do Francês. The town is well worth a visit, for its delightful crumbling buildings and expansive lake, as well as its relaxed atmosphere. It's built on a hill, overlooking Lake Manguaba. Boat trips can be organized through tour guides such as Del (see What to do, page 76).

The town is named after Marechal Deodoro da Fonseca, the charismatic general who founded the Brazilian republic after the deposition of Emperor Dom Pedro II. The modest townhouse where he grew up is now the **Museu Marechal Deodoro** ① *R Marechal Deodoro, daily 0800-1700, free*. It offers an interesting insight into the simplicity of life in Brazil at the end of the 19th century, even for those in the upper middle classes. Marechal Deodoro's large family lived in a few simple rooms; it is easy to imagine them dining together by oil lamp around the plain hard-wood table, watched over by the family patriarch. Typical northeastern *macramé* lace can be bought outside the museum in the adjacent houses.

The town is very pleasant to wander around, which takes all of 20 minutes. The cobbled streets are lined with attractive colonial houses, some of which have been converted into modest restaurants and *pousadas*. These lead to a series of squares watched over by impressive if decrepit Portuguese churches. Some are almost beyond repair, but the most impressive, the **Igreja Matriz de Nossa Senhora da Conceição** (1783), has undergone full restoration, returning to its full baroque glory. Be sure to have a peek inside.

The 17th-century **Convento de São Francisco**, on Praça João XXIII, has another fine baroque church, **Santa Maria Magdalena**, with a superb wooden altarpiece that has been badly damaged by termites. Adjoining it is the **Museu de Arte Sacra** ① *Mon-Fri 0900-1300, US$1.10 guided tours available, payment at your discretion*.

It is easy to visit Marechal on a day trip from Maceió and still have time left over to enjoy the sun and surf on **Praia do Francês**. It is one of southern Alagoas's most beautiful beaches, pounded by glass-green surf at one end, protected by a fringing reef at the other and shaded by towering coconut palms along its entire length. There are plenty of *barracas*, restaurants and bars selling drinks and seafood.

There are more beaches beyond Francês, including **Barra de São Miguel**, entirely protected by the reef. It gets crowded at weekends. Several good, cheap *barracas* serve food and drink and there are some decent places to stay. **Carnaval** is very lively here.

Listings Marechal Deodoro

Tourist information

For more information see www.praiado frances.net and www.turismo.al.gov.br.

Where to stay

$$ Capitães de Areia
R Vermelha 13, Praia do Francês,
100 m from the beach, T082-3260 1477,
www.capitaesdeareia.com.br.
A terracotta-coloured block with terraces of rooms near the beach, a pool and a restaurant. Good low season discounts.

$$ Pousada Bougainville e Restaurant Chez Patrick
R Sargaço 3, T082-3260 1251,
bougainvillepousadamar.com.br.
A pretty little *pousada* near the beach with a/c, rooms with TVs, a pool, seafood and a good French and seafood restaurant cooking.

$$ Pousada Le Soleil
R Carapeba 11, Praia do Francês, T082-3260 1240, www.pousadalesoleil.com.br.
An anonymous concrete block of a hotel with balconies close to the beach. Decent breakfast. Wi-Fi.

Penedo

a kind of forgotten Ouro Preto, and barely a tourist in sight

A more interesting crossing into Alagoas than the usual arrival, along the coast from north or south, can be made by frequent ferry crossings from Neópolis (Sergipe) to Penedo (Alagoas), some 35 km from the mouth of the Rio São Francisco.

Penedo (population 57,000) is a delight, sweltering in the tropical heat on the banks of the sluggish Rio São Francisco, just across the water from Sergipe. Its colonial streets clamber up a series of hills from the banks of the river and are lined with wonderful old buildings. There's a stunning baroque church at every other turn.

The town was founded in 1565; it was overthrown by the Dutch (who built a fort here) in 1637, and then re-taken by the Portuguese shortly after. It developed as a trading port in the 17th and 18th centuries and grew rich from the gold and diamonds transported down the Rio São Francisco from the interior of Bahia and Minas.

Very few of the long two-masted sailing vessels that used to cruise on the river can be seen now, although there are plenty of smaller craft. Boats travel down the river to a series of beautiful white-sand beaches in both Sergipe and Alagaoas; these include **Arambipe** and **Peba**. The latter (in Alagoas) is also reachable by road. Either side of the river mouth are turtle nesting grounds, which are protected.

Sights

The most impressive building in the city is the church of **Nossa Senhora da Corrente** ① *Praça 12 de Abril s/n, Centro, Tue-Sun 0800-1700,* (1784), named 'Our Lady of the Current' presumably in homage to the river, which ran swiftly and powerfully past the town until the construction of the Rio São Francisco dam in the late 20th century. It is one of the finest pieces of Portuguese baroque in Northeastern Brazil, built on an intimate scale like those in Ouro Preto, rather than being grand like the churches of Olinda or Salvador. The simple façade hides a rich interior covered in gold leaf and centred on a splendid painted and gilt altarpiece replete with blue and rose marble. The nave is lined with masterful *azulejo* panels, and paintings by the Pernambucan Portuguese artist Libório Lázaro Lial, who was also responsible for much of the ecclesiastical decoration in the city. According to legend, fugitive slaves were hidden inside the church by a trap door behind one of the side altars.

On Praça Barão de Penedo is the neoclassical **Igreja Matriz** (closed to visitors) and the 18th-century **Casa da Aposentadoria** (1782). East and a little below this square is the Praça Rui Barbosa, where you'll find the **Convento de São Francisco** (1783) and the church of **Nossa Senhora dos Anjos** ① *Praça Rui Barbosa s/n, Centro, Tue-Fri 0800-1100 and 1400-1700, Sat and Sun 0800-1100,* whose façade is topped with typically Portuguese baroque filigree flourishes. As you enter the church, the altar on the right depicts god's eyes on the world, surrounded by the three races (indigenous, black and white). The church has a fine trompe l'oeil ceiling (1784), also by Libório Lázaro Lial, which recalls Mestre Atahyde's ceiling in the Igreja São Francisco de Assis in Ouro Preto. The convent is still in use.

The church of **Rosário dos Pretos** ① *Praça Marechal Deodoro,* (1775-1816), is open to visitors, as is **São Gonçalo Garcia** ① *Av Floriano Peixoto, Mon-Fri 0800-1200, 1400-1700,* (1758-1770). The latter has a particularly fine baroque interior. Lively markets are held outside on weekdays. A wander around them feels like a trip back in time to an older Alagoas. Fishermen sell estuary bream straight out of the wheelbarrow, hacked up bits of cow hang unrefrigerated from meat-hooks in the heat next to stalls offering everything from baskets of home-made soap to pocket calculators. Vast sacks of grain, rice, flour and beans sit next to little hand-drawn carts in front of algae-covered walls of 400-year-old buildings and, above, the flurry and fluster megaphones blare out special offers and political slogans, broken by the occasional peel of a baroque church bell.

On the same street is the pink **Teatro 7 de Setembro** ① *Av Floriano Peixoto 81, Mon-Fri 0800-1200, 1400-1730, Sat morning only,* with a lovely little conch-shaped auditorium dating from 1884. There are river views from the **Rocheira** just behind **Pousada Estylos**. Before the construction of the São Francisco dam, the river used to wash against the stones immediately below the parapet; you can still see the tide mark, some 4 m higher than it is today.

There are two museums. The most interesting is the **Paço Imperial** ① *Praça 12 de Abril 9, Centro, T082-3551 2498, Tue-Sat 1100-1700, Sun 0800-1200.* Emperor Dom Pedro II stayed in this handsome mansion in 1859 and the building has been trading on the glory ever since. It now preserves a wonderful ceiling painting by Francisco Lopes Ruis, as well as furniture and artefacts that once belonged to the Portuguese high society families and church art. There are great views out over the river from the second floor. The **Casa de Penedo** ① *R João Pessoa 126, signs point the way up the hill from Floriano Peixoto, T082-551 2516, Tue-Sun 0800-1200 and 1400-1800,* displays photographs and books on, or by, local figures.

Tourist information

Tourist office
Praça Barão de Penedo 2, T082-3551 3907.
Mon-Fri 0730-1330.
Very friendly and helpful, with useful maps of
the city marked with all the principal sights,
hotels and restaurants. They can organize
guided tours of the baroque buildings,
sometimes in English.

Where to stay

$$ Pousada Colonial
Praça 12 de Abril 21, 5 mins' walk from the bus
station, T082-3551 2355.
A converted colonial building with creaky
wooden floors and huge rooms – the best
with views out over the river. All are fan-
cooled but for the suites. Friendly, efficient
reception staff.

$$ São Francisco
Av Floriano Peixoto, T082-3551 2273,
www.hotelsaofrancisco.tur.br.
A big, ugly 1970s block with boxy little
balconied rooms all with a/c, TV and
fridge. Showing its age far more than
the colonial hotels.

$ Pousada Imperial
Praça Comendador Peixoto 49, T082-3551 4749.
Simple a/c and fan-cooled rooms with a
bath, fan and hot water. The best are on
the upper floors and have river views.
Cheaper for single rooms and doubles
with shared bathrooms.

$ Pousada Styllus I
Praça Jácome Calheiros 79, T082-3551 2465.
A modest modern hotel near the river with
a range of a/c and fan-cooled rooms. Open
sporadically, but always in high season.

Shopping

There is a daily **market** on the streets off
Av Floriano Peixoto, with good hammocks.
Ceramics are on sale outside **Bompreço**
supermarket, on Av Duque de Caxias.

Transport

Bus The *rodoviária* is on the riverfront
on Av Beira Rio, near the service station.
Daily slow buses to **Salvador** (11 hrs) via
Aracaju (4½ hrs). Book in advance as the
route is very popular with locals. It is
quicker to take the ferry across the river
to Neópolis and take a **Coopetaju**, www.
coopetaju.com.br, microbus from there
to **Aracaju** (3½ hrs). To **Maceió**, 115 km,
4 buses a day in either direction, 3-4 hrs,
US$9, and *combis*, 0500-1620.

Ferry Frequent launches for foot
passengers and bicycles across the river
to **Neópolis**, 10 mins, US$0.70, for
connections by bus to **Aracaju**. The dock
in Penedo is on Av Duque de Caxias, below
Bompreço. The ferry makes 3 stops in
Neópolis, the 2nd is closest to the *rodoviária*
(which is near the **Clube Vila Nova**, opposite
the Texaco station). There is also a car ferry
(every 30 mins, US$3.50, take care when
driving on and off).

long stretches of creamy white, coconut-shaded sand washed by a gentle sea

São Miguel dos Milagres and the northern Alagoas beaches

This tiny colonial town, some 110 km north of Maceio near the state border with Pernambuco, is a sleepy little place with huddles of terracotta houses around a crumbling Portuguese church (the second oldest in Alagoas). It lies close to some of the best beaches in Northeast Brazil, with fringing reef within paddling distance of the shore.

Praia do Patacho, **Praia do Toque** and **Praia do Riacho** are increasingly popular with the São Paulo jet set and celebrities after rustic chic. All are backed by a string of modish but low-key boutique beach *pousadas*. The area is as yet fairly 'undiscovered' as public transport connections remain poor, however the next few years could see it become the new Trancoso with prices going through the roof.

The Tatuamunha River near São Miguel is the best place in the world to see West Indian manatees. The **Santuario do Peixe Boi** ⓘ *Projeto Aribama, R Luiz Ferreira Dorta, s/n, Porto de Pedras, T082-9108 0906, daily 1000-1600, US$10*, on the river is devoted to the rehabilitation of the marine mammals, who are subsequently released into the estuary. A trip to the centre will pretty much guarantee a visit and is easily organized through any of the *pousadas*.

Essential São Miguel dos Milagres

Access

The road from Maceió is pocked with potholes. There are no buses along this route but minivans leave from Maceio's main bus terminal when full (approximately every two hours) in daylight hours. The journey takes three hours. From Recife, take a bus to Maragogi (see Transport, below), 38 km north of São Miguel, and then a taxi (US$24) or a *combi* van onward to the *pousada* of your choice. *Pousadas* can arrange transfers from Macéio or Recife airports (around US$42 and US$63 respectively).

Maragogi

Although it is becoming increasingly popular, this little beach town has preserved something of its local character. Outside the high season, when Maragogi gets crowded, life goes on pretty much as it has done before tourists began to arrive in the 1980s. The beach is glorious: a seemingly infinite stretch of broad, fine sand washed by a turquoise sea. Some 6 km offshore, a fringing reef reveals a series of deep swimming pools at low tide. The current is rich with sergeant majors and wrasse and with the occasional visiting turtle. Trips out there are easy to organize (expect to pay around US$10).

Where to stay

São Miguel dos Milagres beaches

$$$$ Pousada Amendoeira
Praia do Toque, Rota Ecológica s/n, T082-3295 1213 www.amendoeira.com.br.
This delightful *pousada*, decorated with a real sense of style and flair, with rustic chic cabins set next to the beach, is one of the few genuine eco-hotels on the Brazilian coast. Water and rubbish are recycled, fruit and vegetables are grown in the hotel kitchen garden, and the owners run several projects devoted to supporting the local community.

$$$$ Pousada Patacho
Praia do Patacho, Rota Ecológica s/n, Porto de Pedras, T082-3298 1253, www.pousadapatacho.com.br.
Faux-Provençale rooms and chalets decorated with a designer touch by the French owner and set in a shady tropical garden right next to the beach. Quiet and private.

$$$ Pousada Riacho dos Milagres
Praia do Riacho 1, T082-3295 1206, www.riachodosmilagres.com.br.
This welcoming, family-run hotel sits right on the beach on sweeping Riacho Bay. A/c rooms some of which are large enough for families come with satellite TVs and DVD players and are set in corridors around the pool or the garden. Generous breakfasts.

$$$ Pousada Xué
Praia do Patacho, Porto de Pedras, T081-3298 1197, www.pousadaxue.com.br.
This intimate beach boutique has a handful of bright, spacious cabins facing the rising sun on beautiful Patacho Beach. Each comes with a large bathroom, flatscreen TV and DVD player. The beach is literally at the end of the garden and the warm and welcoming owners run one of the best restaurants in Northeast Brazil (see Restaurants, below), manned by the ebullient virtuoso chef and owner Guido Migliorini.

$$$ Vila do Patacho
Praia do Patacho s/n, T081-9925 7744, patachobrasil.wordpress.com.
This lovely little *pousada*, sitting right under the palms on Patacho Beach, welcomes guests with open arms. The owners Veronica and Gui go out of their way to be friendly and accommodating. Cabins which were designed with the help of prestigious Gaucho architect Jorge Francisconi are decorated with a personal touch by Veronica.

Maragogi

$$ Jangadeiros
R Palmeira, s/n, Centro, Beira Mar, T082-3296 2167, www.pousadadosjangadeiros.com.br.
Plain but modern tile-floor and whitewash rooms in a concrete hotel a block from the beach 5 mins north of the town centre. A little pool and good breakfast. Friendly staff.

$$ Pousada Água de Fuego
Rodovia AL 101 Norte, T082-3296 1326, www.aguadefuego.com.
Good *pousada* with a range of spacious tile-floor rooms overlooking the beach. Uruguayan owner, great breakfast and a pool. In a quiet area 15 mins' walk south of town along the beach.

$ O Tempo e o Vento
Trav Lourenco Wanderley 22, T082-3296 1720, www.pousadaotempoeovento.com.
Tiny little rooms right near the beach. The best are closest to the seafront. Those overlooking the town *praça* can be noisy. Single rooms cheaper.

Restaurants

São Miguel dos Milagres

$$$ No Quintal
R de acesso a Praia do Toque, T082-9910 7078.
Decent seafood dishes and Brazilian comfort cooking, much of it made from

ingredients grown in the restaurants organic kitchen garden.

$$$ Xuê
Praia do Patacho, T081-3298 1197.
Superb Italian-Brazilian cooking from **DOM**-trained chef Guido Migliorini. Dishes are made with ultra-fresh ingredients straight from the sea or the *pousada*'s organic kitchen garden and served alfresco next to the beach and under a canopy of stars.

Transport

Maragogi
To **Maceió** and **Recife** there are 7 buses a day with **Real Alagoas**, 3 hrs. Frequent *combis* to the *rodoviária* in **Maceió**.

Fortaleza
& the
Far Northeast

Bahia may have Brazil's prettiest coastline but the Northeast has some of the most dramatic. In Rio Grande do Norte, striated cliffs and imposing dunes tower above the wild and deserted beaches of Natal, Genipabu, Pipa and Areia Branca.

In neighbouring Ceará the coast becomes touristy again, especially around the state capital, Fortaleza, a sunny, planned city whose charm is sullied by cheap package tours. Just to the north is the Western hemisphere's kitesurfing capital, Cumbuco.

Beyond the state border at Jericoacoara is the wilderness of Delta do Parnaíba, the largest delta in the Western hemisphere. The wetlands of Rio Parnaíba comprise islands and narrow channels, hiding some of Brazil's least spoilt beaches. The coastal desert of Lençóis Maranhenses in Maranhão state is a huge sea of coastal dunes, with deserted beaches and forgotten fishing villages. Further north, and almost inaccessible, the swamps of Reentrâncias Maranhenses preserve the largest bank of coral in Atlantic South America, Marinho do Parcel Manoel Luís, a new diving destination.

Maranhão's capital, São Luís, is famous for its Bumba-Meu-Boi festival and historic centre, with decaying baroque churches, and colonial buildings. It's one of two World Heritage Sites in the region. The other is Serra da Capivara National Park, whose bizarre honeycomb domes tower over canyons with ancient rock painting.

Ceará

Ceará calls itself the 'Terra da Luz' (Land of Light) and much of its 573-km coastline and bone-dry interior is baked under permanent sunshine. It could just as well be called the Land of Wind: kitesurfers and windsurfers are quickly discovering that there is nowhere better in the world for their sports. Locations such as Cumbuco and Jericoacoara are blown by strong winds almost 365 days a year, and the Atlantic Ocean offers varied conditions from glassy flat through to rolling surf. Ceará boasts some beautiful beaches, too, with long, broad stretches of sand backed by ochre cliffs or towering dunes.

Unfortunately, many of the little fishing villages that lay undiscovered for decades are losing their character to ugly condos and concrete hotels. In places like Canoa Quebrada, Jericoacoara and Cumbuco, other European languages are spoken as much as Portuguese, but there are still pristine and limpid stretches of coast and sleepy fishing villages of *jangada* fishermen, where life continues much as it did before the age of television and the internet.

The state capital, Fortaleza, is a sunny, relaxed city with good food and famous night life, and its once tawdry image has been improved by more vigilant policing and fewer disreputable foreign tourists.

Fortaleza (population 2.1 million) is a stretch of concrete towers along a series of white-sand beaches behind a gloriously misty green-and-blue Atlantic dotted with rusting wrecks. The water temperature is permanently in the high 20s and there's a constant sea breeze. The sea is surprisingly clean, even in Iracema near the centre, but the best beaches for swimming are further east and west.

Fortaleza has a long history and a number if sights of historic interest. However, most tourists visit only in passing, on their way to the beach towns to the south and the north. Fortaleza's reputation for lively nightlife and friendly locals has been tarnished in the last few years by the crime statistics, which have consistently shown the city to be Brazil's most violent. While tourists visiting for a day or two are unlikely to encounter any problems (most crime is restricted to the suburbs), it is wise to be careful in the city – especially at night; see Safety, opposite, for more information.

Sights

Fortaleza has a handful of sights of historic interest. The **Fortaleza Nossa Senhora da Assumpção** ⓘ *Av Alberto Nepomuceno, T085-3255 1600, telephone in advance for permission to visit, daily 0800-1100, 1400-1700,* originally built in 1649 by the Dutch, gave the city its name. Near the fort, on Rua Dr João Moreira, is the 19th-century **Praça Passeio Público** (or Praça dos Mártires), a park with old trees and statues of Greek deities.

West of here a neoclassical former prison (1866) houses a fine tourist centre, the **Centro de Turismo do Estado (Emcetur)** ⓘ *Av Senador Pompeu 350, near the waterfront, T0800-991516, closed Sun,* with museums, theatre and craft shops. It is home to the renovated **Museu de Arte e Cultura Populares** and the **Museu de Minerais** ⓘ *T085-3212 3566.* Further west along Rua Dr João Moreira, at **Praça Castro Carreira** (commonly known as Praça da Estação), is the handsomely refurbished train station, **Estação João Felipe** (1880), which runs commuter services.

The **Theatro José de Alencar** ⓘ *Praça José de Alencar, T085-3229 1989, Mon-Fri 0800-1700, hourly tours, some English-speaking guides, US$1.50, Wed free,* was inaugurated in 1910 and is worth a visit. It is a magnificent iron structure imported from Scotland and decorated in neoclassical and art nouveau styles. It also houses a library and art gallery. The **Praça dos Leões**, or Praça General Tibúrcio, on Rua Conde D'Eu has bronze lions imported from France. Around it stand the 18th-century **Palácio da Luz** ⓘ *T085-3231 5699,* former seat of the state government, and the **Igreja Nossa Senhora do Rosário**, built by slaves in the 18th century. Also here is the former provincial legislature, dating from 1871, which houses the **Museu do Ceará** ⓘ *R São Paulo, next to Praça dos Leões, T085-3251 1502, Tue-Fri 0830-1730, Sat 0830-1400, US$1.* The museum has displays on history and anthropology. To get there, take a bus marked 'Dom Luís'.

The new **cathedral** ⓘ *Praça da Sé,* completed in 1978, in ungainly Gothic style constructed out of concrete with beautiful stained glass windows, stands beside the new semi-circular **Mercado Central**.

There are several worthwhile museums to visit in and around Fortaleza. The **Museu do Maracatu** ⓘ *Rufino de Alencar 231,* at Theatro José (see above), has costumes of this ritual dance of African origin. The exciting **Centro Dragão do Mar de Arte e Cultura** ⓘ *R Dragão do Mar 81, Praia de Iracema, T085-3488 8600, www.dragaodomar.org.br,*

Essential Fortaleza

Finding your feet

International and domestic flights arrive at **Aeroporto Pinto Martins**, 6 km south of the centre.

Buses No 64 (Corujão/Aeroporto/Centro/Rodoviária) and No 404 (Aeroporto/Benfica/Rodoviária) run from the airport to Praça José de Alencar in the centre, and the *rodoviária*, US$1. Taxis to the centre, Avenida Beira Mar or Praia do Futuro charge around US$12, or US$20 at night (30 minutes, allowing for traffic).

Interstate buses arrive at the **Rodoviária São Tomé**, 6 km south of the centre. Many city buses run to the centre (US$1) including No 78, which goes to Iracema via the Centro Dragão do Mar. If in doubt, the tourist information booth will point you in the right direction. A taxi to Praia de Iracema or Avenida Abolição costs around US$8. Buses to Jericoacoara leave twice a day from the *rodoviária*, in the early morning and early evening. See Transport, page 94.

Getting around

The city is spread out, with its main attractions in the centre and along the seashore; transport from one to the other can take a long time. The city bus system is efficient if a little rough; buses and vans cost US$1 per journey. The cheapest way to orientate yourself within the city is to take the 'Circular 1' (anti-clockwise) or 'Circular 2' (clockwise) buses which pass Avenida Beira Mar, the Aldeota district, the university (UFC) and cathedral via Meireles, Iracema, Centro Dragão do Mar and the centre, US$1. Alternatively, take the new *Top Bus* run by **Expresso Guanabara**, T0800-991992, US$2, an air-conditioned minibus starting at Avenida Abolição. For more details see www.fortalbus.com.

When driving outside the city, have a good map and be prepared to ask directions frequently as road signs are non-existent or are placed after junctions.

Safety

Fortaleza has become progressively violent over the last five years. Tourists should be wary walking even in the tourist areas at night and avoid the following areas at all times: Serviluz favela between the old lighthouse (Avenida Vicente de Castro), Mucuripe and Praia do Futuro; the favela behind the railway station; the Passeio Público at night; and Avenida Abolição at its eastern (Nossa Senhora da Saúde church) and western ends. Catch a cab to the beaches, ordered through the hotel or taken at a designated taxi rank.

Tue-Thu 1000-1730, Fri-Sun 1400-2130, US$1 for entry to each museum/gallery, free on Sun, hosts concerts, dance performances and exhibitions of art and photography. It has various entrances, from Rua Almirante Barroso, Rua Boris, and from the junction of Monsenhor Tabosa, Dom Manuel and Castelo Branco. The latter leads directly to three museums: on street level, the **Memorial da Cultura Cearense**, with changing exhibitions; on the next floor down is an art and cultural exhibition; in the basement is an excellent audio-visual museum devoted to the world of the *vaqueiro* – the *sertão* cowboys. Also at street level is the **Livraria Livro Técnico**. There is a **planetarium** with a whispering gallery underneath. The centre also houses the **Museu de Arte Contemporânea do Ceará**. This area is very lively at night.

Some 15 km south of the centre, the **Museu Artur Ramos** ⓘ *in the Casa de José de Alencar, Av Perimetral, Messejana, T085-3229 1898, Mon 1400-1730, Tue-Sun 0800-1200, 1400-1700,* displays artefacts of African and indigenous origin collected by the anthropologist Artur Ramos, as well as documents from the writer José de Alencar.

Beaches

The urban beaches between Barra do Ceará (west) and Ponta do Mucuripe (east) are polluted and not suitable for swimming.

Heading east from the centre, **Praia de Iracema** is one of the older beach suburbs, with some original early 20th-century houses. It is not much of a sunbathing beach as it has little shade or facilities and swimming is unsafe, but at night it is very lively. The Ponte Metálica or **Ponte dos Ingleses**, nearby, was built by the British Civil engineering firm Norton Griffiths & Co in 1921 as a commercial jetty for the port. It was never completed due to lack of funds but instead reopened as a promenade pier in imitation of English seaside piers. It was and is now a very popular spot for watching the sunset and the occasional pod of visiting dolphins.

East of Iracema, the **Avenida Beira Mar** (Avenida Presidente Kennedy) connects **Praia do Meireles** (divided into **Praia do Ideal**, **Praia dos Diários** and Praia do Meireles itself) with Volta da Jurema and Praia do Mucuripe; it is lined with high-rise buildings and most luxury hotels are located here. A *calçado* (walkway), following the palm-lined shore, becomes a night-time playground as locals promenade on foot, rollerskates (which can be hired on the beach), skateboards and bicycles and there are volleyball courts, bars, open-air shows and a **crafts fair**.

Praia do Mucuripe, 5 km east of the centre, is Fortaleza's main fishing centre, where *jangadas* (traditional rafts with triangular sails) bring in the catch; there are many restaurants serving *peixada* and other fish specialities. The symbol of this beach is the statue of Iracema, the main character of the romance by José de Alencar. From the monument there is a good view of Mucuripe's port and bay. At Mucuripe Point is a **lighthouse** built by slaves in 1846, which houses the **Museu de Fortaleza** (now sadly run down and not a safe area, according to the tourist office). There is a lookout at the new lighthouse, good for viewing the *jangadas*, which return in the late afternoon, and the sunset.

Praia do Futuro, 8 km southeast of the centre, is the most popular bathing beach. It is 8 km long with strong waves, sand dunes and freshwater showers, but no natural shade. Vendors in straw shacks serve local dishes such as crab. On Thursday nights it becomes the centre for the city's nightlife, with people enjoying live music and *forró*. The south end of the beach is known as **Caça e Pesca**; water here is polluted because of the outflow of the Rio Cocó. Much of Praia do Futuro is backed by large resort hotels. Be careful on the beach at night away from the *barracas*.

At **Praia de Sabiaguaba**, 20 km southeast of the centre, is a small fishing village known for its seafood; the area has mangroves and is good for fishing.

Some 29 km southeast of the centre is **Praia Porto das Dunas**, a pleasant beach that is popular for watersports, such as surfing. Buggies and microlight tours can be arranged. The main attraction is **Beach Park** ① *R Porto das Dunas, 273, T085-4012 3000, www.beachpark.com.br*, one of the largest water parks in South America, with pools, water toboggans, sports fields and restaurants.

Listings Fortaleza *map below*

Tourist information

If you have problems, contact the **tourist police** (R Silva Paulet 505, Aldeota, T085-3433 8171).

Emcetur
See page 87.

Posta Telefônica Beira Mar
Av Beira Mar, almost opposite Praiano Palace Hotel.
Provides information, sells *combi* tickets to Jericoacoara, and has postcards, clothes and magazines.

Fortaleza

Where to stay ⊜
Abrolhos Praia **1** *B6*
Backpackers **21** *B3*
Casa Blanca **2** *B4*

Casa de Praia **3** *A4*
Gran Marquise **7** *B6*
Ideal Praia **10** *B5*
Luzeiros **13** *B6*

Ponta Mar **6** *B6*
Pousada do Suiço **12** *A4*
Pousada Salinas **22** *B6*
Seara Praia **20** *B6*

Setur

Secretária do Turismo do Estado do Ceará, Av General Afonso Albuquerque Lima, T085-3101 4688, www.setur.ce.gov.br.
The main office of the state tourism agency has maps and brochures and can help book hotels and tours. There are also information booths at the airport and *rodoviária*, and at the **Farol de Mucuripe** (old lighthouse), open 0700-1730.

Where to stay

Almost all hotels offer reduced prices in the low season. There are many *pousadas* in the Iracema/Meireles area, but they change frequently. Most hotels in Fortaleza have a strict policy of not accepting overnight visitors without prior reservations.

City centre and around

$ Backpackers
R Dom Manuel 89, T085-3091 8997, www.backpackersce.com.br.
Central, basic, shared bathrooms, no breakfast, linen, toilet paper or towels but free Wi-Fi, a helpful owner and a lively mixed foreign and Brazilian crowd. 10-min walk from the beach.

Beaches

$$$$ Gran Marquise
Av Beira Mar 3980, Mucuripe, T085-4006 5000, www.granmarquise.com.br.

Villamaris **4** *B6*

Colher do Pau **5** *A3*
Ideal **9** *B5*
La Fiorentina **8** *B6*
Romagna Mia **7** *A4*

Sobre O Mar **3** *A3*

Restaurants 🍴
Amici's **1** *A2*

Bars & clubs 🍸
Pirata **6** *A3*

The best of Fortaleza's many tower block hotels. With modern rooms renovated in 2014, decked out in wood panelling and neutral tones and with large windows featuring ocean views. Good breakfast and modern business facilities. Some 8 km east of Iracema.

$$$$ Luzeiros
Av Beira Mar 2600, Meireles, T085-4006 8585, www.hotelluzeiros.com.br.
This tall tower built at the turn of the millennium couldn't be better located – in a safe area right on Meireles beach next to the bus stop which runs along the coast north and south. Rooms are functional with design touches, the best have sweeping sea views, and there's a pool and sauna. There are plenty of restaurants and bars nearby and the area around the hotel is lively at night (especially on weekends), so ask for an ocean-facing room on the upper floors for the best sleep.

$$$$ Seara Praia
Av Beira Mar 3080, Meireles, T085-4011 2200, www.hotelseara.com.br.
30% cheaper in low season, smart, upper-end hotel in need of a fresh lick of paint, with pool, gym and a restaurant.

$$$ Casa Blanca
R Joaquim Alves 194, T085-3219 0909, www.casablancahoteis.com.br.
The best rooms on the upper floors of this tall tower have wonderful sweeping ocean views. All are a/c, well-appointed (if anonymous) and have international TV.

$$$ Ponta Mar
Av Beira Mar 2200, Meireles, T085-4006 2200, www.pontamar.com.br.
A mid-range business hotel in a safe location right on the beach with cafés and restaurants nearby. Ask for one of the newly renovated rooms on the upper floors and avoid those close to reception.

$$ Abrolhos Praia
Av Abolição 2030, 1 block from the beach, Meireles, T085-3248 1217, www.abrolhospraiahotel.com.br.

Pleasant, TV, fridge, hot shower, a/c, rooms look a bit sparse but no different from others in this category, soft beds, discount in low season, internet.

$$ Casa de Praia
R Joaquim Alves 169, T085-3219 1022, www.hotelcasadepraia.com.br.
Well-kept, modest a/c rooms in warm colours and with international TV, Wi-Fi. The best are above the 4th floor and have partial ocean views. There's a little rooftop pool.

$$ Ideal Praia
R Antonele Bezerra 281, T085-3248 7504, www.hotelideal.com.br.
A mock-colonial hotel in a quiet little back street offering 2 kinds of rooms. Those on the ground floor are decorated with mock-marble tiles and have little windows. Those on the upper floors have ocean views and little terraces.

$$ Pousada do Suiço
R Antônio Augusto 141, Iracema, T085-3219 3873, www.pousadadosuico.com.br. Be sure to reserve Oct-Feb.
A justifiably popular, well-kept and well-run budget hotel in an excellent location near the beach. It is quiet, discreet and on one of the less noisy streets. There are a variety of rooms, some more spacious than others.

$$ Pousada Salinas
Av Zezé Diogo 3300, Praia do Futuro, T085-3234 3626, www.pousadasalinas.com.br.
$ in low season, popular, Well-kept, modest beachside *pousada* with a decent breakfast and parking. Rooms set around a shady garden courtyard.

$$ Villamaris
Av Abolição 2026, Meireles, T085-3248 0112, www.hotelvillamaris.com.br.
Plain, simple a/c rooms with cream painted, crinkle concrete walls, a tiny work table and international TV. Good location.

Restaurants

Iracema and Dragão do Mar

These are 2 good areas for restaurants, with plenty of variety. There are many eateries of various styles at the junction of Tabajaras and Tremembés, mostly smart.

$$ Amici's
R Dragão do Mar 80.
Pasta, pizza and lively atmosphere in music-filled street, evenings only. Some say it's the best at the cultural centre.

$$ Colher de Pau
Ana Bilhar 1178, Meireles, T085-3267 6680. Daily from 1830.
Hearty and varied *sertaneja* food, seafood, in a very pleasant, airy indoor and outdoor dining area.

$$ Romagna Mia
R Joaquim Alves 160.
Very good fresh seafood, pasta and genuine thin crust Italian pizza made by an Italian ex-pat resident of at least 20 years. Meals are served in a little garden shaded by vines tiled with mock-Copacabana dragon's tooth paving.

$$ Sobre O Mar
R dos Tremembés 2, T085-3219 6999, www.sobreomardiracema.com.br.
The perfect vantage point for watching the sky fade from deep red through to lilac over the pier and the green sea at the end of the day. Sit with an icy *batida* in hand (the *vodka com abacaxi* is excellent) or a petit gateau with chocolate sauce under your spoon. But eat your main course elsewhere.

Beaches

Several good fish restaurants at Praia de Mucuripe, where the boats come ashore 1300-1500. R J Ibiapina, at the Mucuripe end of Meireles, 1 block behind the beach, has pizzerias, fast food restaurants and sushi bars.

$$$-$$ La Fiorentina
Osvaldo Cruz 8, corner of Av Beira Mar, Meireles.
Some seafood expensive, but there's also fish, meats and pasta. Unpretentious,

attentive waiters, good food, frequented by tourists and locals alike.

$$$-$ Ideal
Av Abolição e José Vilar, Meireles. Open 0530-2030.
Bakery serving lunches, small supermarket and deli, good, handy.

Bars and clubs

Fortaleza's famous nightlife isn't what it used to be, but the city still boasts 'the liveliest Mon night in the world'. *Forró* is the most popular dance and there is a tradition to visit certain establishments on specific nights.

The most popular entertainment areas are the large **Dragão do Mar** arts complex (see page 87) and the bars just east of the Ponte dos Ingleses and around O Pirata (R dos Tabajaras 325, T085-4011 6161, www.pirata.com.br).

Festivals

6 Jan Epiphany.
Feb Ash Wed.
19 Mar São José.
Jul Last Sun in Jul is the **Regata Dragão do Mar**, Praia de Mucuripe, with traditional *jangada* (raft) races. During the last week of Jul, the out-of-season Salvador-style carnival, **Fortal**, takes place along Av Almte Barroso, Av Raimundo Giro and Av Beira Mar. In Caucaia, 12 km to the southeast, a **vaquejada**, traditional rodeo and country fair, takes place during the last weekend of Jul.
15 Aug, the local *umbanda terreiros* (churches) celebrate the **Festival of Iemanjá** on Praia do Futuro, taking over the entire beach from noon till dusk, when offerings are cast into the surf. Well worth attending (members of the public may '*pegar um passo*' – enter into an inspired religious trance – at the hands of a *pai-de-santo*). Beware of pickpockets and purse-snatchers.

ON THE ROAD

Kitesurfing, windsurfing and surfing

Ceará is one of the best places in the world for kitesurfing and windsurfing (www. kitesurfbrazil.com provides a useful overview). The major centres are Jericoacoara, Cumbuco and Canoa Quebrada (though winds are not as reliable here). Rental equipment can be found at all three. In Fortaleza, equipment for kitesurfing and windsurfing can be rented at some of the popular beaches, such as Porto das Dunas. Surfing is popular on a number of Ceará beaches.

Mid-Oct Ceará Music, a 4-day festival of Brazilian music, rock and pop, is held in Marina Park.

Shopping

Handicrafts

Fortaleza has an excellent selection of locally manufactured textiles, which are among the cheapest in Brazil, and a wide selection of regional handicrafts. The local craft specialities are lace and embroidered textile goods; hammocks (US$15-100); fine alto-relievo woodcarvings of northeast scenes; basket ware; leatherwork; and clay figures (*bonecas de barro*). Bargaining is acceptable at the **Mercado Central**, Av Alberto Nepomuceno (closed Sun), and the **Centur Centro de Turismo** in the old prison. Crafts also available in shops near the market, while shops on R Dr João Moreira 400 block sell clothes. Every night (1800-2300) there are stalls along the beach at Praia Meireiles. Crafts also found in the commercial area along Av Monsenhor Tabosa.

Shopping centres

The biggest is **Iguatemi**, south of Meireles on way to Centro de Convenções; it also has modern cinemas. Others are **Aldeota** and **Del Paseo** in Aldeota, near Praça Portugal.

What to do

Kitesurfing and windsurfing

Bio Board, *Av Beira Mar 914, T085-3242 1797, www.bioboard.com.br*. A windsurfing and kitesurfing school. Will look after equipment.

Tour operators

Many operators offer city and beach tours. Others offer adventure trips further afield, the most common being off-road trips along the beaches from Natal in the east to the Lençois Maranhenses in the west. For transfers to Jericoacoara see also What to do, page 105.

Ceará Saveiros, *Av Beira Mar 4293, T085-3055 4449, www.cearasaveirostur.com.br*. Saveiro and yacht trips, daily 1000-1200, 1600-1800 and with advance group booking at moonlight at 2000 from Praia de Mucuripe.

André Pinto Expedições, *T085-99981 0717, andrepinto70@ig.com.br*. Private driver transfers to Jericoacoara (cheaper than a taxi) and tours of the Serra da Ubijara, Parque Nacional das Sete Cidades, Delta do Parnaíba and all the way from Jericoacoara to Cabure in the Lençóis Maranhenses. Excellent value for small groups. English-speaking.

Jericoacoara Travel, *T085-4042 2219, www. jericoacoara.travel*. Tours throughout Ceará, to Morro Branco, Canoa Quebrada and Jericoacoara with hotel pick-ups from Fortaleza.

Transport

Air

International and domestic flights arrive at **Aeroporto Pinto Martins**, Praça Eduardo Gomes, 6 km south of the centre, T085-3392 1200, www.aeroportofortaleza.net. The airport is modern and well-run with has a **tourist office**, T085-3477 1667, car hire, a food hall, internet facilities, bookstore, **Bradesco** and **HSBC** (for international

ATMs) – on the 2nd floor. Fortaleza is the principal international transport hub for North Eastern Brazil. There are flights to **Europe** (via Lisbon with TAP, via Milan with Meridiana and via Frankfurt with Condor), to the USA (via Miami with TAM) and to **Colombia** (via Bogota with Avianca) as well to destinations throughout Brazil, including **São Luís** and **Belém**, as well as the **Guianas**.

For details of Transport from the airport to the centre, see box, page 88.

Bus

Local Many city buses run to the *rodoviária* (US$1), including 'Aguanambi' 1 or 2 which go from Av Gen Sampaio, 'Barra de Fátima-Rodoviária' from Praça Coração de Jesus, 'Circular' for Av Beira Mar and the beaches, and 'Siqueira Mucuripe' from Av Abolição.

For the eastern beaches near Fortaleza (**Prainha, Iguape, Barro Preto, Batoque**) and towns such as **Aquiraz, Eusêbio, Aracati, Canoa** or **Pacajus**, take São Benedito buses (www.gruposaobenedito.com.br) from the *rodoviária*. To **Beberibe**, 10 a day, US$8. To **Morro Branco**, 4 daily, US$10. To **Canoa Quebrada**, 4 daily, US$12, 3 hrs; more via Aracati. There are regular buses to the western beaches near Fortaleza, including **Cumbuco**, from the *rodoviária*.

Long-distance Interstate buses arrive at the **Rodoviária São Tomé**, Av Borges de Melo 1630, Fátima, 6 km south of the centre, T085-3256 2100. Information is available from the *Disque Turismo* booth, open 0600-1800, which also has lockers for storing luggage. Opposite the *rodoviária* is **Hotel Amuarama**, which has a bar and restaurant; there's also a *lanchonete*.

Fretcar buses to **Jericoacoara** run from the *rodoviária* 4 times daily between 0730 and 1820 (most comfortable buses at 0750 and 1445), 6-7 hrs, US$20.

Nordeste to **Mossoró**, 6 a day, US$12. To **Natal**, 6 daily, US$25, 6 hrs. To **João Pessoa**, 1 daily, US$25, 7 hrs. To **Recife**, 3 night buses including a *leito* daily, US$35-50, 12 hrs, book early for weekend travel. To **Belém**, 3 daily, US$75, 24 hrs. To **São Luís**, 3 daily, US$45, 18 hrs. To **Sobral**, numerous daily, US$8, 4 hrs. To **Ubajara**, 2 daily, 6 hrs, US$8. To **Piripiri** for **Parque Nacional de Sete Cidades**, US$20, 9 hrs, a good stop en route to Belém. To **Quixadá**, 5 daily, US$7, 3 hrs. To **Redentora**, at 0600 and 1200, US$12.50, via **Baturité**, 4 hrs.

Car hire

There are many car hire agencies at the airport.

The coast southeast of Fortaleza
beautiful beaches backed by towering orange and red sand cliffs

Ceará's southeastern coast is lined with beaches and cliffs, which have been sculpted into craggy forms (or eroded altogether into shifting dunes) by the prevailing wind. Clusters of little villages and towns lie behind the beaches – like the little resort town of Morro Branco, the full-scale resort of Canoa Quebrada, or the delightful village of Prainha do Canto Verde where locals still fish on the high seas using *jangadas* – built to a design that has endured for centuries.

It's possible to stay with local communities through the inspiring **Rede Tucum** initiative (see page 99), and even to hike along much of the eastern coast dropping in on settlements along the way (bring plenty of water and sun protection). Where there are rivers to cross, there is usually a boatman and, in the few places where there is no hotel, fishing villages offer home-based accommodation or hammock space.

There are regular buses to the beaches and to the city of Aquiraz from the *rodoviária* in Fortaleza. For further information on the area, including accommodation and restaurants, visit www.aquiraz.ce.gov.br (in Portuguese only).

Aquiraz and around

Some 31 km east of Fortaleza, Aquiraz (population 61,000) was the original capital of Ceará. It retains several colonial buildings and has a religious art museum. It is also the access point for a number of beaches.

Some 6 km east of Aquiraz, **Prainha** is a fishing village and weekend resort with a 10-km beach and dunes. The beach is clean and largely empty and the waves are good for surfing. You can see *jangadas* in the late afternoon. The village is known for its lacework; women using the *bilro* and *labirinto* techniques can be seen at the **Centro de Rendeiras**. In some of the small restaurants it is possible to see displays of the *carimbó*, one of the north Brazilian dances. Just south of Prainha is **Praia do Presídio**, with gentle surf, dunes, palms and *cajueiros* (cashew trees).

About 18 km southeast of Aquiraz is **Praia Iguape**, another fishing village known for its lacework. The beach is a large, elbow-shaped sandbank, very scenic especially at Ponta do Iguape. Nearby are high sand dunes where sand-skiing is popular. There is a lookout at Morro do Enxerga Tudo; a one-hour *jangada* trips cost US$25. Lacework is sold at the **Centro de Rendeiras**. Locals are descendants of Dutch, Portuguese and indigenous peoples; some traditions such as the *coco-de-praia* folk dance are still practised. Some 3 km south of Iguape is **Praia Barro Preto**, a wide tranquil beach, with dunes, palms and lagoons.

Cascavel

Cascavel, 62 km southeast of Fortaleza, has a Saturday crafts fair by the market. It is the access point for the beaches of Caponga and Águas Belas, where traditional fishing villages coexist with fancy weekend homes and hotels. **Caponga**, 15 km northeast of Cascavel, has a wide 2-km-long beach lined with palms. *Jangadas* set sail in the early morning; arrangements can be made to accompany fishermen on overnight trips, or a 90-minute ride costs US$25 for up to five people. There is a fish market and crafts sales (ceramics, embroidery and lacework) on the beach. A 30-minute walk south along the white-sand beach leads to **Águas Belas**, at the mouth of the Rio Mal Cozinhado, offering a combination of fresh and saltwater bathing (access also by road, 15 km from Cascavel, 4 km from Caponga). The scenery here, and 5 km further east at Barra Nova, changes with the tide. A walk north along the beach for 6 km takes you to the undeveloped **Praia do Batoque**, which is surrounded by cliffs and dunes.

Morro Branco and Praia das Fontes

Beberibe, 78 km from Fortaleza, is the access point for two of the most beautiful beaches on the southeast coast.

About 4 km from Beberibe, **Morro Branco** has the most spectacular beach in southern Ceará with coloured craggy cliffs cut by a narrow valley, sweeping dunes and beautiful views. *Jangadas* leave the beach at 0500, returning 1400-1500 with catches of lobsters and reef fish. Coloured sands from the dunes are bottled into beautiful designs and sold alongside other crafts such as lacework, embroidery and straw goods in the village. *Jangadas* may be hired for sailing (one hour for up to six people, around US$40). Beach buggies are also available for hire.

South of Morro Branco and 6 km from Beberibe is **Praia das Fontes**, which also has coloured cliffs with freshwater springs. There is a fishing village and, at the south end, a lagoon. Near the shore is a cave, known as **Mãe de Água**, visible at low tide. Buggies and microlights can be hired on the beach. A luxury resort complex has been built here, making the area expensive.

South of Praia das Fontes are several less developed beaches including **Praia Uruaú** or **Marambaia**, about 6 km from Praia das Fontes along the beach or 21 km by road from Beberibe, via Sucatinga on a sand road. The beach is at the base of coloured dunes; there is a fishing village with some accommodation. Just inland is **Lagoa do Uruaú**, the largest in the state and a popular place for watersports. A buggy from Morro Branco costs US$50 for four people.

About 50 km southeast of Beberibe is **Fortim**. From here, boats run to **Pontal de Maceió**, a reddish sand point at the mouth of the Rio Jaguaribe, from where there is a good view of the eastern coast. In the winter the river is high and there is fishing for shrimp; in the summer it dries up, forming islands and freshwater beaches. There's a fishing village about 1 km from the ocean with bars, restaurants and small *pousadas*.

Prainha do Canto Verde

Some 120 km east of Fortaleza, in the district of Beberibe, is Prainha do Canto Verde, a small fishing village on a vast beach, which has an award-winning community tourism project run by **Rede Tucum** (see page 99). There are guesthouses or houses for rent (see Where to stay, below), restaurants and a handicraft cooperative. Each November there is a **Regata Ecológica**, with *jangadas* from up and down the coast competing. *Jangada* and catamaran cruises are offered, as well as fishing and a number of walking trails. This a simple place, where people make their living through artisanal fishing, without the use of big boats or industrial techniques. The village has built up its tourism infrastructure without any help from outside investors, and has been fighting the foreign speculators since 1979. The people are friendly and visitors are welcome to learn about the traditional way of life.

To get to Prainha do Canto Verde, take a São Benedito bus to Aracati or Canoa Quebrada, buy a ticket to Quatro Bocas and ask to be let off at Lagoa da Poeira, two hours from Fortaleza. If you haven't booked a transfer in advance, Márcio at the **Pantanal** restaurant at the bus stop may be able to take you, US$1.75. The website www.prainhadocantoverde. org is the best source of information.

Aracati

Situated on the shores of the Rio Jaguaribe, Aracati (population 62,000) is the access point for Ceará's most southeasterly beaches. The city is best known for its **Carnaval** (the liveliest in the state) and for its colonial architecture, including several 18th-century churches and mansions with Portuguese tile façades. There is a **Religious Art Museum** (closed lunchtime and Sunday afternoon), a Saturday morning **crafts fair** on Avenida Coronel Alexandrino, and a number of simple *pousadas* ($$-$) on the same street.

Canoa Quebrada

Canoa Quebrada, 10 km from Aracati, is on a beautiful long sandy beach backed by crumbling, multi-coloured sandstone cliffs (sadly blighted by ugly and illegal *barracas* and an unsightly metal walkway) and extending to a long point. It remained an isolated fishing village until 1982, when a road was built. It is now a very popular resort, with many package hotels, busy bars and restaurants (most of them gathered along a central strip known as Broadway). The nightlife is very vibrant in season, especially over Christmas, New Year and Carnaval, when it can be very difficult to find a room. Canoa is famous for its *labirinto* lacework, coloured sand sculpture and beaches. Sand-skiing is popular on the dunes and there is good windsurfing and kitesurfing on the Jaguaribe estuary, just outside town, with plenty of options for lessons and equipment rental (see What to do, below).

Local fishermen have their homes in **Esteves**, a separate village also on top of the cliff. Rides on *jangadas*, buggy tours, sandboarding and ziplining can be organized in town or on the beach, though visitors should be aware that excessive buggy trips have damaged the delicate dunes near the resort.

Wear shoes or sandals to avoid biting insects and *bicho do pé* (burrowing fleas that breed on dirty beaches).

South of Canoa Quebrada

Heading south from Canoa Quebrada, **Porto Canoa** is a resort town that opened in 1996, fashioned after the Greek islands. It includes beach homes and apartments, shopping areas, restaurants and hotels, and there are facilities for watersports, horse riding, microlight flights, buggy and *jangada* outings.

South of here, **Majorlândia** is a very pleasant village with multi-coloured sand dunes (used in bottle pictures and cord crafts) and a wide beach with strong waves that are good for surfing. The arrival of the fishing fleet in the evening is an important daily event; lobster is the main catch. It is a popular weekend destination with beach homes for rent and plenty of *pousadas*. Unlike many beach locations in Ceará, the area is predominantly Brazilian. **Carnaval** here is quite lively, but you will have no trouble finding a room outside the peak season. The town is easy to find your way around.

About 5 km south along the beach from Majorlândia is the village of **Quixaba**, on a beach surrounded by coloured cliffs, with offshore reefs and good fishing. At low tide you can reach the popular destination of **Lagoa do Mato**, some 4 km south. The *lagoa* can also be reached by buggy from Canoa Quebrada Beach (US$20 for four people). There's a hotel, restaurant and pristine beach surrounded by dunes, cliffs and palms.

Ponta Grossa

Ponta Grossa, 30 km southeast of Aracati near Icapuí, is the last municipality before Rio Grande do Norte (access from Mossoró) and is reached via a sand road just before Redonda. It's a very pretty place, nestled at the foot of the cliffs, with a beautiful beach.

Ponta Grossa has its own tourism development initiative. The fishing community has many members of Dutch origin, following a shipwreck in the 19th century, and many people have fair hair. It is also one of the few places where *peixe boi marinho* (manatees) can be spotted. There's a good lookout from the cliffs and a delightful walkway extending over the placid warm ocean into an area of pristine mangrove forest.

Beach trips go from Canoa Quebrada (see above) to Ponta Grossa for lunch, but it is possible to stay here through **Rede Tucum** (see page 99). Be sure to visit the Terra Mar institute where you can buy guidebooks to the local flora and fauna, arts and crafts and cosmetics made from seaweed harvested from the ocean near the village.

To the south are the beaches of **Redonda**, another very pretty place, and **Barreiras**, which is good for surfing and has a handful of hotels.

Listings The coast southeast of Fortaleza

Tourist information

Canoa Quebrada
For more information, including extensive accommodation listings, visit www.portalcanoaquebrada.com.br.

Where to stay

Aquiraz and around
In Águas Belas, there are simpler rooms available in private houses.

$$ Kalamari
Av Beira Mar, Porto das Dunas Beach,
T085-3361 7500, www.kalamari.com.br.
Small beach hotel with balconied rooms
overlooking a smart pool. Equidistant between
Fortaleza and Aquiraz. Tours organized.

$$ Pousada Mama Rosália Via Local 19
Porto das Dunas Beach T085-3361 7491,
www.pousadamamarosalia.com.br.
Family-run beach hotel with simple
tile-floor and whitewash rooms with
en suites, a restaurant and a pool.

$$ Pousada Villa Francesa
Av Beira Mar, Prainha, 1.5 km from the beach,
T085-3361 5007, www.villafrancesa.com.
Tiny 8-room, French-run beach hotel. Rooms
are gathered around a smart pool and the
hotel offers tours and internet.

Morro Branco and Praia das Fontes
Rede Tucum (www.tucum.org) has good
accommodation options with members of the
community and in small *pousadas* in Morro
Branco (eg **Casa Cangulo** or **Vila Marésia**).
Note that prices rise by 30% for the regatta
and over Christmas and Semana Santa.

$$ Das Falésias
Av Assis Moreira 314, Praia das Fontes, T085-
3327 3052, www.hotelfalesias.com.br.
Pleasant German-owned cliff-side *pousada*
with a pool and tidy rooms.

$$ Pouasda dos Hibiscos
Morro Branco, T085-98526 8668,
www.pousadadoshibiscos-ce.com.br.
Annexes of modest sparsely furnished rooms
fronted with hammock-slung terraces.
Generous breakfasts, nice little pool.

$$ Recanto Praiano
Morro Branco, T085-3338 7233.
Peaceful little *pousada* with a good breakfast.
Recommended.

Prainha do Canto Verde
See www.prainhadocantoverde.org for a list
of *pousadas* and facilities in the village.

$ Refugio da Paz Dona Mirtes
T085-9222 6683.
Simple, very spacious fan-cooled brick rooms
with mosquito nets, marine murals on the
walls, tile floors and a great breakfast of
tapioca, cuscus, fruit, cakes and cereals.

Canoa Quebrada
Villagers will let you sling your hammock
or will put you up cheaply. **Verónica** is
recommended, European books exchanged.
Sr Miguel rents good clean houses for US$10
a day. The websites www.canoabrasil.com
and www.portalcanoaquebrada.com.br have
lists of hotels and restaurants in English.

$$$ Tranqüilândia
R Camino do Mar, T088-3421 7012,
www.tranquilandia.it.
A range of thatched roofed, a/c chalets
around a smart pool in a lawned tropical
garden. Decent restaurant. Italian-owned
and with facilities for kitesurfers.

$$ Pousada Alternativa
R Francisco Caraço, T088-3421 7278,
www.pousada-alternativa.com.br.
Rooms with or without bath. Centrally
located and recommended.

$$ Pousada Azul
R Dragão do Mar (Broadway) s/n,
T088-9932 9568 (mob), www.
portalcanoaquebrada.com.br.
Very simple, small concrete and blue tile a/c
or fan-cooled boxes, a sunny upper deck,
miniature pool and warm service from the
owner, Saméa.

$$ Pousada Latitude
R Dragão do Mar (Broadway), T088-3241
7041, www.pousadalatitude.com.br.
Large a/c 2-storey bungalows in a large
complex off the main street. Not intimate
but with decent service.

$$ Pousada Lua Estrela
R Nascer do Sol 106, 20 m off R Dragão
do Mar, T088-3421 7040, www.
pousadaluaestrela.com.

A smart hostel/*pousada* with with fan-cooled rooms with great sea views, fridges and hot showers and a/c rooms without views in the garden.

$$ Pousada Oásis do Rei
R Nascer do Sol 112, T088-3421 7081, www.pousadaoasisdorei.com.br.
Simple rooms around a pool in a little garden, with polished concrete or tiled floors; some with sea views and some with bed space for 3 or 4.

$$ Pousada Via Láctea
Just off R Dragão do Mar (Broadway), T088-3421 7103, www.pousadavialactea.com.
This chunky brick building may not be beautiful, but the views are and the beach is only some 50 m away. English spoken and tours organized. Highly recommended.

$ Hostel Ibiza
R Dragão do Mar (Broadway) 360, T088-3421 7262 (mob), www.hostelpousadaibiza.com.
Tiny, boxy but astonishingly cheap and fairly spruce doubles and dorms in a bright, hostel decorated with dozens of international flags, and with a party atmosphere 200 m from the beach.

Festivals

Canoa Quebrada
Jul In the 2nd half of the month is the **Canoarte** festival, which includes a *jangada* regatta and music festival.

What to do

Canoa Quebrada
The websites www.canoabrasil.com and www.portalcanoaquebrada.com.br have lists of local tour companies and kitesurf schools which are all very similar.

Transport

Canoa Quebrada
There are regular buses to **Fortaleza**. Very frequent *combi* vans connect to **Aracati** (which is served by hourly buses from Fortaleza) from where there are connections into **Rio Grande do Norte**.

The coast northwest of Fortaleza

where Fortaleza takes its weekend beach escapes

The beaches immediately northwest of Fortaleza are the city's weekend-spill-over. They're pretty much empty during the week though, and are easily reached on a day trip (by cab or with your own transport) or for a quick overnight stop if you don't have days free to reach Jericoacoara. There is excellent kitesurfing in the international resort of Cumbuco, which has sadly lost much of its uniquely Brazilian character.

Praia Barra do Ceará
This long beach lies 8 km northwest of the centre of Fortaleza where the Rio Ceará flows into the sea (take a 'Grande Circular 1' bus) near a down-at-heel neighbourhood ridden with favelas. The ruins of the 1603 **Fortaleza de Nossa Senhora dos Prazeres** (the first Portuguese settlement in the area which gives the city its name) lie on the coast, partially covered by dunes. They are a good spot from which to can watch the beautiful sunsets (though be vigilant in this area).

The palm-fringed beaches west of here on the other side of the Rio Ceará are cleaner but have strong waves. An iron bridge has been built across this river, making the area more accessible and open to development, which has been exploited more at the **Praia** de Icaraí, 22 km to the northwest, and **Tabuba**, 5 km further north, both of which have many *barracas*, guesthouses and simple restaurants and are busy at weekends.

Cumbuco

Cumbuco is a long, white-sand beach backed by foreign-owned hotels and condominiums, a few palms and a handful of little beach shacks; the area has a problem with rubbish. The beach itself is nothing special – unless you're a kitesurfer. Cumbuco is one of the best places in Brazil to learn how to kitesurf; ideal conditions can be guaranteed almost every day of the year. Sadly, as Cumbuco is largely European-owned and locals can no longer afford to buy property here, the town has almost entirely lost its Brazilian personality. Portuguese is rarely heard and the only locals that remain work in the hotels or restaurants. As well as kitesurfing and windsurfing, there are buggies, horse riding and *jangadas*, as well as dune-surfing (known locally as *skibunda*), during which you can slide down into the freshwater **Lagoa de Parnamirim**. A buggy tour costs around US$12 per person.

Cumbuco is served by regular buses from Fortaleza. Allow one to two hours for the journey. For more information visit www.kite-surf-brazil.com.

Listings The coast northwest of Fortaleza

Restaurants

Cumbuco
Accommodation can be organized through **Hi Life** (www.kiteboarding.com; see What to do, below).

What to do

Cumbuco
Hi Life, *Av Dos Coqueiros s/n, Cumbuco, Caucaia, T085-3318 7195, http://www. ikiteboarding.com/user/1062/about*. One of the leading kitesurf schools in Ceará. Can arrange full tours from Europe and organize hotels in Cumbuco, and transfers.

Jericoacoara and around

a delightful little resort nestled in dunes with world-class kite- and windsurfing

Jeri – as it is known to locals – is 300 km northwest of Fortaleza. Up until the 1990s tourism was almost unknown here and the locals eked their living fishing from *jangadas* and renting rooms to the occasional visiting surfer from São Paulo. Now the little sandy streets and the main *praça* are busy with visiting southern Brazilians and Europeans and the shacks have been replaced with modish hotels, restaurants and little boutiques selling fashionable beachwear from Rio and São Paulo designers.

Many visitors to Jeri come for the kitesurfing, which is about as good as it gets anywhere in the world, with a constant prevailing wind and a choice of lake and ocean locations. There are a handful of kitesurf schools/rental shops in town. Other visitors prefer to wander the beaches, sandboard or do stand-up paddle boarding, or take a buggy tour to the lakes and dunes nearby.

Tip...
A Jeri ritual is to climb the big dune south of town to watch the sunset with a caipirinha in hand, bought from one of the vendors who make the trek. This is one of the only spots in Brazil where the sun sinks into the sea on the horizon.

ON THE ROAD

Environmental issues

Jeri had become crowded with hotels and buggies by the turn of the millennium and the delicate dune systems were becoming badly damaged. Today buggies cannot enter the town and buggy rides are carefully controlled by a cooperative. For now Jeri seems safe from the predatory tourism which has damaged so many of the little fishing villages along the Brazilian coast.

If you would like to keep it this way avoid staying in the larger hotels (many of which have been illegally or insensitively built out onto the beach) and be sure to book tours only through the cooperative, thus ensuring that the descendants of the local fishing community are not marginalized and can earn a living in the town their ancestors have occupied for over 400 years. We list only hoteliers and businesses which are sensitive to Jeri's environment and local community.

There are no banks in town; most *pousadas* and restaurants accept Visa but it is wise to bring plenty of reais.

Around Jericoacoara

The nearby beaches offer superb conditions for kitesurfing and windsurfing – both practices that do little to damage the environment – and there is excellent walking and cycling along the long flat beaches to beauty spots like the crumbling chocolate-coloured rock arch at **Pedra Furada** (also visited on buggy tours). Sandboarding is popular on the dune south of town, though it is prohibited within the national park area. The park protects some 9000 ha of coastline, delicate dunes, *restinga* and perched dune lakes around Jericoacoara. The scenery is magnificent.

Buggy rides off the main paths are prohibited. Some of the most popular locations include the solar-powered lighthouse (*farol*) for sunrise and full moon, the Lagoas Azul and Paraiso (blue-water lakes surrounded by dunes), Mangue Seco (a tiny village in the dunes, see below), Serrote (a small range of rocky hills with bizarrely eroded crags) and Tatajuba (where you can see some of the most impressive and largest of all the dunes including the enormous Duna do Funil). See Transport, page 105.

Heading west along the beach takes you through a succession of sand dunes and coconut groves; the views are beautiful. After 2 km is the beach of **Mangue Seco**, and 2 km beyond this is an arm of the ocean that separates it from **Guriú** (across the bridge), where there is a village on top of a fixed dune. There is good birdwatching here and if you wish to stay hammock space can be found. The village musician sings his own songs in the bar. It's a four-hour walk from Jericoacoara, or take a boat across the bay.

The pebbly **Praia de Malhada is** reachable either by walking east along the beach or by cutting through town. A 3- to 4-km walk to the east takes you to the **Pedra Furada**, a stone arch sculpted by the sea, one of the landmarks of Jeri, only accessible at low tide (check the tide tables at the Casa do Turismo). Swimming is dangerous here as waves and currents are strong. In the same direction but just inland is **Serrote**, a large hill with a lighthouse on top; it is well worth walking up for the magnificent views.

The best kitesurfing and windsurfing beaches are beyond Jeri, some 15 km east of town (43 km by road via Jijoca and Caiçara), at **Praia do Preá** and **Praia de Guriú**. Both beaches are reachable on buggy day tours for around US$20 if you have your own kitesurfing equipment. Tours including equipment (US$40) can be arranged in Jeri through any of the local kite shops and there is designated kitesurfer accommodation on Preá, with stay-and-surf packages. See www.kite-prea.com for more information. It is also possible to visit the **Pedra da Seréia**, a rock pocked with natural swimming pools.

Some of the best scenery in the area is around **Nova Tatajuba**, about 35 km west of Jerí. One Toyota a day passes through the town on the way to the ferry point at Camocim and almost all buggy tours visit. There are simple *pousadas* and restaurants and the village is far smaller and less touristy than Jeri. See Where to stay, below.

Some 10 km beyond Praia do Preá (62 km by road) is the beach of **Barrinha**, with access to the picturesque **Lagoa Azul**. From here it's 10 km inland through the dunes (20 km along the road) to **Lagoa Paraíso** or **Jijoca**, a turquoise, freshwater lake, great for bathing (buggy US$10 per person).

Cruz

Some 40 km east of Jijoca is Cruz, an obligatory stop if travelling by bus from Sobral to Jericoacoara. It is a small pleasant town, surrounded by a *carnauba* palm forest (used in making brooms). At the south end is a large wooden cross dating from 1825, nearby is a statue to São Francisco. There is a lively market on Sunday when, at dawn, *pau d'arara* trucks, mule carts and bicycles converge on the town. There are two very basic hotels.

Listings Jericoacoara and around

Where to stay

Jericoacoara
There are crowds at weekends mid-Dec to mid-Feb, in Jul and during Brazilian holidays. Many places are full in low season too. For New Year's Eve, 4- to 5-day packages are available. Prices rise by as much as 40% in peak season (New Year and Carnaval).

$$$$ Vila Kalango
R das Dunas 30, T088-3669 2289,
www.vilakalango.com.br.
The smartest option in town with well-appointed rooms in stilt house cabins in a tree-filled garden just set-back from the beach. Lovely pool and bar area, a decent restaurant and excellent facilities for kitesurfers and windsurfers. There's a sister kitesurfer hotel, **Rancho do Peixe** (see below), on Praia da Preá. Shuttle buses to/from Fortaleza.

$$$ Espaço Nova Era
R do Forró s/n, T088-3669 2056,
www.novaerapousada.com.br.
A mock-Mediterranean lobby house leads to a set of circular a/c or fan-cooled cabins in

terracotta brick and polished concrete. These sit in an Italianate garden shaded by trees and coloured with tropical flowers. Room for 5 in the larger cabins making this an economical option. Italian-owned.

$$ Barão
R do Forró 433, T088-3669 2136,
www.recantodobarao.com.
Duplex rooms in 2 corridors strung with hammocks. All overlook the corridors and *pousada* gardens and the brightest and best-kept rooms are on the upper floors. The *pousada* has a small pool and attractive sitting areas furnished with sun beds. There is a popular *churrascaria* next door. The owners are from São Paulo.

$$ Cabana
R das Dunas 297, T085-99635 8197,
www.pousadacabana.com.br.
Rows of colourful, well-appointed barn-door cabins with hammock terraces set in a tree-shaded garden filled with heliconia flowers. Tiny pool. Large breakfast.

$$ Papagaio
Trav do Forró s/n, T088-3669 2142,
www.pousadapapagaio.com.br.
Attractive, stone-floored a/c rooms with
pretty pebble-dash bathrooms and
hammock-strung verandas overlooking a
courtyard garden shaded by prickly pears
and with a tiny pool. Brazilian-owned.

$$ Pousada Tirol
R São Francisco 202, T088-3669 2006,
www.jericoacoarahostel.com.br.
HI-affiliated hostel with dorms (**$** per person)
with hot water showers and scrupulously
clean but tiny doubles (cheaper in low
season; the best are at the far end of the
corridors) with barely room for a double
and a single bed. Very friendly and popular
with party-loving travellers. Free Wi-Fi, little
hammock-slung garden.

$$ Pousada Zé Patinha
R São Francisco s/n, T088-3669 2081,
www.pousadazepatinha.com.
Simple, a/c or fan-cooled tiled rooms and
plain white rooms in 2 parallel corridors.
No outside windows, just overlooking the
corridor. Cool in the heat of the day, quiet,
with decent mattresses and locally owned.
Sandboard rental.

Around Jericoacoara

$ Rancho do Peixe
Praia do Preá, T088-9966 2111,
www.ranchodopeixe.com.br.
Chic bungalows set right on the beach
next to a long pool. All have hammock
verandas and are fan-cooled. Special
rates and excellent facilities for kitesurfers
and windsurfers.

Tatajuba
There are a handful of very simple *pousadas*
in this village between Camocim and
Jericoacoara. There are plenty of simple
seafood restaurants, the most famous of
which is the **Barraca de Dona Delmira**.

$ Pousada Brisa do Mar
T088-9961 5439, www.
pousadabrisadomartatajuba.blogspot.com.
Spartan and very basic rooms, some
with en suites.

Restaurants

Jericoacoara
The town has a good choice of small
restaurants, many of them low-lit with
hanging lights or candlelight at night.

$$ Bistrogonoff
Beco do Guaxelo 60, T088-3669 2220.
Fish and meat combinations, stroganoffs
and a healthy selection of pastas. Convivial
atmosphere, very popular in the evenings.
The owners are from São Paulo.

$$ Na Casa Dela
R Principal, T088-3669 2024.
Northeastern Brazilian and Bahian cooking,
including delicious sun-dried meat with
onions, manioc flour, rice and puréed squash.
The dining is intimate with tables mood-lit
and sitting in the sand under their own
private *palapa*.

$$ Tamarindo
R Ismael. Open for dinner only.
Lovely evening atmosphere with soft lit
round raw wood tables set in a garden.
Varied menu of fish dishes, pasta and
Brazilian standards.

$ Do Sapão
R São Francisco s/n, T088-9905 8010.
Good-value *prato feito*, set meals including a
delicious vegetarian pizzas and pastas. Live
music. Named in homage to the giant toads
that appear everywhere in Jeri after dark.

$ Kaze Sushi
R Principal.
Decent, fresh sushi and sashimi, miso soups
and fruit juices.

Bars and clubs

Jericoacoara

The liveliest bars are Samba Rock (R Principal at the Praça) and the Tortuga (R São Francisco) which are especially full on Fri and Sat. About once a week in high season there is a folk dance show that includes *capoeira*. There is nightly *forró* in high season at the **Casa do Forró** (R do Forró, a couple of blocks inland from the beach, low season on Wed and Sat only); starts about 2200.

What to do

Jericoacoara

Buggy tours cost US$30 for a buggy to all the sites; contact the **Associação de Bugueiros (ABJ)** or head to the buggy park at the back end of town. **Vila Kalango** (see Where to stay, above) is orientated to kitesurfers and organizes some of the best kitesurf trips in Jeri. **Clube dos Ventos**, *R das Dunas, T088-3621 0211, www.clubventos.com.* Windsurfing and kitesurfing at Preá and Lagoa Jijoca. Equipment hire, courses and transfers.

Transfers and tours

A private transfer to Jericoacoara and Fortaleza or to Caburé in the Lençóis Maranhenses, with stop-offs at beaches and sights along the way makes a great trip. The scenery between Ceará and Maranhão is particularly spectacular. Expect to pay between US$145 and US$225 for a car transfer between Fortaleza and Jericoacoara by road (3-4 hrs) or beach (5-6 hrs) respectively and US$200-300 for transfers to Caburé. Cars have space for between 4 and 6. Most of the bigger *pousadas* in Jeri can arrange a pick-up from Fortaleza on request. **André Pinto**, *T085-99981 0717, andrepinto70@ ig.com.br.* Good-value transfers and tours from Fortaleza to Jeri, to the Lençóis Maranhenses and to the spectacular Sete Cidades national park in comfortable 4WDs. **Eco Dunas**, *T011-9902 9149, www.ecodunas. tur.br.* By far the best option for multi-day transfer tours between Jericoacoara and

the Lençóis with options for visiting the wild locations in Piauí like the Sete Cidades National Park, the Delta do Parnaíba and the Serra da Capivara. Better value, more reliable and with more modern cars than other operators. Book ahead and mention that you were recommended by the *Footprint Handbook* for the best prices.

Litoral, *T088-9921 7532, www.litoraltur.com.* Offer tours and transfers by road or beach between Fortaleza and Jericoacoara. Also airport pick-ups.

Transport

Jericoacoara

Bus Twice daily buses from **Fortaleza** to Jijoca (catch a *jardineira*, or Toyota pickup, from Jericoacoara for the 45-min connection). Be sure to take a *VIP* or *executivo* bus to/from Fortaleza as the journey takes 5-6 hrs (or even 7-8 hrs on some buses). In high season more comfortable a/c *combis* also run to **Fortaleza** via Jijoca, US$30, 4 hrs. Book through *pousadas* in Jeri or agencies in Fortaleza.

If heading to **Belém** or other points north and west, take the *jardineira* to **Jijoca**, from where buses run to **Cruz**. In Cruz, you can change for **Sobral**; there is only one bus a day Cruz–Sobral, US$15, 3-4 hrs, but **Redenção** runs from Cruz to **Fortaleza** several times daily, US$32.50.

To get to **Parnaíba**, take a Toyota to **Camocim** (US$15). Enquire at the *pousada* for times; most leave at around 0900; book through your hotel or ask around for buggy or *jardineira* (US$25 per person). There are regular connections between Camocim and Parnaíba (3 hrs, US$10). Be sure to arrive in Camocim as early as possible for the best connections.

Cruz

Bus The bus to **Jijoca** goes through town at about 1400, US$15 (US$22.50 to Jericoacoara); the bus meets the *jardineira* for **Jericoacoara** (US$7.50); wait for the bus at 1330. Alternatively, take an *horário* pick-up from Cruz to Jijoca.

Chapada de Ibiapaba

An area of tablelands, caves, rock formations, rivers and waterfalls, most of which is unprotected, the Chapada de Ibiapaba lies in the heart of the Chapada de Ibiapaba mountains in the far northwest of the state. There are many small towns and places to visit: **Tianguá** is surrounded by waterfalls; 3 km to the north is Cachoeira de São Gonçalo, a good place for bathing; 5 km from town are natural pools at the meeting place of seven waterfalls; and about 16 km from town, on the edge of the BR-222, is **Cana Verde**, a 30-m-high waterfall surrounded by monoliths and thick vegetation.

Some 30 km north of Tianguá is **Viçosa do Ceará**, a pretty colonial town also within the *chapada*, known for its ceramics, hang-gliding, food and drink. Climb to the **Igreja de Nossa Senhora das Vitórias**, a stone church on top of the 820-m-high **Morro do Céu** (reachable by walking up 360 steps), for a good view of the town, the surrounding highlands and the *sertão* beyond. Near the town are interesting rock formations, such as the 100-m-wide **Pedra de Itagurussu** with a natural spring. There is good walking in the area.

Basic walking maps are available at the **Secretaria de Turismo**, near the old theatre to the right of the *praça* on which the church stands. Ask about visiting the community that makes sun-baked earthenware pots. There are five buses a day from Fortaleza via Sobral.

Parque Nacional Ubajara

Some 250 km southwest of Fortaleza, at an altitude of 840 m, Parque Nacional Ubajara has 563 ha of native highland and *caatinga* brush. The park's main attraction is the **Ubajara Cave** on the side of an escarpment. Some 15 chambers, extending for a total of 1120 m, have been mapped, of which 360 m are open to visitors. Access is along a 6-km footpath and steps (two to three hours, take water) or by a **cable car** ① *T088-3634 1219, 0900-1430, US$4*, which descends the cliff to the cave entrance.

Essential Parque Nacional Ubajara

Access

There are six buses daily from Fortaleza to Ubajara town. From Jericoacoara it is necessary to change buses in Sobral (which is itself reachable from Jijoca). In Sobral is **$$$ Beira Rio**, across from the *rodoviária*, T088-3613 1040, www.beirariohotel.com.br.

Visiting the cave

Visiting the cave is by guided tour. At the park entrance is an **ICMBio office**, 5 km from the caves, T085-3634 1388, www.icmbio.gov.br. A bar by the entrance serves juices, snacks and drinks. In the park there is a new easy walkway through the woods with stunning views at the end. Start either to the left of the park entrance or opposite the snack bar near the cable-car platform.

There is a good 8-km trail to the park from Araticum (7 km by bus from Ubajara). This route is used by locals and passes through *caatinga* forest.

Park information

For information, including accommodation, see http://portalubajara.com.br and www.ubajara.ce.gov.br.

Lighting has been installed in nine caverns of the complex. The cave is completely dry and home to 14 types of bat. Several rock formations look like animals, including a horse's head, caiman and a snake; a fact which guides spend much of the tour explaining. In 1979 a speleological expedition found a giant skull in one of the caves, belonging to what was later identified as a previously unknown species of bear related to the Andean spectacled bear, and suggesting that the *serra* was far colder 10,000 years ago than it is today.

Listings Western Ceará

Where to stay

Chapada de Ibiapaba

$$$ Serra Grande
About 2 km from town, BR-222, Km 311, T088-3671 1818, www.serragrandehotel.com.
All the usual amenities, good.

Parque Nacional Ubajara

The website www.portalubajara.com.br has an overview of the area including information on *pousadas* and hotels.

$$ Pousada Gruta da Ubajara
50 m from the entrance to the park, T088-3634 1375, www.pousadagruta.com.br.
With a dozen lemon and orange concrete chalets, some with room for 4 people, and a restaurant serving spit-roast meat, stewed chicken and the owner's potent, home-made *cachaça*.

$$ Pousada Sítio do Alemão
Estrada do Teleférico, near the park, 2 km from town, T088-9961 4645, www.sitio-do-alemao.20fr.com.
Take Estrada do Teleférico 2 km from town, after the **Pousada da Neblina** turn right, signposted, 1 km to Sítio Santana/Klein (Caixa Postal 33, Ubajara, CEP 62350-000, T088-9961 4645). 5-chalet *pousada* sits in an old coffee and banana plantation surrounded by beautiful cloudforest. The chalets vary in size. The largest has 2 bedrooms; the smallest and cheapest have shared bathrooms. A generous breakfast is included in the price.

What to do

Parque Nacional Ubajara
Birdwatching
Ciro Albano Birding Brazil, *T085-9955 5162, www.nebrazilbirding.com.* The best and most experienced birdwatching guide in the northeast of Brazil, offering bespoke and scheduled trips to the Maciço de Baturité and other locations in Ceará, as well as further afield in Bahia, Alagoas, Pernambuco, Sergipe and Minas. Speaks English and will pick up from airports in Fortaleza or Salvador and organize transport and accommodation as part of an all-inclusive package.

Hang-gliding
Sítio do Bosco, *T088-9444 8967, www.sitiodobosco.com.br.* Hang-gliding from the Serra de Ibiapaba near Ubajara.

Transport

Parque Nacional de Ubajara
Bus 6 daily to and from **Fortaleza** to Ubajara town, US$12. From **Jericoacoara** take a *combi* to Jijoca and then to Sobral from where there are buses to both Ubajara and Tinguá. 2 buses daily to and from **Teresinha** (onward to São Luís and Belém), 3 to and from **Parnaíba** and buses every hour from Tinguá to Ubajara. 5 buses a day between Sobral (with connections to Jijoca (for Jericoacoara) and Fortaleza) and Viçosa do Ceará (6 hrs, US$21).

Piauí

But for a sliver of coast Piauí is dry *sertão*, pocked with jagged hills, cut by canyons and dotted with weather-worn ancient mounds of rock. Few tourists stop here, but those who do seldom regret it. Torrid Teresina is a friendly and well-planned capital where foreigners are a curiosity, Parnaíba is a pretty colonial river port, and the dry interior is broken by a number of stunning and intriguing state and national parks. These include the enigmatic Serra da Capivara, Sete Cidades and the almost inaccessible Serra dos Confusões, beehive mounds sticking up out of the desert whose canyon walls are daubed with some of the oldest rock art in the Americas. And while Piauí's coast is tiny it includes the magnificent Delta do Parnaíba: one of the largest river deltas in the world, replete with mangrove swamps and tiny islands fringed with golden beaches and home to traditional communities who seldom see tourists.

After neighbouring Maranhão, Piauí is the poorest state in Brazil. Its population is about 2.7 million, but many leave to seek work elsewhere. The economy is almost completely dependent upon agriculture and livestock, both of which in turn depend on how much rain, if any, falls.

BACKGROUND

Piauí

Piauí's wineskin shape derives from its history and the state's delineation along the course of the Parnaíba River, which winds 1480 km through the arid *sertão* to the coast: Piauí is the only Brazilian state to have been founded from the interior rather than as a coastal port. It was initially explored from Bahia and Pernambuco through the *sertão* by 18th-century ranchers looking for fresh pasture land. Long forgotten colonial towns such as Oerias date from this period. Other towns sprung up along the Parnaíba River, like Floriano, Amarante and, in 1852, Teresina. The latter remains the only northeastern capital to lie inland. The river's delta eventually became the coastal frontier of the state.

Until the early 19th century Piauí was under the control of neighbouring Maranhão. At Independence, there was bitter, bloodthirsty fighting between supporters of the Portuguese colony and the Brazilians who sought their freedom. Well into the 20th century Piauí maintained a strong tradition of Portuguese-inspired *Coronelismo* (the dominance of wealthy landowners over rural communities), whose vestiges persist to this day.

Teresina

Brazil's hottest state capital with friendly locals and a pleasant riverside setting

Piauí's capital Teresina (population 716,000) lies about 350 km from the coast, at the confluence of the Rio Poti and the Rio Parnaíba. It is flat with a grid of streets, some of which are lined with handsome terracotta roofed 19th-century buildings. There are more than 30 urban parks, and the usual gamut of Brazilian concrete apartment blocks. Teresina has a lively cultural scene and a famously vibrant nightlife. The city itself is reputed to be the hottest after Cuiabá, with temperatures up to 42°C and an annual mean of around 30°C.

The city was founded in the 18th century as the Vila do Poti and was renamed in honour of the empress of Brazil and wife of Dom Pedro II, Teresa Cristina, who had supported the idea of moving the capital from Oreias.

Sights

Praça Pedro II lies at the heart of the city and is the hub of Teresina life. There are many bars and restaurants in the surrounding streets, where diners are frequently serenaded by *violeiros* (Brazil's equivalent of *mariachis*). Many *violeiros* also congregate at the **Casa do Cantador** ⓘ *R Lucia 1419, Vermelha, T086-3211 6833, 1400-2000, Wed is the best night*, a little *boteco* outside the city centre surrounded by mangroves. There is live poetry, a gallery of art and shows at the **Oficina da Palavra** ⓘ *R Benjamin Constant 1400, Centro, T086-3223 4441, www.oficinadapalavra-pi.com.br, Mon-Fri 0800-1200 and 1400-2000, Sat and Sun 0800-1200*. The centre has some attractive buildings including the **Teatro 4 Setembro** and the old art deco cinema, the **Rex**. There's a decent crafts market at the **Central do Artenasato**, which is well known for its opals, carved wood and hammocks. The **Museu do Piauí** ⓘ *Praça Marechal Deodoro s/n, Tue-Fri 0730-1730, Sat and Sun 0800-1200, US$1.50*, is in a mansion house dating from 1859 and has been completely refurbished. It preserves a collection of sacred art by local artists from the 19th century, as well as impressive woodcarvings by Mestre Dezinho Nonato de Oliveira and an extensive collection of frowsty fossils. The **Palácio de Karnak** ① *just west of Praça Frei Serafim, T086-3221 9820, Mon-Sat 0800-1800 (visits to the inside of the palace by appointment only)*, is a grand neoclassical edifice set in pretty gardens landscaped by Roberto Burle Marx, and has been the governor's palace since 1926. Inside is a collection of period furniture and artefacts and a rare set of lithographs of the Middle East in 1839 by the Scottish artist David Roberts, famous for his depictions of unexcavated temples throughout the Middle East and most notably in Egypt. The **Casa da Cultura** ① *R Rui Barbosa 348, Centro, T086-3215 7849, Mon-Fri 0800-1900, Sat 0900-1300, Sun 1300-1600*, is devoted to the history of the city and to the lives of famous ex-residents such as the journalist Carlos Castelo Branco and the photographer Jose de Medeiros. The reception desk has a programme of cultural events taking place in Teresina.

Every morning along the picturesque river, with washing laid out to dry on its banks, is the *troca-troca* (market), where people buy, sell and swap. Most of the year the rivers are low, leaving sandbanks known as *coroas* (crowns). The confluence of the two rivers is at the **Parque Encontro dos Rios** ① *Av Boa Esperanca s/n, Poti Velho, T086-3217 5020, daily 0800-1800*, where there is a statue of the Cabeça de Cuia river demon, Crispim. Canoes are available for hire on the river.

Listings Teresina *map below*

Tourist information

The website www.teresina.pi.gov.br is a useful source of information (in Portuguese only).

Ana Turismo
R Álvaro Mendes 1961, Centro, T086-3221 2272.

Piemtur
R Álvaro Mendes 2003, Caixa Postal 36; R Magalhães Filho, next to 55 N; and R Acre, Convention Centre, T086-3221 7100.
There are also kiosks at the *rodoviária* and the airport.

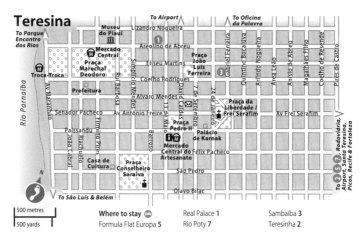

Where to stay	Real Palace **1**	Sambaíba **3**
Formula Flat Europa **5**	Rio Poty **7**	Teresinha **2**

Sindicato dos Guiás de Turismo de Piauí (Singtur)
R Paissandu 1276, T086-3221 2175.
Information booths at the Centro de Artesanato, Praça Dom Pedro II (helpful, friendly), the Encontro das Águas, Poty Velho and on the shores of the Rio Poty.

Where to stay

There are many cheap places on R São Pedro and R Alvaro Mendes. The cleanest and best is **Glória**, No 823, blocks 800 and 900. There are other cheap hotels and *dormitórios* around Praça Saraiva.

$$$ Rio Poty
Av Mcal Castelo Branco 555, Ilhota, T086-3367 2200, www.riopoty.com.
5 stars. One of the better options in town with rooms in a large concrete Benidorm-style block overlooking a big swimming pool.

$$ Formula Flat Europa
R José Olímpio de Melo 3330, Ilhotas, T086-3223 7100, www.formulaflateuropa.com.br.
Bright, modern and well-appointed flats with microwaves, kitchenettes and living areas. Space for up to 3 people making this an **$** option per person.

$$ Real Palace
R Areolino de Abreu 1217, T086-2107 2700, www.realpalacehotel.com.br.
Business orientated hotel with a range of old-fashioned rooms and suites and a small business centre.

$$ Sambaíba
R Gabriel Ferreira 230-N, T086-3222 3460.
A functional 2-star with very simple a/c rooms.

$ Hotel Teresinha
Av Getúlio Vargas 2885, opposite the rodoviária, T086-3211 0919.
With a/c or fan, clean, friendly.

Transport

Air Senador Petrônio Portela Airport, 5 km from the centre, Av Centenário s/n, T086-3133 6270, has flights to **Fortaleza**, **Brasília**, **Rio de Janeiro**, **São Paulo**, **Goiânia** and **São Luís**. Outside the airport, buses run straight into town and to the *rodoviária*.

Bus The *rodoviária* is 4 km from the centre. Buses run into the town every few minutes. The bus journey to **Fortaleza** is scenic and takes 9 hrs (US$13.50). There are direct bus connections with Fortaleza (a scenic 9-hr journey), **Belém** (US$23.40, 13 hrs), **Recife** (US$27, 16 hrs) and **São Luís** (US$12, 7 hrs).

Parque Nacional de Sete Cidades
eerie outback wilderness with some of the strangest rock formations on Earth

Lost in the scrub and thorn bush of the Sertão 205 km northeast of Teresina, dotted with bizarre domed hills and crumbling canyons and home to puma, caves and unique birdlife, this 6221-ha national park can be visited on a long detour between Jericoacoara and the Lençóis Maranhenses. If you visit on a weekday you are almost certain to have it entirely to yourself.

The park is named after seven eroded rock formations which, from the ground, look like a medley of weird monuments – shallow cupula-shaped hills encrusted with hexagons, wind-sculpted rocks with odd cylindrical bars running through them, canyons and overhangs, beehive domes

Tip...
The best view is from Segunda Cidade, especially in the late afternoon when the golden light brings out the panoply of colours on the rocks and casts haunting shadows.

Essential Parque Nacional de Sete Cidades

Access

The park is 26 km northeast of the little town of Piripiri on the BR-343. There are buses to Piripiri from Parnaíba and Teresina as well as Fortaleza, Ubajara and São Luís (though these buses have many stops). From Piripiri there is an **Instituto Chico Mendes de Conservação da Biodiversidade (ICMBio)** bus direct to the park at 0700 daily, from by the Telemar office in front of the Praça da Bandeira (it is ostensibly for employees, but usually possible to hitch a ride). The bus passes in front of the **Hotel Fazenda Sete Cidades** at 0800, reaching the park 10 minutes later; it returns at 1630. *Mototáxis* in Piripiri charge (US$10) to the park, or a standard taxi costs US$12.

If coming from Parnaíba, Barreirinhas (in the Lençóis Maranhenses) or Jericoacoara, agencies such as **Eco Dunas** (see page 129), offer trips often as part of an interstate transfer. You can also visit with a private driver like André Pinto (see page 94).

Opening hours

The park is open daily 0800-1700.

and scrub-covered shallow valleys. The hills are grouped into *cidades* (cities), each of which is unique, and a few of which have sweeping views out over the dry forest of the Brazilian outback, or Sertão.

The rocks are covered in prehistoric art – which has yet to be archaeologically dated but which is thought to be from between 5000 and 10,000 years old. There are various unlikely theories for their origins, including one which links them with the Phoenicians and another from Argentine Professor Jacques de Mahieu which suggests they are Nordic runes left by the Vikings.

With 22 springs, the park is an oasis in the dry surroundings and forms a transition zone between *caatinga* vegetation and *cerrado*. There is abundant wildlife including white-tailed deer, paca, various armadillos, puma, tamandua anteaters and well over 100 bird species, some of them rare *sertão* endemics. Large iguanas descend from the trees in the afternoon.

The park spans 12 km and can be walked across in a day, beginning at the Portaria Sul (south gate) and finishing at the Portaria Norte (north gate). Trails are well signposted, but beware of rattlesnakes when hiking. Guides from the visitor centre will drive you to the various trailheads in a tour of a few hours for a modest fee. Try and be here in the early morning (0800) or late afternoon (1500-1700) for the best light and to see the wildlife.

Listings Parque Nacional de Sete Cidades

Tourist information

Instituto Chico Mendes de Conservação da Biodiversidade (ICMBio)
Av Homero Castelo Branco 2240, Teresina, T086-3343 1342, www.icmbio.com.br.
For information and maps.

Where to stay

Piripiri, 26 km from the park, is a cheap place to break the Belém–Fortaleza journey. There is accommodation right next to the park gates (see below) and in Piripiri town. As well as those listed, there are other options near bus offices and behind the church.

$$-$ Fazenda Sete Cidades
Right next to the park gates, T086-3276 2222.
A converted farmhouse with large
though simple fan-cooled and a/c rooms,
horse riding, river water swimming pools
and a play area for kids.

$ Hotel California
R Dr Antenor de Araujo Freitas 546, Piripiri,
T086-3276 1645, www.hotelcaliforniapiripiri.
com.br.
There's plenty of room in the Hotel California,
with 32 rooms all with a/c and en suites.
24-hr reception so you can check out any
time you like and even leave. Convenient for
the 0700 bus to the park from nearby Praça
da Bandeira.

$ Instituto Chico Mendes de ICMBio
(Ibama) Hostel
In the park, T086-3343 1342. Price per person.
Rooms with bath, pleasant, good
restaurant, natural pool nearby, camping.
Recommended. Not open all year round,
so book ahead or check with **Instituto
Chico Mendes de Conservação da
Biodiversidade (ICMBio)** (www.icmbio.
com.br, in Portuguese only), in Teresina.

What to do

Tours can be arranged with **Eco Dunas**
(see page 129) as well as most agencies
in Jericoacoara (see page 105).

Parnaíba and around
relaxed, friendly place, with a pretty colonial centre by Parnaíba River

Parnaíba (population 133,000) makes a good break in the journey north or south. If
crossing the delta, buy all provisions here. There are beaches at Luís Correia, 14 km
from Parnaíba, with radioactive sands.

About 18 km from Parnaíba is **Pedra do Sal**, with dark blue lagoons and palm trees. At
Lagoa de Portinho, 12 km from Parnaíba, there are bungalows, a bar, restaurant and
canoes for hire; it is possible to camp. **Praia do Coqueiro** is a small fishing village with
natural pools formed at low tide. Seafood is good at **Alô Brasil** and **Bar da Cota**.

Delta do Parnaíba
The Delta do Parnaíba, which separates Piauí from Tutóia (see page 126) and the
spectacular Lençóis Maranhenses (see page 126) in neighbouring Maranhão, is one of the

Essential Delta do Parnaíba

Access

Crossing the delta is no longer possible by
public ferry, but it's possible to charter a
launches (US$ 90-150 depending on the
number of people; the maximum is 12) at
the Porto dos Tatus (also called Porto da
Barca), 10 km north of Parnaíba or in Tutóia.
Alternatively, take a boat from Parnaíba to
the crab-fishing village of Morro do Meio on
Ilha das Canarias (Monday at high tide, usually
in the small hours). It is sometimes possible
to hitch a lift from Ilha das Canarias to Tutóia

with a crab fisherman. It's more interesting
and better value to cross the delta rather than
returning to the same place, but allow plenty
of time. See Transport, page 115.

Tours

The Delta do Parnaíba can be visited as part
of a tour between Jericoacoara and the
Lençóis Maranhenses, with **Eco Dunas** (see
page 129). Short day trips also run from Porto
dos Tatus, on a huge boat full of noisy people
(around US$7 with snacks and a drink).

largest river deltas in the world. It's a watery labyrinth of mangroves, broad rivers and narrow creeks, with unspoilt tropical islands fringed by gorgeous deserted beaches. The interiors of these islands are home to largely unstudied wildlife, including many rare birds, and traditional Caiçara fishing communities, who seldom see tourists.

Renting hammock space with them is straightforward and simple makeshift *pousada* accommodation can be arranged. Many people in this region live as they have done for generations, in adobe houses, on a diet of fresh fish cooked in baked-earth ovens. Illiteracy is the norm. There is no mains electricity and the nearest shopping is at Parnaíba or Tutóia.

Listings Parnaíba and around

Where to stay

Parnaíba

$$$ Pousada dos Ventos
Av São Sebastião 2586, Universidade, T086-3322 2555, www.pousadadosventos.com.br.
The best business hotel in town, a 10-min taxi ride from the centre, with spacious, simple rooms and an attractive breakfast area next to the pool.

$$ Casa Santo Antonio
Praça Santo Antônio, 988, www.mvchoteis decharme.com.br, T086-3322 1900.
The best in town with rooms a refurbished belle époque town house and adjacent annexes. Garden and a small pool.

$$ Pousada Chalé Suiço
Av Padre R J Vieira 448, Fátima, T086-3321 3026, www.chalesuico.com.br.
Cheaper without a/c or breakfast, bar, laundry, pool, tours arranged, windsurfing, sandboarding, buggies and bikes.

$$ Pousada Vila Parnaíba
R Monsenhor Joaquim Lopes 500, T086-3323 2781, www.pousadavilaparnaiba.com.br.
Brightly painted *pousada* in the historical town centre near the river, with simple tiled floor rooms gathered around a small pool.

$ Residencial
R Almirante Gervásio Sampaio 375, T086-3322 2931, www.residencialpousada.com.br.
Very plain, simple doubles, dorms and plusher en suites with cold water showers gathered around a plant-filled courtyard.

There are many other basic hotels nearby in the centre.

Delta do Parnaíba

$$$ Pousada Ecológica Ilha do Caju
Contact: Av Presidente Vargas 235, Centro, Parnaíba, T086-3321 1179, www.ilhadocaju.com.br.
Comfortable rustic cabins, each has its own hammock outside, but inside there is a huge bed, handmade by the same craftsmen who made much of the *pousada*'s highly individual furniture. The owner, Ingrid, and senior staff speak English and are helpful and welcoming. Children must be aged 14 or over. The *pousada* will organize all transfers.

$ Ilha das Canarias
Morro do Meio Caiçara Comunidade.
Bring a hammock and ask at the **Raimundo Aires** restaurant (US$15 per person per night) great fish in the restaurant and idyllic beaches nearby. Very simple, no showers – just the river.

Transport

Parnaíba
Boat About 14 km from the town centre, on the Parnaíba River, is the Porto dos Tatus, where boats leave for the delta.

Bus The *rodoviária* is 5 km south of centre on BR-343, T086-3323 7300. Buses marked Praça João Luíz run to the centre; taxi US$6.
If travelling west up the coast from Parnaíba, there are 3 buses a day to **Tutóia**

(US$8, 2½ hrs) with **Nazaré** at 0700, 1200 and 1400. From Tutóia, Toyotas leave when full from the dock area for **Paulinho Neves** (US$6, 1 hr), further Toyotas leave from here to **Barreirinhas** (US$10, 2 hrs) near the **Parque Nacional Lençóis Maranhenses**.

It's also possible to take a bus inland to **São Luís** (4-6 hrs, US$20 – a very bad road, better to go via Tutóia) and from there to **Barreirinhas** (Cisne Branco, 4 per day, US$12, 3-3½ hrs on a new road). See São Luís transport, page 126.

If travelling east down the coast to **Jericoacoara** take a bus to **Camocim** (2 daily with **Guanabara**, US$12, 1½-2 hrs). To avoid getting stuck in Camocim, take the early bus at around 0700. This connects with the 1100 Toyota to **Jericoacoara** (US$10, 2 hrs) via the ferry (US$1 per foot passenger) across the river separating Piauí and Ceará, and the village of Tatajuba.

Parnaíba is connected to **Fortaleza** (US$50, 10 hrs) and **Teresina** (US$50, 6 hrs). Buses for the **Porto da Barca** (Tatuís) leave from the *rodoviária* every hour and take 10 mins. Taxis cost around US$10. There are also buses to Piripiri (for Parque Nacional da Sete Cidades).

Delta do Parnaíba

Boat Boats can be chartered from **Tutóia** (connected to Barreirinhas and Caburé in the Lençóis Marnahenses, via Paulino Neves, and direct to São Luís) or at **Porto dos Tatus** (also called Porto da Barca), 14 km north of Parnaíba.

Southern Piauí

colonial town and UNESCO-listed park with ancient rock paintings

Oeiras

The old capital of Piauí, 320 km from Teresina, is a pretty colonial treasure almost completely unknown to most Brazilians – let alone international tourists. The state government is restoring some of the colonial buildings, such as the bishop's palace and the church of Nossa Senhora da Vitória. There are some impressive celebrations during holy week, including a huge fireworks display and costumed parade on Maundy Thursday, serenaded by local mandolin players.

Parque Nacional Serra da Capivara

35 km from São Raimundo Nonato. The agency Trilhas da Capivara, T089-3582 1294, trilhascapivara@uol.com.br, runs excursions from US$40. For the most up-to-date information on transport and logistics, contact Fundham, below.

About 500 km south of Teresina is this 130,000-ha park, on the UNESCO World Heritage list. Some 30,000 prehistoric rock paintings on limestone have been found, dating from between 6000 and 12,000 years ago. The paintings are of daily life, festivities and celebrations, as well as hunting and sex scenes. Excavations by Brazilian and French archaeologists have uncovered fossilized remains of extinct animals such as the sabre-toothed tiger, giant sloths larger than elephants and armadillos the size of a car.

Nearly 400 archaeological sites have been identified in the park since research began in 1970. About 22 of them have been set up to receive tourists. Roads and all-weather paths allow visitors to view the sites with ease. Specially trained guides are available. The area is good for hiking in the *caatinga*, with its canyons and *mesas*. It is also possible to see much of the *caatinga* wildlife, in particular the birds.

Much investment has gone into the park, not just for visitors' facilities, but also to educate the local population about protecting the paintings and to establish a bee-keeping project to provide income in times of drought.

São Raimundo Nonato

São Raimundo Nonato is best known as the administration centre and access point for the Parque Nacional Serra Da Capivara, and for the remote and spectacular Serra dos Confusões further to the south. The **Fundação Museu do Homem Americano (Fundham)** ⓘ *Centro Cultural Sérgio Motta, Bairro Campestre, T089-3582 1612, www.fumdham.org.br*, has a fascinating collection of artefacts found in the *serra*. These are well displayed, though the information in English is poor. In September, the city hosts the **Festival Internacional Serra da Capivara** with music, theatre and parades.

There are bus connections with Teresina (a bumpy 540-km journey) and Petrolina in Pernambuco (300 km away).

Listings Southern Piauí

Where to stay

Oeiras

$ Pousada do Cônego
Praça das Vitórias 18, Centro, T089-3462 1219.
Very simple hotel housed in a large and somewhat decrepit town house and a small pizza restaurant with tables on the sunny veranda under the shade of tropical trees.

Parque Nacional Serra da Capivara

$ Serra da Capivara
Estrada PI-140 exit for Teresina, Km 2, T089-3582 1389.
Intimate country hotel near the park, with a pool and 18 a/c cabins and a restaurant.

São Raimundo Nonato

$ Pousada Lelinha
R Dr Barroso 249, Aldeia, T089-3582 2993.
One of the better options in the town with large, airy rooms the biggest of which have room for up to 5. Breakfasts are generous and the staff can give advice on visiting the *serra*.

$ Pousada Zabelê
Praça Major Toinho 280, Centro, T089-3582 2726.
Simple standard town hotel with a range of fan-cooled and a/c rooms. Helpful staff.

What to do

Parque Nacional Serra da Capivara
Trips can be organized via **Trilhas da Capivara**, T089-3582 1294, and **Cariri Ecotours** (see page 47) in Natal. Contact **Fundação Museu do Homem Americano (FUMDHAM)**, T089-3582 1612, www.fumdham.org.br, for further information.

Transport

Oerias
Bus The *rodoviária* is on Av Transamazônica s/n, T089-3462 2006. Buses to **Teresina** (310 km), **São Raimundo Nonato** (280 km) and connections to **Tocantins**.

Parque Nacional Serra da Capivara
Bus The *rodoviária* is at R Cândido Ferraz, T089-3582 1266. There are buses to **Teresina** (530 km) and connections to **Pernambuco**.

Maranhão

Maranhão is one of Brazil's most fascinating states with spectacular natural sights and a rich traditional culture based on a strong African heritage. The capital, São Luís, was founded by the French but built by the Portuguese, their azulejos and ornate baroque flourishes once graced the elegant buildings of its colonial centre which have sadly been allowed to deteriorate by the municipal and state government. Every Friday and Saturday night Sao Luís erupts with the riotous rhythms of cacuriá, and in June the city becomes the backdrop for one of the most colourful spectacles in the Northeast: the Bumba-Meu-Boi pageant.

The city is enclosed on both sides by natural beauty. To the southeast are the Lençóis Maranhenses, a 155,000-ha coastal desert of vast shifting dunes and isolated communities, cut by broad rivers and in the rainy season (between June and September), pocked with lakes, whose clear reflective waters are a vivid sky blue against brilliant white sand. To the northwest are the little-explored deltas of the Reentrâncias Maranhenses, which preserve the largest concentration of mangrove forest in Brazil, and which are fringed by the south Atlantic's longest coral reef.

Inland, Maranhão is remote and desperately poor but filled with fascinating forgotten villages and wilderness areas such as the Chapada das Mesas in Carolina: a forest-shrouded escarpment dripping with waterfalls that forms the transition zone between the hot, dry Northeast and the wet and warm Amazon.

The capital and port of Maranhão state, founded in 1612 by the French and named after St Louis of France, stands upon São Luís island between the bays of São Marcos and São José. It was once a beautiful city rivalling Recife and Salvador for colonial charm, but following more than a decade of neglect by the local authorities the UNESCO-protected colonial centre is in a dreadful state. The famous townhouses on Rua do Giz have been stripped of their beautiful 18th- and 19th-century *azulejo* tiles, which were some of the most striking in Brazil and are rumoured to have been sold off. Historic mansions and churches have been allowed to fall into a shocking state of disrepair.

Like both cities, São Luís (population 870,000) was a slaving port, initially for indigenous Amazonians who were brought in here in huge numbers to grow sugar cane, and subsequently for Africans. São Luís retains an African identity almost as strong as Salvador and Recife. The city is as Amazonian as it is northeastern and is subject to heavy tropical rains. However, a large proportion of the surrounding deep forest has been cut down to be replaced by *babaçu* palms, the nuts and oils of which are the state's most important products.

Sights

The old part of the city, on very hilly ground with many steep streets, is replete with colonial art nouveau and art deco buildings which are now falling apart (despite ostensibly being protected on a municipal, state and federal level). This has apparently gone unnoticed by UNESCO who still include the historic centre on the World Heritage List, rather than on the List in Danger. São Luís's damp climate encouraged the use of ceramic *azulejo* tiles for exterior walls. *Azulejos* are a common sight in Portugal but their civic use is relatively rare in Brazil; until a few years ago São Luís had a greater quantity and variety than anywhere else in the country, with historic tiles from Porto, Holland and France. Most have since been replaced by drab paint and are rumoured to have been auctioned off.

A good place to start a tour of the centre is **Avenida Dom Pedro II**. This was the heart of the original Tupinambá island village of Upaon Açu. When the French arrived in 1612, captained by Daniel de la Touche, they planted a huge wooden cross in the ground and, with a solemn Mass, decreed the land for France. La Touche renamed the village after Louis XIII, the emperor of France, and declared it the capital of the new land of 'France Equinoxiale' (Equinoctial France). There is a bust of La Touche in the 17th-century **Palácio de la Ravardière** ① *Av Dom Pedro II s/n, T089-3212-0800, Mon-Fri 0800-1800.*

Essential São Luís

Finding your feet

Marechal Cunha Machado Airport is 13 km from the centre. *Colectivo* mini-vans run from outside the terminal to Praça Deodoro in the city centre (every 40 minutes until 2200, US$1, 40 minutes). A taxi to the centre costs US$12.

From the *rodoviária*, 12 km from the centre on the airport road, the bus marked 'Rodoviária via Alemanha' runs to Praça João Lisboa in the centre (US$1).

Ferries cross the bay from Alcântara to the São Luís docks, **Terminal Hidroviário**, on Rampa Campos Mello, Cais da Praia Grande. See also Transport, page 125.

Part of the original wall of the French fort still remains in the bulwarks of the **Palácio dos Leões** ① *Av Dom Pedro II, T089-3214 8638, Mon, Wed and Fri 1500-1800, US$3*, which was extensively embellished by the Portuguese after they re-conquered the city in 1615. When Maranhão became part of the newly independent Brazil in the 19th century, the palace was

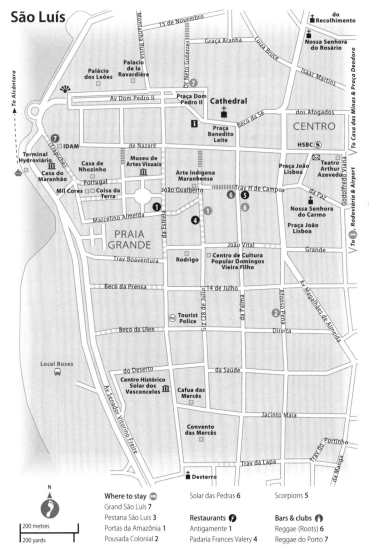

São Luís

Where to stay
Grand São Luís **7**
Pestana São Luis **3**
Portas da Amazônia **1**
Pousada Colonial **2**

Solar das Pedras **6**

Restaurants
Antigamente **1**
Padaria Frances Valery **4**

Scorpions **5**

Bars & clubs
Reggae (Roots) **6**
Reggae do Porto **7**

taken over by the governor. The rooms are furnished with period antiques from Portugal, France and the UK, with a series of paintings by artists including Vitor Meirelles, who was responsible for Imperial Brazil's most famous painting: *A Batalha*

Tip...
Visit Palácio dos Leões for marvellous views from the terrace.

de Guararapes. The building is replete with stunning tropcial dark *jacarandá* wood and light *cerejeira* polished floors; visitors are required to use carpet slippers.

Together with neighbouring Belém, Portuguese São Luís was the centre of a voracious slave trade. *Banderiante* expeditions roamed far into the interior capturing indigenous men, murdering their wives and children and bringing the prisoners to Maranhão to work on the cane fields. Entire Amazon civilizations, including the Omagua, were wiped out in this way. The Jesuits were appalled by the cruelty and their most famous politician-priest, Antônio Vieira, came to São Luís as a missionary to protest against the slave trade in 1653: "At what a different price the devil buys souls today compared with what he used to offer for them! There is no market in the world where the devil can get them more cheaply than in our own land … In Maranhão … what a cheap market! An Indian for a soul! That Indian will be your slave for the few days that he lives; but your soul will be enslaved for eternity… Break the chains of injustice and free those whom you hold captive and oppressed! … It is better to live from your own sweat than from the blood of others". The naves of São Luís's churches once echoed with his hell fire sermons, including the simple **Catedral da Sé** ① *Praça Dom Pedro II, s/n, T089-3222 7380, daily 0800-1900, free*, (1629), with its beautiful 19th-century baroque altarpiece! **Nossa Senhora do Carmo** ① *Praça João Lisboa 350, T098-3222 6104, daily 0700-1115 and 1430-1800, free* (1627), which has an extraordinary, elaborate façade; and the **Igreja do Desterro** ① *Largo do Desterro s/n, daily 0800-1130 and 1500-1830, free*, which was perhaps the first church built in the city. Vieira was eventually driven out of the city and went to Pará where he met with similar failure.

Before he left, Vieira inaugurated the **Convento das Mercês** ① *R da Palma 506, T098-3211 0062, Mon-Fri 0800-1800, Sat 0800-1400*, which houses copies of his 17th-century sermons, along with numerous rare Portuguese and French books (available on request). The main body of the convent is given over to exhibits devoted to Brazilian presidency of Jose Sarney, a former Maranhão senator of dubious repute, whose dynasty continues to rule over Brazil's poorest state with an iron hand, and reap the benefits.

Miraculously some indigenous groups managed to avoid the ravages of the slave trade and still survive in Maranhão. Their cultures are touched upon, from an old-fashioned anthropological perspective, in the **Casa de Nhozinho** ① *R dos Portugueses s/n, T098-3218 9951, 0900-1900, free*. There are also exhibitions devoted to Maranhão *caboclo* life. Nhozinho, who came from Curupuru and gives the house its name, was a famous local wooden toy maker in the mid-20th century.

When the indigenous people had died from exhaustion and the slave trade ran dry, Maranhão and the rest of Brazil turned to Africa for their slaves, thus beginning the world's largest skin trade. Like Salvador and Recife, this has resulted in a strong African heritage, which is celebrated most powerfully in the city's exuberant music and festivals. São Luís is famous for reggae, but this is just the commercial tip of a huge musical iceberg. The exuberance and variety of music can be sampled on any weekend night throughout the year with *cacuriá* dancing and live shows, but becomes most obvious in May and June during the local festivals of **Bumba-Me-Boi** in São Luís, and the syncretistic **Festo do Divino** in Alcântara.

ON THE ROAD
Bumba-Meu-Boi

Throughout the month of June the streets of São Luís are alive to the sound of *tambores* and dancers recreating the legend of Catirina, Pai Francisco and his master's bull. Although this mixture of African, indigenous and Portuguese traditions exists throughout the north, it is in Maranhão that it is most developed, with around 100 groups in São Luís alone. Here there are various styles called *sotaques*, which have different costumes, dances, instruments and *toadas*. These are **Boi de Matraca da Ilha** and **Boi de Pindaré** (both accompanied by small percussion instruments called *matracas*), **Boi de Zabumba** (marked by the use of a type of drum) and **Boi de Orquestra** (accompanied by string and wind instruments). Although there are presentations throughout June the highlights are the 24th (São João) and the 29th (São Pedro) with the closing ceremony lasting throughout the 30th (São Marçal), particularly in the *bairro* João Paulo. The shows take place in an *arraial*, which are found all over the city, with the ones at Projeto Reviver and Ceprama being more geared towards tourists (however be aware that a livelier more authentic atmosphere is to be found elsewhere in other *bairros*, such as Madre Deus). The **Centro de Cultura Popular Domingos Vieira Filho** at Rua do Giz 221, Praia Grande, is the place to learn more about these variations as well as many other local festivals and traditions such as *tambor de crioula* or *cacuriá*, both sensual dances derived from Africa. A good location to see these dances as well as *capoeira* is **Labouarte**, Rua Jansen Muller, Centro (Cacuriá de Dona Tetê is particularly recommended, with participation encouraged).

The **Centro de Cultura Popular Domingos Vieira Filho** (**Casa da Festa**) ① *R do Giz 225, T098-3218 9924, Tue-Sun 0900-1900*, has exhibitions on the **Festa do Divino**, together with the African-Brazilian *Tambor-de-Mina* spirit religion (similar to *candomblé*), and Christmas festivities. The old customs building, **Casa do Maranhão** ① *R do Trapiche s/n, Praia Grande, on the waterfront at the far end of R Portugal*, houses a museum devoted to the **Bumba-Meu-Boi** festival (see box, above) and Maranhão music. Downstairs is an exhibition hall with artefacts, costumes and video shows of previous Bumba festivals. Upstairs is a series of rooms devoted to a different Bumba-Meu-Boi African-Brazilian rhythm and instruments associated with the festival.

The centre of the African slave trade in the city was the **Cafua das Mercês** ① *R Jacinto Maia 54, Praia Grande, Mon-Fri 0900-1800*. It is now a museum of African-Brazilian culture with an extensive collection of musical and religious instruments, clothing and cultural artefacts. The **Casa das Minas** ① *R do Sol 302, T098-3221 4537, Tue-Sun 0900-1800*, is one of the oldest sacred spaces in Brazil for African-Brazilian religions and is an important centre of black culture in São Luís.

There are numerous other buildings of interest. Although the prettiest and liveliest colonial streets are **Rua Portugal** and **Rua do Giz** (28 de Julho), it is Caixa Econômica Federal in the 19th-century **Edifício São Luís** ① *R da Nazare at R do Egíto*, that preserves what is probably the largest *azulejo*-fronted building in the Americas. It now houses a bank. The **Teatro Arthur de Azevedo** ① *R do Sol 180, T089-3232 0299, daily 1500-2000 or when there are shows*, is a very handsome 19th-century theatre restored to its original spendour in the 1990s. Some of the city's best performances are held here. The **Centro Histórico Solar dos Vasconcelos**

ⓘ *R da Estrela 462, Praia Grande, T098-3231 9075, Mon-Fri 0800-1900, Sat and Sun 0900-1900, free*, is a fine colonial town house devoted to the history of the city with many interesting paintings, photographs and exhibits. The first floor of the **Museu de Artes Visuais** ⓘ *R Portugal 293, Praia Grande, T098-3231 6766, Tue-Fri 0900-1900, Sat and Sun 0900-1800*, has a collection of some of the city's most precious and intricate European *azulejos*, mostly from Portugal but with some pieces from England, Holland and Belgium. Upstairs is a collection of important Brazilian art including pieces by Tarsila do Amaral, Cícero Dias and Alfredo Volpi.

Trips from São Luís

Calhau is a huge beach, 10 km away. **Ponta D'Areia** is nearer to São Luís but more crowded. **Raposa**, a fishing village built on stilts, is a good place to buy handicrafts; there are a few places to stay on Avenida Principal. To get there, take a bus from the Mercado Central in São Luís (one hour with **Viação Santa Maria**, every 30 minutes). Another fishing village, **São José de Ribamar**, has a church dedicated to the patron saint and is a centre for *romeiros* in September. Many bars on the seafront serve local specialities such as fried stonefish. It is a 30-minute bus ride with **Maranhense** from the market in São Luís.

Alcântara

The former state capital, Alcântara (population 22,000), is on the muddy mainland bay of São Marcos, 22 km by boat from São Luís across the turbid Rio Bacanga. It's a sleepy, but beautifully preserved colonial town with one of the largest and least modified groups of 17th- and 18th-century colonial buildings in Brazil, whose terracotta roofs and brightly painted façades sit under a baking sun. The town is another of Maranhão's UNESCO World Heritage Sites.

During the sugar boom, Alcântara was the preferred retreat of Portuguese plantation owners. The crop was initially harvested by enslaved Indians captured from the Amazon. Most were wiped out by cruelty and disease in the 17th century, and it is the descendants of the African slaves brought in to replace their numbers who give contemporary Alcântara its distinctive Afro-Brazilian culture and cuisine. The town is renowned for its *cacuriá* dancing (from which lambada is derived), its spicy food and the practice of the *candomblé* spirit religion.

The town clusters around a pretty grassy square called the **Praça da Matriz**, which retains a pillory at its centre. Some 50 of the city's few hundred houses, civic buildings and churches are protected by the federal heritage bureau, IPHAN, and many have been restored. The **Museu Histórico** ⓘ *Praça da Matriz, s/n, daily 0900-1400*, houses some fine *azulejos* and colonial miscellanea, including a bed which was built especially for a scheduled, but cancelled, visit by the Emperor Dom Pedro. It has never been slept in. Another small museum, the **Casa Histórica** ⓘ *Praça da Matriz, Mon-Fri 1000-1600*, has some 18th-century English furniture and porcelain imported by the Alcântara aristocracy.

Essential Alcântara

Access

Launches run to Alcântara from the Terminal Hidroviário (Rampa Campos Mello, Cais da Praia Grande, São Luís) at around 0700 and 0930 (US$12), returning to São Luís at about 1630, depending on the tide. The journey takes about an hour. The sea can be very rough between September and December. Catamaran tours can be booked in São Luís. See What to do, page 125.

There is a ruined fort on the southern edges of town and a number of crumbling churches and mansions, These include the 17th-century. **Igreja de Nossa Senhora do Carmo** ① *Praça da Matriz, Mon-Fri 0800-1300, 1400-1800, Sat and Sun 0900-1400, free,* with a finely carved rococo interior, the ruined **Matriz de São Matias** (1648), and colonial mansions, such as the **Casa** and **Segunda Casa do Imperador**. These sit alongside numerous old plantation aristocracy mansions with blue, Portuguese-tile façades.

Canoe trips go to **Ilha do Livramento**, where there are good beaches and walks around the coast. It can be muddy after rain, and watch out for mosquitoes after dark. A rocket-launching site has been built nearby.

Listings São Luís and around *maps p119 and below*

Tourist information

São Luís

Central de Servicos Turísticos
*Praça Benedito Leite, T098-3212 6211,
www.turismo.ma.gov.br.*
Look out for Corbis photographer Barnabás Bosshart's masterfully photographed map-guides to São Luís and Alcântara.

Where to stay

São Luís

Although many Brazilians opt to stay on the beach the sand is not as beautiful as it is in Piauí and Ceará. The far more interesting but sadly neglected city centre can be sketchy at night. Cheap hotels can be found in **R das Palmas**, very central, and **R Formosa**.

Alcântara

Where to stay 🛏
Pousada Bela Vista **2**
Pousada da Josefa **4**
Pousada dos Guarás **1**

Sítio Tijupá **3**

Restaurants 🍴
Bar do Lobato **1**

$$$ Grand São Luís Hotel
Praça Dom Pedro II 299, T098-2109 3500, www.grandsaoluis.com.br.
A 1960s grand dame with plain rooms, the best of which have sea views. Business facilities, pool and gym.

$$$ Pestana São Luís
Av Avicência, Praia do Calhau, T098-2106 0505, www.pestana.com/en/hotel/pestana-sao-luis.
A resort hotel housed in a former 1970s grand hotel. This is the best option for families or business travellers.

$$ Portas da Amazônia
R do Giz 129, T098-3222 9937, www.portasdaamazonia.com.br.
Tastefully converted wood-floor rooms in a colonial building in the the heart of the centre. Smart and well run. Internet.

$$ Pousada Colonial
R Afonso Pena 112, T098-3232 2834.
Clean, well-kept rooms set in a beautiful restored, tiled house, a/c, comfortable, quiet.

$$-$ Solar das Pedras
R da Palma 127, T098-3232 6694, www.ajsolardaspedras.com.br.
This HI-affiliated hostel is by far the best backpacker option in town, well run, with tidy 4- to 6-person dorms ($ pp) and doubles, internet, lockers and a little garden.

Trips from São Luís
In Raposa there are hotels on Av Principal.

$$ Hotel Sol e Mar
Av Gonçalves Dias 320, São José de Ribamar.
With a restaurant.

Alcântara

$$ Pousada dos Guarás
Praia da Baronesa, T098-3337 1339.
A beachfront *pousada* with a series of bungalows with en suites, a good restaurant, canoe hire and advice on excursions around the town.

$ Pousada Bela Vista
Vila Jerico s/n, Cema, T098-3337 1569, danniloalcantara@ig.com.br.
Cabins and pretty suites with great views out over the bay and a restaurant with delicious Maranhense food.

$ Pousada da Josefa
R Direita, T098-3337 1109.
A friendly, family-run restaurant and *pousada* right in the centre with a range of very simple, plain rooms. Look at several.

$ Sítio Tijupá
R de Baixo s/n at the Post Office, T098-3337 1291.
Tiny simple *pousada* with 4 small but well-kept, fan-cooled rooms.

Restaurants

São Luís
Street stalls provide simple home cooking, although most are found away from the centre and beaches. Typical dishes are *arroz de cuxá* and *torta de camarão* and desserts or liqueurs made from local fruits. Try the local soft drink *Jesús* or *Jenève*. **R da Estrela** has many eating places with outdoor terraces. **R dos Afogados** has good places for lunch. There is further choice in the **São Francisco** district, just across bridge. The centre is very lively on Fri and Sat but on Sun most people go to **Praia Calhau**.

$$$-$$ Antigamente
R da Estrela 210.
Portuguese and Brazilian standards, decent fish and pizza in this restaurant decorated with local art, colourful bottles and bric-a-brac. Lively on weekends and Mon-Fri after 0800.

$ Padaria Frances Valery
R do Giz (28 de Julho) 164.
Delicious cakes, eclairs, quiches, tropical fruit juices and coffee, friendly.

$ Scorpions
R da Palma 83.
Great-value per kilo with a good choice of stews, salads and *pratos feitos*. Near the HI.

Alcântara

$ Bar do Lobato
Praça da Matriz.
Pleasant with good simple food, fried
shrimps highly recommended.

Bars and clubs

São Luís
There is *cacuriá* dancing, drum parades
and buzzing nightlife every Fri and Sat
along the north end of **R do Giz** and
along **R João Gualberto**.

Antigamente
Praia Grande.
Live music Thu-Sat.

Reggae Bar do Porto
R do Portugal 49, T098-3232 1115.
One of the best reggae bars in the city with a
broad range of live acts and DJs and a vibrant
crowd at weekends.

Reggae (Roots) Bar
R da Palma 86, T098-3221 7580.
Live reggae and Maranhão roots music most
nights. Especially lively at weekends.

Festivals

São Luís
24 Jun Bumba-Meu-Boi, see box, page 121.
For several days before the festival, street
bands parade, particularly in front of São
João and São Benedito churches. There are
dances somewhere in the city almost every
night in Jun and a whole string of smaller
Boi-related festivals and very lively *cacuriá*
and reggae at weekends all year round,
especially on R Giz.
Aug São Benedito, at the Rosário church.
Oct Festival with dancing, at **Vila Palmeira**
suburb (take a bus of the same name).

Alcântara
Jun Festa do Divino, at Pentecost
(Whitsun). On 29 Jun is **São Pedro** saint day.
Aug São Benedito.

Shopping

São Luís
Arts and crafts
IDAM, **Coisa da Terra** and **Mil Cores Rua
Portugal**, on R Portugal, sell wicker and weave
work, pottery and figurines from Maranhão.
Arte Indígena Maranhense, *R do Giz at João
Gualberto, T098-3221 2940.* Sells Maranhão art
made by indigenous peoples.

Music and books
Poeme-Sé, *R João Gualberto 52, Praia Grande,
T098-3232 4968.* Cosy little bookshop and
cybercafé with a selection of Maranhão music.
Rodrigo CDs Maranhenses, *R João Vital
s/n between Estrela and Giz, T098-3232
4799.* Sells a huge selection of Maranhão
and northeastern roots, traditional and
contemporary music. This is one of the
best music shops in Northeast Brazil.

What to do

São Luís
See **Eco Dunas**, page 129, for information
on tours of Lençóis Maranhenses, in
and around São Luís, and Alcântara.

Transport

São Luís
Air The shoddy **Marechal Cunha Machado
Airport**, Av Santos Dumont, T098-3217 6100,
has been in the process of being rebuilt
for the past 10 years but never quite got
there. Minivans run to the airport from Praça
Deodoro in the centre, every 40 mins until
2200, US$1, 40-60 mins, depending on traffic.
As well as local flights, there are connections
through **Belém**, **Parnaíba**, **Teresina** or
Fortaleza to the rest of Brazil and international
flights to the **Guianas** and **Portugal**. Gol, Azul
and **Tam** have offices in the terminal, and there
is car rental, a tourist office (daily 0800-2200),
banks with ATMs and a sprinkling of shops.

Boat Boats to **Alcântara** leave from the
Terminal Hidroviário, Rampa Campos Melo
s/n, Cais da Praia Grande, São Luís, T098-3232

0692. There are departures in the morning usually at 0700 and 0930 but times vary according to the tide. The trip takes 1 hr, US$4.

Bus To **Fortaleza**, 4 a day, US$60, 18 hrs. To **Belém**, US$20, 13 hrs, **Transbrasiliana** at 1900 and 2000 (no *leito*). Also to **Recife**, 25 hrs, US$70, all other major cities and local towns. To **Barreirinhas**, US$10, 3 hrs. More comfortable on a private bus, US$20 – organize through **Eco Dunas** (see page 129) or your hotel.

Ferry Ferries cross the bay from Alcântara to the São Luís docks, **Terminal Hidroviário**, Rampa Campos Mello, Cais da Praia Grande, US$4 foot passenger, US$25 car, usually in the afternoon. To check ferry times call T098-3222 8431.

Alcântara
Boat Boats from Alcântara to **São Luís** leave daily at 0830 and 1600.

Parque Nacional Lençóis Maranhenses
coastal desert of brilliant-white dunes, seasonal lakes and turtle-nested beaches

Northeastern Brazil's windswept coast is broken by extensive dunes all the way from Natal to the Amazon. In eastern Maranhão they become so vast that they form a coastal desert stretching for some 140 km between Tutóia on the Delta do Parnaíba and Primeira Cruz, east of São Luís. The Parque Nacional Lençóis Maranhenses, which encloses only a part of the *lençóis*, covers an area of 1550 sq km. The sand extends up to 50 km inland and is advancing by as much as 200 m a year. Dumped by the sea and blown by the wind, it forms ridges 50 m high in long flowing patterns that change constantly. From the air the undulating, talcum powder-white dunes look like giant wrinkled bed sheets ('lençóis' in Portuguese). Between December and June the dunes are pocked with freshwater lakes that shine a brilliant blue under the tropical sky and provide a startling contrast with the brilliant white sand.

The coast of the Lençóis Maranhenses provides a refuge for severely endangered species including manatee. Leatherback and green turtles come here to lay their eggs in late summer, while in the forests and scrubland around the Rio Preguiças there are resident puma, jaguar and spectacled caiman. The Lençóis are home to numerous rare species of fish and shoals of huge game fish like *camurupim* (tarpon) live in the estuaries and rivers. The dunes are a breeding ground for migratory birds such as the lesser yellowlegs, which come all the way from the Arctic to feed here. Recent studies have shown the sparse vegetation to include grasses that are unknown elsewhere.

Excavations begun in 1995 on the supposed site of a Jesuit settlement which, according to local rumour, was buried intact by a sandstorm.

The *lençóis* are not difficult to visit. Travellers who have a few days to spare are rewarded by an amazing panorama of dunes reaching from horizon to horizon, deserted beaches washed by a powerful surf, boat rides on the **Rio Preguiça** (Lazy River), and tiny, quiet towns and hamlets where strangers are still a relative novelty.

Visiting the park
The *lençóis* are divided into two areas. To the west of Rio Preguiça is the park proper and the **Grandes Lençóis**, which stretch between Ponta Verde in the far west and the town of **Barreirinhas** on the banks of the Preguiça.

Essential Parque Nacional Lençóis Maranhenses

Access

There are four buses a day to Barreirinhas from São Luís (US$7, four hours) and numerous transit *combis* and Toyotas bookable through São Luís hotels.
There is Toyota transport east between Barreirinhas and Paulino Neves and further connections from here to the scruffy port town of Tutóia and the Delta do Parnaíba, or onward buses to Parnaíba town for the rest of Piauí and Jericoacoara and Fortaleza in Ceará.

Rubbish

Be careful of broken glass – especially in Caburé where rubbish is buried rather than collected. Many of the towns along the route have a bad wind-blown rubbish problem and their streets are littered with billowing plastic bags and the corpses of discarded bottles.

Traversing the Pequenos Lençóis

It is possible to walk or cycle along the coast in front of the Pequenos Lençóis between Caburé and Tutóia in either direction; allow about three days. Camping is permitted, but you must take all supplies with you including water, since some dune lakes are salty. The area is very remote and you may not see another person for the duration of the walk. Because of the hot and sandy conditions, this is a punitive trek, only for the very hardy. Do not try the treacherous hike inland across the dunes or a hike into the Grandes Lençóis without a guide. The dunes are disorientating and there have been a number of cases of hikers becoming lost and dying of heat exposure or starvation.

Park information

See www.parquelencois.com.br for useful information on the park (in Portuguese only).

Barreirinhas is the tourist capital for the region and has plenty of *pousadas* and restaurants and tour operators, such as **Eco Dunas**, offering trips into the park. From here it is easy to arrange tours and transfers along the Rio Preguiça both up and downstream and onwards through the Delta do Parnaíba to Jericoacoara.

The dunes east of the Rio Preguiça form the **Pequenos Lençóis**, which extend to **Tutóia**. These are easier to travel through than the Grandes Lençóis but less easy to visit on an organized tour. **Paulino Neves**, on the Rio Cangata, is just south of a series of large dunes at the eastern end of the *lençóis*.

There are several small, friendly settlements in the Pequenos Lençóis. Most lie on the Rio Preguiça. The two-shack town of **Vassouras** is literally at the feet of the *lençóis*; its makeshift huts are watched over by a spectacular, looming dune whose crest affords wonderful views. Further downstream at **Mandacaru** there is a lighthouse with great views out over the coast and some craft shops selling Buriti palm-weave work and carvings.

Atins and **Caburé** are miniature beach resorts sandwiched between a rough and windy Atlantic and the lazy blue waters of the Preguiça. Both are surrounded by a bleak sea of sand and Atins is fronted by a superb beach, one of the best for kitesurfing in Brazil. The sleepy charm of the village, the proximity to the national park and the sky filled with stars make Atins the best place to stay in the Lençóis. You can walk into parts of the Grandes Lençóis from Atins and into the Pequenos Lençóis from Caburé (see box, above). Many of the overland tours from Jericoacoara finish in Caburé.

Where to stay

Barreirinhas

Most hotels can organize tours. Bring a hammock for flexibility; in the smaller hamlets it is always possible to rent space in a beach bar or restaurant for a few dollars.

$$$ Buriti
R Inácio Lins s/n, T098-3349 1800, www.pousadadoburiti.com.br.
Corridors of large, plain rooms with concrete terraces near a pool and breakfast area. Simple but the best in the centre of town.

$$ Belo Horizonte
R Joaquim Soeiro de Carvalho 245, T098-3349 0054, www.bhmirante.com.br.
Well-kept tiled and whitewashed rooms near the central square. The quietest are at the front. Good service from the welcoming owner, Albino, and a pleasant rooftop breakfast area.

$$-$ Pousada Igarapé
R Coronel Godinho 320, T098-9111 0461.
Small, boxy fan-cooled or a/c doubles set in corridors opposite the Assembleia de Deus church, which has noisy hellfire sermons at weekends.

$ Tia Cota
R Coronel Godinho 204, T098-3349 0159, Facebook: Pousada Tia Cota.
Simple fan or a/c whitewashed rooms, with decent beds and mattresses, ranging from phone box-sized with shared baths to more spacious en suite doubles.

Caburé, Vassouras, Mandacaru and Atins

It is possible to rent hammock space in the restaurant shacks in Vassouras or Mandacaru for around US$12 per day, with food included. All the towns are so tiny it's impossible to get lost. None have more than 3 streets. There are other options in Caburé apart from the *pousada* below, and rooms are always available outside peak season.

$$$ Cajueiro
R Principal, Atins, T098-99204 0222, www.pcatins.com.br.
This place has 9 simple suites with hammock-slung balconies and a palm-tatch public restaurant area. Tours and kitesurfing can be organized through the *pousada*. Decent food, friendly service.

$$$ Rancho do Buna
R Principal s/n, Atins, T098-3349 5005, www.ranchodobuna.com.br.
Attractive *pousada* set on the river at the back of town. Small rooms are situated in a brick annexe in front of a fish-filled lake, there's a pool and pleasant, airy public areas.

Barreirinhas

Pousada Igarapé **2**
Tia Cota **3**

Restaurants ⑦
Barlavento Carlão **1**
Bona Mesa Pizzaría **3**
Maré Mansa Mineiro **4**
Paladar **5**

Where to stay ◉
Belo Horizonte **4**
Buriti **1**

Excellent food and tours available to the Lençóis and the beaches.

$ Pousada do Paulo
(aka Pousada Lençóis de Areia)
Praia do Caburé, T098-9143 4668.
Well-kept *pousada* with rooms for up to 4 people. The owner was the first to settle here and named the town after a local bird. They serve the best food in the village. Watch out for glass on the vast, sweeping Atlantic beach.

Barreirinhas

$$-$ Barlavento Carlão
Av Beira Rio s/n, T098-3349 0627.
Fillet of fish in passion fruit sauce, açai pulp with guarana and various simple meat and poultry dishes and fresh juices.

$ Bona Mesa Pizzaria
R Inacio Lins s/n.
Wide choice of pizzas cooked in a traditional wood-fired oven and delicious *doce de buriti* dessert.

$ Maré Mansa Mineiro
Rio Preguicas at Joaquim Diniz.
A floating restaurant, bar and dance club with live reggae every Wed and Sat. Very busy after 2300 with a crowd ranging from 18-80 years old.

$ Paladar
Coronel Godinho 176.
Very cheap but hearty *prato feitos* with meat, chicken or fish options, rice, beans, vegetables and salad.

Barreirinhas

There is an arts and crafts market next to the river selling *buriti* palm weavework bags, mats and homeware. Light and excellent value.

Barreirinhas

Eco Dunas, *R Inácio Lins 164, T011-4654 1200, www.ecodunas.tur.br.* The best option for tours of Lençóis Maranhenses, Sete Cidades, the delta and tours all the way from São Luís to Jericoacoara or vice versa. Excellent guides, infrastructure and organization. English spoken and flights organized. Can arrange wonderful scenic flights over the Lençóis with pilot Amirton for around US$100. The company also runs 1-day tours around São Luís, trips to the Parque Nacional das Sete Cidades and visits to Alcântara.

Atins

Nativos Kite Surf, *available on the beach or through Rancho do Buna; see Where to stay, above.* The best option for board rental and classes and the only school run by locals.

Parque Nacional Lençóis Maranhenses
Hotels in São Luís can book minivan trips for the same price as the bus. See page 123. A regular boat service plies the river between **Barreirinhas** and **Caburé** and/or **Atins** stopping at **Vassouras** and **Mandaracu** on the way. Boats leave daily at 1000-1100 from the end of the *orla* next to the town dune (to Caburé or Atins; both 4 hrs, US$8); the boat returns with the tide. Speedboats can be organized at Barreirinhas through **Eco Dunas** (see page 129), and it is possible to reach both **Paulino Neves** or even **Tutóia** by boat.

pretty colonial town, gateway to the Chapada das Mesas National Park

Carolina

Carolina (population 23,000) is made up of whitewashed houses and terracotta roofs on the banks of the Tocantins River. The climate is hot and damp, the sunsets over the river spectacular and the town is set in the midst of the **Parque Nacional Chapada das Mesas**, a vast area of some 160,000 ha of waterfalls and escarpments covered in a mix of *cerrado* and tropical forest and replete with wildlife. Guides and transport to the **Parque Nacional Chapada das Mesas** cost US$12-30 per half day and can be organized through *pousadas*.

> ## Essential Carolina
>
> ### Access
>
> Carolina lies 221 km south of Imperatriz on a road which joins the BR-010. There are frequent buses. The *rodoviária* (T099-3531 2076) is in the centre. A ferry connects the town with Filadelfia in Tocantins on the opposite bank of the river (10 minutes).

The **Cachoeira da Pedra Caída**, on the Rio Farinha just off the BR-010, 35 km outside town is one of the Northeast's most beautiful: a three-tiered waterfall that plunges into a rocky gorge. The **Cachoeiras do Itapecuru** off the BR-230, 33 km from Carolina, are two conjoined falls that fall into a huge swimming hole surrounded by pretty white-sand beaches. The Rio Farinha, a tributary of the Tocantins, has a further series of spectacular falls including the **Cachoeira São Romão** – a thundering curtain of water more than 100 m – and **Farinha** itself which falls into wide, deep and clear plunge pool. You'll need a guide with a 4WD to visit them. But come soon as they are threatened by a hydroelectric project.

The **Cachoeira da Prata**, 40 km from town, are next to the **Morro das Figuras**, which is covered with rock inscriptions thought to have been carved by the ancestors of the Tupi people. Access is by unsealed road from the BR-230, requiring a 4WD. The Chapada das Mesas has a series of other table-top mountains, including the **Morro do Portal**, which affords wonderful views and is easy to reach from Carolina.

Between June and August the Tocantins River is low and lined with beaches, the best of which are on the opposite side of the river in the little town of **Filadélfia**, in Tocantins. The city's goes out at night on the **Ilha dos Botes**, a river island 5 km from town filled with simple bars and restaurants.

Listings Southern Maranhão

Tourist information

Carolina

Secretaria de Turismo
*R Duque de Caxias 522, T098-3731 1613.
Mon-Fri 0800-1300.*

Where to stay

Carolina

There are a handful of very simple *pousadas* near the bus station.

$$ Chalés da Pedra Caída
*Praça do Estudante 460, T099-3531 2318,
www.pedracaida.com.*
Chalets with fan, restaurant, natural pool and 3 neighbouring waterfalls.

$$-$ Pousada do Lajes
Estr por Riachão (BR-230), Km 2, T099-3531 2452, www.pousadadolajes.com.br.
Chalets with a/c gathered around a little pool outside town with a restaurant and a small play area for kids.

Rio Grande
do Norte

The state of Rio Grande do Norte, east of Fortaleza Ceará, is famous for its beaches and dunes, especially around Natal where there are a string of resorts including Ponta Negra and Genipabu, which are essentially city suburbs and Pipa, a low-key resort town just to the south. The coastline begins to change here, becoming gradually drier and less green, as it shifts from running north–south to east–west. The vast sugar cane plantations and few remaining stands of Mata Atlântica (coastal forest) are replaced by the dry *caatinga* vegetation and *caju* orchards. The people are known as 'Potiguares', after an indigenous tribe that once resided in the state.

Natal and around

state capital with popular beaches nearby

The state capital of Natal (population 713,000), located on a peninsula between the Rio Potengi and the Atlantic Ocean, is pleasant enough but has few sights of interest. Most visitors head for the beaches to the north and south. During the Second World War, the city was, somewhat bizarrely, the second largest US base outside the United States and housed 8000 American pilots.

Sights
No-one comes to Natal for sightseeing, but the city is not without culture. The oldest part is the **Ribeira** along the riverfront, where a programme of renovation has been started. This can be seen on Rua Chile and in public buildings restored in vivid art deco fashion, such as the **Teatro Alberto Maranhão** ⓘ *Praça Agusto Severo, T084-3222 9935*, built 1898-1904, and the **Prefeitura** ⓘ *R Quintino Bocaiuva, Cidade Alta*. The **Cidade Alta**, or Centro, is the main commercial centre and Avenida Rio Branco its principal artery. The main square is made up by the adjoining *praças*, **João Maria**, **André de Albuquerque**, **João Tibúrcio** and **7 de Setembro**. At Praça André de Albuquerque is the old **cathedral** (inaugurated 1599, restored 1996). The modern cathedral is on Avenida Deodoro. The

Essential Natal

Finding your feet

Flights arrive at **Augusto Severo International Airport** in Parnamirim, 18 km south of centre, and 10 km from the beach and tourist hub of Ponta Negra. **Trampolim da Vitória** microbuses run from the airport to Petrópolis and the city centre of Natal via **Shopping Natal** (0500-2330, US$1), from where there are connections to Ponta Negra (bus No 66), and Pipa (with **Expresso Oceano**). Taxis from the airport to Ponta Negra cost US$12, or US$20 to the centre.

Interstate buses arrive at the new **Rodoviária Cidade do Sol** on Avenida Capitão Mor Gouveia 1237, Cidade da Esperança, 6 km southwest of the centre. A taxi to Ponta Negra costs around US$12; to the Via Costeira around US$15. Alternatively, take bus No 66 to Ponta Negra; this passes close to the hotel strip while not taking Avenida Erivan Franca (the street that runs along the seafront). For Praia do Meio Beach and the Via Costeira take bus No 40 and alight at Praia do Meio for an easy walk to any of the hotels on that beach or Praia dos Artistas. Or take any of the 'Via Costeira' buses.

Buses from the south pass Ponta Negra first, where you can ask to alight. The city buses 'Cidade de Esperança Avenida 9', 'Areia Preta via Petrópolis' or 'Via Tirol' run from the new *rodoviária* to the centre. See Transport, page 137.

Getting around

Unlike most Brazilian buses, in Natal you get on the bus at the front and get off at the back. The **Old Rodoviária** on Avenida Junqueira Aires, by Praça Augusto Severo, Ribeira, is a central point where many bus lines converge. Buses to some of the nearby beaches also leave from here. Taxis are expensive compared to other cities (eg four times the price of Recife); a typical 10-minute journey costs US$7.50. However, buses are the best option for getting around. Route 54 and 46 connect Ponta Negra with the city, the former via Via Costeira and the old *rodoviária*.

church of **Santo Antônio** ⓘ *R Santo Antônio 683, Cidade Alta, Tue-Fri 0800-1700, Sat 0800-1400*, dates from 1766, and has a fine, carved wooden altar and a sacred art museum.

The **Museu Câmara Cascudo** ⓘ *Av Hermes de Fonseca 1440, Tirol, T084-3212 2795, www.mcc.ufrn.br, Tue-Fri 0800-1130, 1400-1730, Sat and Sun 1300-1700, US$2.50*, has exhibits on *umbanda* rituals, archaeological digs, and the sugar, leather and petroleum industries. There is also a dead whale.

The 16th-century **Forte dos Reis Magos** ⓘ *T084-3211 3820, daily 0800-1600, US$1.50,* www.turismo.natal.rn.gov.br, is at Praia do Forte, the tip of Natal's peninsula. Between the fort and the city is a military installation. Walk along the beach to the fort for good views (or take a tour, or go by taxi).

At Mãe Luiza is a **lighthouse** with beautiful views of Natal and surrounding beaches (take a city bus marked 'Mãe Luiza' and get the key from the house next door).

Avoid walking in Natal city at night. Crime has risen over the last few years.

There are three urban beaches in Natal: **Praia do Meio**, **Praia dos Artistas** and **Praia de Areia Preta; the first two are** are sheltered by reefs and good for windsurfing. The beachside promenade, **Via Costeira**, runs south beneath the towering sand dunes of **Parque das Dunas** (access restricted to protect the dunes), joining the city to the neighbourhood of Ponta Negra.

Tip...
For great views of the coastline, walk or bike along the cycle path which runs parallel to Via Costeira.

Ponta Negra

The vibrant and pretty Ponta Negra, 12 km south of Natal centre (20 minutes by bus), is justifiably the most popular of Natal's beaches and has many hotels. The northern end is good for surfing, while the southern end is calmer and suitable for swimming. **Morro do Careca**, a 120-m-high sand dune, surrounded by vegetation, sits at its far end. It is crowded on weekends and holidays. The poorly lit northern reaches can be unsafe after dark.

Trips from Natal

The beautiful beaches around Natal – some of which are developed, others are deserted and accessible only by trails – are good all year round for day trips or longer stays. Those north of the city are known as the **Litoral Norte**, where there are extensive cashew plantations; those to the south form the **Litoral Sul**. The areas closest to the city are built-up and get busy during the summer holidays (December to Carnaval), when dune-buggy traffic can become excessive.

Popular tours from Natal include boat trips on the **Rio Potengi**, along the nearby beaches of the Litoral Sul, and to **Barra do Cunhaú**, 86 km south of Natal. The latter goes through mangroves and visits an island and a salt mine, **Passeio Ecológico Cunhaú** ⓘ *T084-9934 0017, www.barradocunhau.com.br.* Other popular pastimes include buggy tours, marlin fishing (11 km from shore, said by some to be the best in Brazil) and microlight flights over the Rio Potengi and sand dunes north of Natal. See What to do, page 137.

The **Centro de Lançamento da Barreira do Inferno** ⓘ *11 km south of Natal on the road to Pirangi, T084-3216 1400, visits by appointment on Wed from 1400*, is the launching centre for Brazil's space programme.

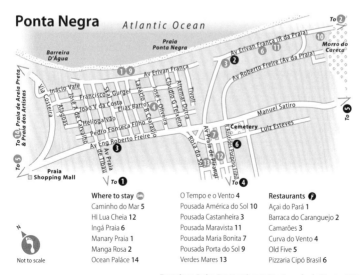

Ponta Negra — map

Where to stay 🛏
Caminho do Mar **5**
HI Lua Cheia **12**
Ingá Praia **6**
Manary Praia **1**
Manga Rosa **2**
Ocean Palace **14**

O Tempo e o Vento **4**
Pousada América do Sol **10**
Pousada Castanheira **3**
Pousada Maravista **11**
Pousada Maria Bonita **7**
Pousada Porta do Sol **9**
Verdes Mares **13**

Restaurants 🍴
Açai do Pará **1**
Barraca do Caranguejo **2**
Camarões **3**
Curva do Vento **4**
Old Five **5**
Pizzaria Cipó Brasil **6**

Not to scale

Tourist information

SETUR
Centro de Turismo R Aderbal de Figueiredo 980, Petrópolis, T084-3211 6149, http:// turismo.natal.rn.gov.br (in Portuguese only). Mon-Sat 0800-1900, Sun 0800-1800.
The state tourist office covers the whole of Rio Grande do Norte state, although their information and English is very limited, and the office is not conveniently located. However, there are **tourist information booths** at the airport, the bus station, on Av Presidente, at **Café Filho** on Praia das Artistas Beach, and **Erivan Franca** on Ponta Negra; all open daily 0800-2100.

Where to stay

Natal
Economical hotels are easier to find in Natal than at the outlying beaches or Ponta Negra, but very few people stay here and what they save by doing so is often spent on public transport to and from the beaches.

The distinction between **Praia do Meio** and **Praia dos Artistas** is often blurred. Most hotels are on the beachfront **Av Pres Café Filho**, the numbering of which is illogical.

The **Via Costeira** is a strip of enormous, upmarket beachfront hotels, which are very isolated, with no restaurants or shops within easy walking distance.

$$$ Bruma
Av Pres Café Filho 1176, T084-3202 4303, www.hotelbruma.com.br.
A small, family-run beachfront hotel with 25 balconied rooms around a little pool. Popular with Brazilian families.

$$$ Imirá Plaza
Via Costeira 4077, Praia Barreira d'Agua, T084-3211 4104, www.imiraplaza.com.br.
A vast, sprawling package resort on the beach and with a pool and tennis court. Popular with families. Cheaper in low season.

Ponta Negra
Ponta Negra is the ideal place to stay, with its attractive beach and concentration of restaurants. The most popular hotels are those right on the beach, on **Av Erivan França** facing the sea, and on **R Francisco Gurgel** behind that street. The latter is quieter.

$$$$ Manary Praia & Amana Spa
R Francisco Gurgel 9067, T084-3204 2900, www.manary.com.br.
The best and most tranquil hotel facing the beach and the only one with a trace of style. The rooms, which are decorated in hardwood and pastel colours, have ample bathrooms and secluded private terraces.

$$$$ Ocean Paláce
Km 11, near Ponta Negra, T084-3220 4144, www.oceanpalace.com.br.
A 5-star with large, comfortable suites, smaller, pokier family rooms and a string of bungalows in a regimented line near the beach. Public areas include a lovely oceanfront pool and terrace. Relaxed and friendly.

$$$ Hotel e Pousada O Tempo e o Vento
R Elias Barros 66, T084-3219 2526, www.otempoeovento.com.br.
Small terracotta and whitewash hotel 2 blocks back from the beach with a range of a/c rooms gathered around a pool. The *luxo* rooms are by far the best, others have a fan and there are low season discounts.

$$$ Manga Rosa
Av Erivan França 240, T084-3219 0508, www.mangarosanatal.com.br.
Well-appointed small rooms with attractive wooden fittings, colourful bedspreads and sea views. Wi-Fi.

$$$ Pousada Castanheira
R da Praia 221, T084-3236 2918, www.pousadacastanheira.com.br.
English/Brazilian owners, comfortable spacious rooms with TV, fridge and safe, set in a little leafy garden, with a small jewel-like

pool, breakfast room with sea view, room service, parking, very helpful staff.

$$ Caminho do Mar
R Dr Ernani Hugo Gomes 365, T084-3215 9707, www.caminhodomarnatal.com.br.
Simple plain rooms and breakfast, a short walk from the beach.

$$ Ingá Praia
Av Erivan França 17, T084-3219 3436, www.ingapraiahotel.com.br.
A pink cube on the beach with comfortable well-kept rooms and a rooftop terrace with a pool. Wi-Fi in all rooms. Those without a sea view are cheapest.

$$ Pousada América do Sol
R Erivan França 35, T084-3219 2245, www.pousadaamericadosol.com.br.
Very simple a/c rooms with pokey bathrooms and TVs. Good breakfast in a terrace overlooking the beach and substantial off-season reductions.

$$ Pousada Maria Bonita 2
Estrela do Mar 2143 at Arabaiana, T084-3236 2941, www.mariabonita2.com.br.
One of the area's first *pousadas* with either a/c or fan-cooled rooms. Most are plain but light, bright and well kept, with tiled floors, flatscreen TVs and little marble writing desks. Right next to the nightlife quarter.

$$ Pousada Porta do Sol
R Francisco Gurgel 9057, T084-3236 2555, www.pousadaportadosol.com.br.
A tranquil pool and breakfast area overlooking the beach and simple rooms with tiled floors small chests of drawers, flatscreen TVs, fridges, Wi-Fi and an excellent breakfast.

$ HI Lua Cheia
R Dr Manoel Augusto Bezerra de Araújo 500, T084-3236 3696, www.luacheia.com.br.
One of the best youth hostels in Brazil; in a 'castle' with a 'medieval' **Taverna Pub** in the basement. The price includes breakfast.

$ HI Verdes Mares
R das Algas 2166, Conj Algamar, T084-3236 2872, www.hostelverdesmares.com.br.
HI youth hostel with attractive public areas decorated with northeastern arts and crafts, and colourfully painted rooms dorms and doubles. Facilities include Wi-Fi, a little pool and gym, breakfast. Discounts in low season.

$ Pousada Maravista
R da Praia 223, T084-3236 4677, www. pousadamaravistanatal.com.br.
Plain and simple but with a good breakfast, English spoken, TV, fridge.

Restaurants

Natal
Prawns feature heavily on menus as Natal is the largest exporter of prawns in Brazil. Check out the beach *barracas* for snacks and fast food. The city centre area of Petrópolis is well known locally for having the best restaurants in the state.

$$ A Macrobiótica
Princesa Isabel 524, Centro.
Vegetarian restaurant and shop. Lunch only.

$$ Peixada da Comadre
R Dr José Augusto Bezerra de Medeiros 4, Praia dos Artistas.
Lively seafood restaurant with popular prawn dishes.

$$-$ Farol Bar
Av Sílvio Pedrosa 105 (at the end of Via Costeira on Praia Areia Preta), Facebook: Farol-Bar e Restaurante.
Overlooking the ocean. The famous dried meat dishes are a local speciality.

Ponta Negra

$$$ Manary
Manary Praia Hotel, R Francisco Gurgel (see Where to stay, above).
The best seafood in the city in a poolside restaurant overlooking Ponta Negra Beach.

$$$ Old Five
Av Erivan França 230, T084-3236 2505.
Romantic and rustic chic beach bar restaurant next to the dunes with outdoor candles, low-light, decent cocktails and a menu of seafood, fish and chicken standards and bar snacks.

$$ Açai do Pará
R das Algas 2151, T084-3219 3024.
Pará dishes including delicious *tacacá frango no tucupi* and *maniçoba*, snacks and a superb selection of juices including *camu camu* and *açai*.

$$ Barraca do Caranguejo
Av Erivan França 1180, T084-3219 5069.
Ultra-fresh prawn and seafood dishes for a decent price, and live music nightly from 2100.

$$ Camarões
Av Eng Roberto Freire 2610, T084-3209 2424, www.camaroes.com.br/.
Also at Natal Shopping Centre. Touristy, but very good seafood.

$$ Casa de Taipa
R Dr M A B de Araujo 130-A, T084-3219 5790, http://casadetaipatapiocaria.com.br.
A brightly painted mock-beach bar with chunky painted wooden tables sitting on a sandy floor under a thatch-palm roof and a big menu of tapioca dishes (including excellent *carne do sol* with *queijo coalho*).

$$ Curva do Vento
R Dr Manoel A B de Araújo 396, T084-2010 4749.
Some of the best pizzas in Ponta Negra, together with all manner of rosti (stuffed with curry, lobster or stroganoff) and a broad selection of ice-cold beers. Lively atmosphere.

$$ Pizzaria Cipó Brasil
R Aristides Porpino Filho, T0800-328 4051, www.cipobrasil.com.br.
Funky little Playa del Carmen-style bar with a jungle theme, 4 levels, sand floors, lantern-lit, very atmospheric. Average food (pizzas, crêpes), good cocktails, live music from 2100.

Bars and clubs

Natal's nightlife hotspots lie in the streets around Dr Manoel A B de Araujo (behind Ponta Negra beach on the other side of Av Eng Roberto Freire). This street and the one that joins it by Taverna/Lua Cheia is known as 'Broadway', and has lots of bars and cafés.

Centro de Turismo (see Tourist information, above) has *Forró com Turista*, a chance for visitors to learn this fun dance on Thu at 2200. There are many other enjoyable venues where visitors are encouraged to join in.

Decky
Av Roberto Freire 9100, Ponta Negra, T084-3219 2471.
Models of Mick Jagger and John Lennon greet you at the entrance of this al fresco rock bar, where live bands play to a buzzing crowd at weekends. Also serves food.

Rastapé
R Aristides Porpino 2198, Ponta Negra, T084-3219 0181, www.rastapecasadeforro.com.br.
Lively faux-rustic *forró* bar with 3 live bands a night and areas for eating, chatting and dancing. Very popular.

Taverna Pub
R Dr Manoel A B de Araújo 500, Ponta Negra, T084-3236 3696, www.tavernapub.com.br.
Medieval-style pub in youth hostel basement. Eclectic (rock, Brazilian pop, jazz, etc.) live music Tue-Sun from 2200, best night Wed, singles night Mon. Recommended.

Festivals

Jan Festa de Nossa Senhora dos Navegantes, when numerous vessels go to sea from Praia da Redinha, north of town.
Mid-Oct Country show, **Festa do Boi** (bus marked Parnamirim to the exhibition centre), gives a good insight into rural life.
Dec Carnaval, the Salvador-style out-of-season carnival, a lively 4-day music festival with dancing in the streets in the 1st week of the month.

What to do

Boat trips

Popular boat trips include the **Rio Potengi** and along the nearby beaches of the Litoral Sul. A 2-hr tour includes hotel pick-up, a snack, and allows time for a swim, US$20 per person. Boat trips to **Barra do Cunhaú**, 86 km south of Natal, go through mangroves, visit an island and a salt mine (**Passeio Ecológico Cunhaú**).

Buggy tours

Buggy tours are by far the most popular activity and can be organized through the hotels. Be sure to check that only shifting dunes are visited; fixed dunes are protected by Brazilian environmental law. It is possible to hire a buggy, or take a tour, all the way to Fortaleza with companies like **Buggy e Compania** (www.buggyecia. com.br); avoid the huge operators who journey in large convoys. **Cariri Ecotours** (see below), can recommend environmentally sensitive operators.

Dromedary rides

Dromedunas, *www.dromedunas.com.br*. Cleide Gomes and Philippe Landry offer dromedary rides on the dunes above Genipabu. Walks last around 30 mins and they make a far more peaceful alternative to buzzing dune buggies. You'll find them on Genipabu Beach from 0900 every day.

Ecotourism

Cariri Ecotours, *R Francisco Gurgel 9067, Ponta Negra, T084-9660 1818, www.cariri ecotours.com.br*. Excellent tours to some of the most interesting sights in the northeastern interior, such as Souza, Cariri and the Serra da Capivara as well as extensive beach itineraries in Rio Grande do Norte, Paraíba and Pernambuco (including Fernando de Noronha). Very professional and personable. One of the best companies in Northeast Brazil.

Transport

Air Flights to **Brasília**, **Fortaleza**, **Recife**, **Rio de Janeiro**, **Salvador**, **São Paulo**; **Belo Horizonte**, **Goiânia**, **São Luís**, **Fernando de Noronha**, **Vitória**, **Porto Alegre** from Natal airport, T084-3087 1200, www.infraero. gov.br. There are international flights to **Lisbon** with **TAP**.

Buggy It's possible to travel all the way to **Fortaleza**, via the stunning Rio Grande do Norte dunes and beaches, but avoid the beach buggy tours, for while they are better controlled than they were a few years ago, buggies are still responsible for erosion damage to the coast. Book a trip through a responsible operator like **Cariri Ecotours** (see above).

Bus Regional tickets are sold on street level of the new *rodoviária* in Cidade da Esperança, T084-3205 4377; interstate tickets are available on the 2nd floor. For transport to and from the *rodoviária* see box, page 132.

To **Tabatinga** (90 mins, US$5) via **Pirangi** (30 mins, US$4), 5 times a day 0630-1815, 3 on Sun 0730, 0930, 1645.

There are 12 buses a day (6 at weekends) to **Pipa** via **Tibau do Sul**, **Goianinha** and **São José de Mipibu**, US$6, 2 hrs. With **Nordeste** to **Mossoró**, US$22.50, 4 hrs. To **Aracati**, US$27.50, 5½ hrs. To **Fortaleza**, 7 a day including 2 night buses, US$47.50, 8 hrs. To **João Pessoa**, every 2½ hrs, US$15, To **Maceió**, 10 hrs, US$40. To **Recife**, 9 daily, 3½ hrs, US$20. To **Salvador**, 2 daily, US$65, 20 hrs.

Combis connect **Pipa** and **Tibau** until around 2300. 12 buses a day to **Natal**'s new *rodoviária*, US$4, 2½ hrs, from Pipa via Tibau do Sul. Minivans also do this run and are easiest to catch from the beach. Buses to **Paraíba** pass through **Goianinha** on the interstate road. Frequent *combis* connect **Goianinha** with Pipa (30 mins, US$4).

Car hire Car hire offices can be found at the airport and in mid- to top-range hotels. **Avis**, at airport, www.avis.com. **Hertz**, airport, www.hertz.com. **Localiza**, Av Nascimento de Castro 1792, www.localiza.com.

The coast north of Natal is is lined with many sand dunes, some reaching a staggering 50 m in height. Genipabu, a weekend resort for the Natal middle classes, is the most famous of these and is only a very short bus ride from the city. The country beyond the resort is well off the tourist trail, with vast long beaches backed by multi-coloured cliffs, dunes and salt lakes. It is dramatic terrain, so much so that it has been used as the backdrop to numerous biblical films. Three crosses stand over the cliffs at Areia Branca, left there by one of the most recent productions, *Maria, A Mãe do Filho de Deus*.

The best way to experience the majesty of the coastal landscape is to walk and listen to the wind on the sand. Buggy tourism has led to the degradation of many of the Northeast's dunes. Fixed dunes are protected and should not be disturbed, but shifting dunes can be visited by buggy, camel or horse. Ask locally for advice.

Genipabu and around

Natal's northernmost beach has very scenic dunes around the **Lagoa de Genipabu**, a lake surrounded by cashew trees. There are many bars and restaurants on the seashore. Buggy rental and microlight flights can be arranged; contact the **Associação dos Bugueiros** (T084-3225 2077). It costs around US$20 for a dune buggy tour. Microlight flights are also available.

North of Genipabu, across the Rio Ceará Mirim, are several beaches with coconut groves and dunes, lined with fishing villages and summer homes of people from Natal; access is via the town of Extremoz. One of these beaches, **Pitangui**, 35 km from Natal, is 6 km long and has a crystalline lake where colourful schools of fish can be seen. **Jacumã**, 49 km from Natal, has a small waterfall and the inland Lagoa de Jacumã, a lake surrounded by dunes where sand-skiing is popular.

Muriú, 44 km from Natal, is known for its lovely green ocean where numerous small boats and *jangadas* anchor; the beach has attractive palms; a buggy tour from Natal, including shifting dunes costs around US$65. About 5 km to the north is **Prainha** or **Coqueiro**, a beautiful cove with many coconut palms and strong waves.

Lovely beaches continue along the state's coastline; as you get further away from Natal the beaches are more distant from the main highways and access is more difficult. Around 83 km north of Natal, in the centre of a region known for its coconuts and lobsters, is the ugly resort town of **Touros**. From here the coastline veers east–west.

Far north

As the coast turns to the west, the terrain becomes more dramatic and bleak. Sheltered coves are replaced by vast beaches stretching in seemingly interminable broad curves. Behind them are pink, brown and red cliffs, or large expanses of dunes. Highlights are the sleepy little village of **Galinhos**, with its sand streets and beautiful, gentle beach washed by a calm sea, and the **Costa Branca** near the little fishing towns of **Areia Branca**, **Ponta do Mel** and **Rosadao**, where huge pink and white dunes converge behind magnificent long beaches.

South of Natal, the Rota do Sol/Litoral Sul (RN-063) follows the coastline for some 55 km and provides access to beaches south of Ponta Negra. From here the coast becomes more remote. Long curves of white sand backed by multi-coloured sandstone cliffs and sweeping dunes; fragments of Atlantic forest alive with rare birds; black tea lagoons; and bays filled with dolphins, make this one of the most popular stretches in the Northeast. Thankfully development is small scale and it still feels relaxed (outside high season). Several species of turtle, including giant leatherbacks, still nest here, although numbers are declining as the popularity of beach buggy tourism grows. The best place to stay along this stretch of coast is Pipa (see below), a lively little town with good *pousadas* and restaurants.

Tibau do Sul and Pipa

The little fishing town of **Tibau do Sul** (population 6124) has cobbled streets and sits high on a cliff between surf beaches and the manatee-filled Lago de Guaraíra. Boat trips can be arranged from here to the *lago* or to see dolphins in the calm waters offshore. Although most tourists head straight for Pipa, which is more developed, the beach *barracas* in Tibau are lively at night with *forró* and MPB. Natal's finest restaurants are also here (see Restaurants, below) and there are a handful of decent *pousadas* in town.

From Tibau, a series of white-sand crescents, separated by rocky headlands and backed by high cliffs crowned with coconut groves and remnant coastal forest, stretches south to **Pipa**. This is one of Natal's most enchanting little tourist towns, whose mix of local fishermen and settlers from all over Brazil has formed an eclectic alternative community. There are excellent *pousadas* and restaurants in all price ranges and the nightlife is animated. The town is becoming increasingly popular and the number of people can feel overwhelming during Carnaval and New Year.

The town beach is somewhat developed, but there are plenty of others nearby. **Praia dos Golfinhos** to the south and **Madeiro** beyond it have only a few hotels, and **Praia do Amor** to the north is surrounded by cliffs and has reasonable surf. Access to the shore is down the steps built by the few cliff-top hotels or by walking along the beach from Pipa at low tide. There are tours to see dolphins from US$8 per person and also around the mangrove-lined **Lagoa Guaraíra** at Tibau, particularly beautiful at sunset.

Just north of town, on a 70-m-high dune, is the **Santuário Ecológico de Pipa** ⓘ *T084-3201 2007, www.pipa.com.br/santuarioecologico, 0800-1700 (last entrance at 1600), US$2.50*, a 60-ha park created in 1986 to conserve the Mata Atlântica forest. There are several trails and lookouts over the cliffs, which afford an excellent view of the ocean and dolphins. Although larger animals like cats and howler monkeys are long gone, this is one of the few areas in the state where important indicator bird species, such as guans, can be found.

Where to stay

Tibau do Sul and Pipa

In Pipa, there are more than 30 *pousadas* and many private homes offer accommodation.

$$$$ Sombra e Água Fresca
Praia do Amor, T084-3246 2144,
www.sombraeaguafresca.com.br.
Cheaper in low season. Tastefully decorated but small chalet rooms and vast luxury suites with separate sitting and dining areas. All with magnificent views.

$$$$ Toca da Coruja
Praia da Pipa, T084-3246 2226,
www.tocadacoruja.com.br.
One of the best small luxury hotels in Northeast Brazil, with a range of chalets set in forested gardens and decorated with Brazilian antiques and art. Beautiful pool and an excellent restaurant.

$$$$ Village Natureza
Canto do Madeiro, Pipa, T084-3246 4200,
http://villagenatureza.com.br.
Beautifully appointed a/c chalets nestled in tropical wooded gardens overlooking the sea and Madeiro Beach. Gorgeous circular pool, pleasant grounds, lovely views and a long series of steep steps leading to the beach.

$$$ Marinas Tibau Sul
Tibau do Sul, T084-3246 4111,
www.hotelmarinas.com.br.
Cabins for 4, pool, restaurant, watersports, horse riding and a boat dock.

$$$ Mirante de Pipa
R do Mirante 1, Praia da Pipa, T084-3246 2055, www.mirantedepipa.com.br.
A/c and fan-cooled chalets with a veranda set in a forested garden.

$$$ Ponta do Madeiro
R da Praia, Estr para Pipa Km 3, T084-3246 4220, www.pontadomadeiro.com.br.
Very comfortable spacious a/c chalets, beautiful pool with bar and spectacular views over the Praia do Madeiro. Excellent service, Wi-Fi and a good restaurant. Transfers into Pipa town throughout the day and until fairly late at night.

$$$ Tartaruga
Av Baía dos Golfinhos, 508, T084-3246 2385,
www.pousadatartaruga.com.br.
Rooms gathered around a pretty little pool with raw tile floor, flower paintings, lovely big mirrors in bamboo frames, heavy wooden furniture and a shady bar and restaurant area. Wi-Fi throughout.

$$ A Conchego
R do Ceu s/n, Praia da Pipa, T084-3246 2439,
www.pousada-aconchego.com.
Family-run *pousada* with simple chalets with red-tiled roofs and terraces, in a garden filled with cashew and palm trees. Tranquil and central. Good breakfast.

$ Pousada da Pipa
R do Cruzeiro s/n, T084-3246 2271.
Small rooms decorated with a personal touch. The best are upstairs and have a large shared terrace with glazed terracotta tiles, sitting areas and hammocks.

Restaurants

Tibau do Sul and Pipa

There are many restaurants and bars along Pipa's main street, Av Baía dos Golfinhos. Almost all restaurants are cash only.

$$$ Camamo Beijupirá
Tibau do Sul, T084-3246 4195,
www.camamo.com.
One of the best restaurants in Brazil with an eclectic mix of fusion dishes like prawns and slices of leek in a spicy cashew sauce with raisins and ginger, served with fervent enthusiasm by owner Tadeu Lubambo. Excellent wine list.

$$$ Toca da Coruja
Praia da Pipa (see Where to stay, above).
Superlative and beautifully presented
regional food in a tropical garden setting.
Intimate and romantic. Highly recommended.

$$$ Vivenda Art & Comer
Av Baía dos Golfinhos 731, Pipa.
One of the town's best seafood restaurants
and a good place to watch the passers-by.

$$$-$$ Espaço Lampião
*Av Baía dos Golfinhos 50, T084-3246 2069,
www.restaurantelampiao.com.br.*
An attractive, open-sided restaurant lit with
faux-Moroccan lamps and built around a
huge Pitumbeira tree, serving standard
Brazilian dishes – from seafood (grilled fish
and *moquecas* to *bacalhau*), steaks, pastas
and *petiscos*.

$$ Quintal
*Av Baía dos Golfinhos 985, lj 1, T084-9631
8771, www.facebook.com/Quintalpipa.*
Savoury and sweet tapiocas, *moquecas*,
grilled fish and *barreado* served on an
open-air deck overlooking the sea.

What to do

Tibau do Sul and Pipa
Pousadas in Pipa can organize dolphin-
watching trips, kayaking on the lagoons,
surf and windsurf classes and board rental
and buggy rides.
Pipa Aventura, *Av Bahia dos Golfinhos 654,
T084-3246 2008, www.pipaaventura.com.br.*
Light adventure trips around Pipa including
zip lining, kayaking and short hikes.

Practicalities

Getting there

Air

The Northeast has two principal international airports: in Recife and 785 km northwest in Fortaleza. Recife's **Gilberto Freyre Airport** at Guararapes (see page 41), 12 km from the city centre near the hotel district of Boa Viagem, has international connections to Lisbon, Frankfurt, Panama City and Buenos Aires as well as São Paulo, Rio, Brasília, Belo Horizonte, Fernando de Noronha and other state capitals. Fortaleza's airport (see page 94), 6 km south of the centre, has connections to **Europe** (via Lisbon with **TAP**, via Milan with **Meridiana** and via Frankfurt with **Condor**), to the **USA** (via Miami with **TAM**) and to **Colombia** (via Bogotá with **Avianca**) as well to destinations throughout Brazil, including all Brazil's major state capitals.

TRAVEL TIP

Packing for Brazil

Bag Unobtrusive sturdy bag (either rucksack or bag with wheels) and an inelegant day pack/bag – to attract minimal attention on the streets.

Clothing Brazilians dress casually. It's best to do likewise and blend in. Avoid flashy brands. Thin cotton or a modern wicking artificial fabric are best. Take lightweight trousers, shorts, a long-sleeved shirt, skirts, cotton or wicking socks, underwear, shawl or light waterproof jacket for evenings and a sun hat.

Footwear Light Gore-Tex walking shoes (or boots if you intend to trek) are best. Buy from a serious, designated outdoor company like Brasher or Berghaus rather than a flimsy fashion brand. Wear them in before you come. Nothing gives a tourist away more than new shoes.

Sponge bag 2% tincture of iodine; Mercurochrome or similar; athlete's foot powder; tea tree oil; antibiotic ointment; toothbrush; rehydration tablets; anti-diarrheals such as Imodium; sun protection (high factor) – this is expensive in Brazil.

Electronics UK, US or European socket adaptor; camera with case to attract minimal attention; torch (flashlight).

Miscellaneous items Ear plugs for surfing, traffic noise and cockerels at dawn; penknife; strong string (3 m); hooks with a screw-in thread (for mosquito net); gaffer tape; sunglasses (with UV filter); money belt; a sealable waterproof bag large enough for camera and clothes.

For rural and beach destinations take a mosquito net impregnated with insect repellent (the bell-shaped models are best) and a water bottle.

What not to pack – to buy there

T-shirts (local brands make you less conspicuous and they are sold everywhere); insect repellent (Johnson's Off! aerosol is best); beachwear (unless you have neuroses about your body – no one cares if their bum looks big in anything in Brazil); flip-flops (Havaianas); painkillers; shampoo and soap; toothpaste; beach sarong (*kanga*); vitamins; hammock and rope.

Prices are cheapest in October, November and after Carnaval and at their highest in the European summer and the Brazilian high seasons (generally 15 December to 15 January, the Thursday before Carnaval to the Saturday after Carnaval, and 15 June to 15 August). Departure tax is usually included in the cost of the ticket.

The best deals on flights within Brazil are available through **Azul** ⓘ *www.voeazul. com.br*; **GOL** ⓘ *www.voegol.com.br*; and **TAM** ⓘ *www.tam.com.br*; and **Avianca** ⓘ *www. avianca.com.br*.

Air passes
TAM and GOL offer a 21-day **Brazil Airpass**, which is valid on any TAM destination within Brazil. The price varies according to the number of flights taken and the international airline used to arrive in Brazil. They can only be bought outside Brazil. Rates vary depending on the season. Children pay a discounted rate; those under three pay 10% of the adult rate. Some of the carriers operate a blackout period between 15 December and 15 January.

Baggage allowance
Airlines will only allow a certain weight of luggage without a surcharge; for Brazil this is usually two items of 32 kg but may be as low as 20 kg for domestic flights; with two items of hand luggage weighing up to 10 kg in total. UK airport staff can refuse to load bags weighing more than 30 kg. Baggage allowances are higher in business and first class. In all cases it is best to enquire beforehand.

Sea

Travelling as a passenger on a cargo ship to South America is not a cheap way to go, but if you have the time and want a bit of luxury, it makes a great alternative to flying. The passage is often only available for round trips.

Cruise ships
Cruise ships regularly visit Brazil. The website www.cruisetransatlantic.com has full details of transatlantic crossings. There are often cheaper deals off season.

Getting around

First time visitors seldom realise how big Brazil is and fail to plan accordingly. The country is the world's fifth largest, making it bigger than the USA without Alaska, or the size of Australia with France and the UK tagged on. The Northeast region alone is bigger than South Africa. Maranhão state is the size of Germany. There is no intercity rail in the Northeast (or elsewhere) and travelling within a state overland can involve long bus or car journeys. Plan for long journey times (overnight buses are good value and save on accommodation) or consider flying between capitals.

Air

Due to the huge distances between places, flying is the most practical option to get around. All state capitals and larger cities are linked with each other with services several times a day, and all national airlines offer excellent service. Deregulation of the airlines has greatly reduced prices on some routes and low-cost airlines offer fares that can often be as cheap as travelling by bus (when booked online). Buy your internal flights before leaving home. Paying with an international credit card is not always possible online within Brazil (as sites often ask for a Brazilian social security number), but it is usually possible to buy an online ticket through a hotel, agency or willing friend without a surcharge. Many smaller airlines go in and out of business sporadically. **Avianca** ⓘ *www.avianca.com.br*, **Azul** ⓘ *www.voeazul.com.br*, **GOL** ⓘ *www.voegol.com.br* and **TAM** ⓘ *www.tam.com.br* operate the most extensive routes.

Road

Bus

Other than flying, the most reliable way of travelling is by bus. Routes are extensive, prices reasonable and buses modern and comfortable. There are three standards of intercity and interstate bus: *Comum*, or *Convencional*, are quite slow, not very comfortable and fill up quickly; *Executivo* are more expensive, comfortable (many have reclining seats), and don't stop en route to pick up passengers so are safer; *leito* (literally 'bed') run at night between the main centres, offering reclining seats with leg rests, toilets, and sometimes refreshments, at double the normal fare. For journeys over 100 km, most buses have chemical toilets (bring toilet paper). Air conditioning can make buses cold at night, so take a jumper; on some services blankets are supplied.

Buses stop fairly frequently (every two to four hours) at *postos* for snacks. Bus stations for interstate services and other long-distance routes are called *rodoviárias*. They are frequently outside the city centres and offer snack bars, lavatories, left luggage, local bus services and information centres. Buy bus tickets at *rodoviárias* (most now take credit cards), not from travel agents who add on surcharges. Reliable bus information is hard to come by, other than from companies themselves. Buses usually arrive and depart in very good time. Many town buses have turnstiles, which can be inconvenient if you are carrying a large pack. Urban buses normally serve local airports.

Car hire

Car hire is competitive with mainland Europe and a little pricier than the USA. But roads are not always well-signposted and maps are hard to come by. Use a Sat Nav only outside the cities. Within a city a Sat Nav offers the shortest routes, which can involve potentially dangerous crossings through peripheral communities. Costs can be reduced by reserving a car over the internet through one of the larger international companies such as **Europcar** ⓘ *www.europcar.co.uk*, or **Avis** ⓘ *www.avis.co.uk*. The minimum age for renting a car is 21 and it's essential to have a credit card. Companies operate under the terms *aluguel de automóveis* or *auto-locadores*. Check exactly what the company's insurance policy covers. In many cases it will not cover major accidents or 'natural' damage (eg flooding). Ask if extra cover is available. Sometimes using a credit card automatically includes insurance. Beware of being billed for scratches that were on the vehicle before you hired it.

Taxi

At the outset, make sure the meter is cleared and shows 'tariff 1', except (usually) from 2300-0600, Sunday, and in December when '2' is permitted. Check that the meter is working; if not, fix the price in advance. The **radio taxi** service costs about 50% more but cheating is less likely. Taxis outside larger hotels usually cost more. If you are seriously cheated, note the number of the taxi and insist on a signed bill; threatening to take it to the police can work. **Mototaxis** are much more economical, but many are unlicensed and there have been a number of robberies of passengers. Taxis vary widely in quality and price but are easy to come by and safe when taken from a *posto de taxis* (taxi rank).

Essentials A-Z

Accident and emergency

Ambulance T192. **Police** T190/197. If robbed or attacked, contact the tourist police. If you need to claim on insurance, make sure you get a police report.

Children

Travel with children is easy in Brazil. Brazilians love children and they are generally welcome everywhere. Facilities are often better than those back home.

Some hotels charge a cheaper family rate. Some will not charge for children under 5 and most can provide an extra camp bed for a double room. A few of the more romantic boutique beach resorts do not accept children. If you are planning to stay in such a hotel it is best to enquire ahead.

Most restaurants provide children's seats and menus as well as crayons and paper to keep them happy. Children are never expected to be seen but not heard.

Children under 3 generally travel for 10% on internal flights and at 70% until 12 years old. Prices on buses depend on whether the child will occupy a seat or a lap. Laps are free and if there are spare seats after the bus has departed the child can sit there for free.

On tours children under 6 usually go free or it may be possible to get a discount.

Disabled travellers

As in most Latin American countries, facilities are generally very poor. Problems are worst for **wheelchair users**, who will find that ramps are rare and that toilets and bathrooms with facilities are few and far between, except for some of the more modern hotels and the larger airports. Public transport is not well geared up for wheelchairs and pavements are often in a poor state of repair or crowded with street vendors requiring passers-by to brave the traffic. The metro has lifts and disabled chair lifts at some stations (but not all are operational). Disabled Brazilians obviously have to cope with these problems and mainly rely on the help of others to get on and off public transport and generally move around. Drivers should bring a disabled sticker as most shopping centres and public car parks have disabled spaces.

Disability Travel, www.disabilitytravel.com, is an excellent US site written by travellers in wheelchairs who have been researching disabled travel full-time since 1985. There are many tips and useful contacts and articles and the company also organizes group tours.

Global Access – Disabled Travel Network Site, www.globalaccessnews.com. Provides travel information for 'disabled adventurers' and includes a number of reviews and tips.

Society for Accessible Travel and Hospitality, www.sath.org. Has some specific information on Brazil.

Brazilian organizations include: **Sociedade Amigos do Deficiente Físico**, T021-2241 0063, based in Rio and with associate memberships throughout Brazil; and **Centro da Vida Independente**, Rio, www.cvi-rio. org.br. There are a number of specialist and general operators offering holidays specifically aimed at those with disabilities. These include: **Responsible Travel**, www.responsibletravel.com; **CanbeDone**, www.canbedone.co.uk; and **Access Travel**, www.access-travel.co.uk.

Nothing Ventured, edited by Alison Walsh (Harper Collins), has personal accounts of worldwide journeys by disabled travellers, plus advice and listings.

TRAVEL TIP
Brazilian etiquette

In his 1941 travel book, *I Like Brazil*, Jack Harding said of Brazilians that "anyone who does not get along with (them) had better examine himself; the fault is his." And perhaps the best writer on Brazil in English, Joseph Page, observed in his 1995 book *The Brazilians* that "cordiality is a defining characteristic of their behaviour. They radiate an irresistible pleasantness, abundant hospitality, and unfailing politeness, especially to foreigners." It is hard to offend Brazilians or to find Brazilians offensive, but to make sure you avoid misunderstandings, here are a few, perhaps surprising, tips.

Public nudity, even toplessness on beaches, is an arrestable offence.

Brazilians will talk to anyone, anywhere. "Sorry, do I know you?" is the least Brazilian sentiment imaginable and no one ever rustles a newspaper on the metro.

Walks in nature are never conducted in silence. This has led many Brazilians to be unaware that their country is the richest in terrestrial wildlife on the planet.

Drug use, even of marijuana, is deeply frowned upon. Attitudes are far more conservative than in Europe. The same is true of public drunkenness.

When driving it is normal, especially in Rio, to accelerate right up the bumper of the car in the lane in front of you on the highway, hoot repeatedly and flash your headlights. It is considered about as rude as ringing the doorbell in Brazil.

The phrase 'So para Ingles Ver' ('just for the English to see') is a common expression that means 'to appear to do something by the rule book whilst doing the opposite'.

This is the land of red tape. You need a social security number to buy a SIM card and fingerprint ID just to go to the dentist.

Never presume a policeman will take a bribe. And never presume he won't. Let the policeman do the presuming.

Never insult an official. You could find yourself in serious trouble.

Brazilians are very private about their negative emotions. Never moan for more than a few seconds, even with justification – you will be branded an *uruca* (harbinger of doom), and won't be invited to the party.

Never confuse a Brazilian footballer with an Argentine one.

Brazilians believe that anyone can dance samba. They can't.

Never dismiss a street seller with anything less than cordiality; an impolite dismissal will be seen as arrogant and aggressive. Always extend a polite "não obrigado".

Brazilian time. Peter Fleming, the author of one of the best travel books about Brazil, once said that "a man in a hurry will be miserable in Brazil." Remember this when you arrive 10 minutes late to meet a friend in a bar and spend the next hour wondering if they've already gone after growing tired of waiting for you. They haven't. They've not yet left home. Unless you specify 'a hora britanica' then you will wait. And wait. And everyone will be mortified if you complain.

Electricity

Generally 110 V 60 cycles AC, but occasionally 220 V 60 cycles AC is used. European and US 2-pin plugs and sockets.

Embassies and consulates

For a list of Brazilian embassies abroad, see http://embassygoabroad.com.

Gay and lesbian travellers

Brazil is a good country for gay and lesbian travellers as attitudes are fairly liberal, especially in the big cities. Opinions in rural areas are far more conservative and it is wise to adapt to this.

Festivals include the nationwide **Mix Brasil festival of Sexual diversity**, www.mixbrasil. uol.com.br.

Health

See your GP or travel clinic at least 6 weeks before departure for general advice on travel risks and vaccinations. Make sure you have sufficient medical travel insurance, get a dental check, know your own blood group and, if you suffer a long-term condition such as diabetes or epilepsy, obtain a **Medic Alert** bracelet (www.medicalalert.co.uk).

Vaccinations and anti-malarials

Confirm that your primary courses and boosters are up to date. It is advisable to vaccinate against polio, tetanus, typhoid, hepatitis A and, for more remote areas, rabies. Yellow fever vaccination is obligatory for most areas. Cholera, diptheria and hepatitis B vaccinations are sometimes advised. Only a very few parts of Brazil have significant malaria risk. Seek specialist advice before you leave.

Health risks

The major risks posed in the region are those caused by insect disease carriers such as mosquitoes and sandflies. The key parasitic and viral diseases are malaria, which is not widespread, South American trypanosomiasis (Chagas disease) and dengue fever. **Dengue fever** (which is present throughout Brazil) is particularly hard to protect against as the mosquitoes can bite throughout the day as well as night (unlike those that carry malaria; see box, page 150, for advice on avoiding insect bites. **Chagas disease** is spread by faeces of the triatomine, or assassin bugs, whereas sandflies spread a disease of the skin called **leishmaniasis**.

While standards of hygiene in Brazilian restaurants are generally very high, **intestinal upsets** are common, if only because many first time visitors are not used to the food. Always wash your hands before eating and be careful with drinking water and ice; if you have any doubts about the water then boil it or filter and treat it. In a restaurant buy bottled water or ask where the water has come from. Food can also pose a problem, be wary of salads if you don't know if it has been washed or not.

There is some risk of **tuberculosis** (TB) and although the BCG vaccine is available, it is still not guaranteed protection. It is best to avoid unpasteurized dairy products and try not to let people cough and splutter all over you.

Cases of **Zika virus** have been reported in Brazil and it is recommended that you check with the Foreign Office (www.gov.uk) before travelling, particularly if you're pregnant or planning to become pregnant, and seek advice from a health professional.

Websites
www.cdc.gov Centres for Disease Control and Prevention (USA).
www.fitfortravel. nhs.uk Fit for Travel (UK), A-Z of vaccine and travel health advice for each country.
www.fco.gov.uk Foreign and Commonwealth Office (FCO), UK.
www.itg.be Prince Leopold Institute for Tropical Medicine.
http://travelhealthpro.org.uk Useful website for the National Travel Health

How to avoid insect bites

Brazilian insects are vectors for a number of diseases including zika, chikungunya, dengue and, in some areas, malaria and yellow fever. These are transmitted by mosquitoes (and some by sandflies) which bite both day and night. Here are a few tips to avoid getting bitten.

- Be particularly vigilant around dawn and dusk when most diurnal and nocturnal mosquitoes bite. Cover ankles and feet and the backs of arms.
- Check your room for insects and spray insecticide before you go out for the day to ensure an insect-free night. Most hotels will have spray, otherwise it can be bought in pharmacies and supermarkets.
- Use insect repellent, especially in beach and forested areas. No repellent works 100%, but most will limit bites. Repellent is available at most pharmacies and supermarkets throughout Brazil. The Off! brand is reliable. If you wish to make your own 'industrial-chemical-free' formula, the author finds the following recipe made with essential oils effective throughout Brazil, including the Amazon: 70% jojoba oil, 30% citronella oil, 10-20 drops of Eucalyptus radiata, 10-15 drops of Wintergreen, 10-15 drops of Cajeput. Do not take this formula internally. This insect repellent also works with sandflies who cannot land on the thick jojoba oil.
- Sandflies are not as widely present in Brazil as in Central America but you will encounter them in some locations (most notably Ilhabela). Many DEET repellents and citronella-based repellents do not work on sandflies. The recipe above, jojoba oil or 'Skin so Soft' baby oil does but you need to apply it thickly.
- Bring a mosquito net. Bell nets are best. Lifesystems do treated models which repel and kill insects. Bring a small roll of duct tape, a few screw-in hooks and at least 5 m of string to ensure you can put the net up in almost all locations.
- Sleep with the fan on when you sleep. Fans are for stopping mosquitoes as much as they are for cooling.
- Consider using insect-repellent treated shirts like those in the Craghoppers Nosilife range. Avoid black clothing. Mosquitoes find it attractive.

Network and Centre (NaTHNaC), a UK government organization.
www.who.int World Health Organization.

Books
Dawood, R, editor *Travellers' health*. Oxford University Press, 2012.
Warrell, David, and Sarah Anderson, editors *Oxford Handbook of Expedition and Wilderness Medicine*. Oxford Medical Handbooks 2008.
Wilson-Howarth, Jane *The Essential Guide to Travel Health*. Cadogan 2009.

Insurance

Always take out travel insurance before you set off and read the small print carefully. Check that the policy covers the activities you intend or may end up doing. Also check exactly what your medical cover includes (eg ambulance, helicopter rescue or emergency flights back home). Also check the payment protocol. You may have to cough up first before the insurance company reimburses you. To be safe, it is always best to dig out all the receipts for expensive personal effects like jewellery or cameras. Take photos of these items and note down all serial numbers.

Internet

Internet usage is widespread. Most hotels offer in-room Wi-Fi (usually free but sometimes at exorbitant rates).

Language *See also page 161.*

Brazilians speak Portuguese, and very few speak anything else. Spanish may help you to be understood a little, but spoken Portuguese will remain undecipherable even to fluent Spanish speakers. To get the best out of Brazil, learn some Portuguese before arriving. Brazilians are the best thing about the country and without Portuguese you will not be able to interact beyond stereotypes and second guesses.

Cactus (www.cactuslanguage.com), **Languages abroad** (www.languages abroad.co.uk) and **Travellers Worldwide** (www.travellersworld wide.com) are among the companies that can organize language courses in Brazil. **McGraw Hill** and **DK** (*Hugo Portuguese in Three Months*) offer the best teach-yourself books. **Sonia Portuguese** (www.sonia-portuguese.com) is a useful online resource and there are myriad free and paid-for Portuguese apps of varying quality.

Money

Currency

£1=R$5.35; €1=R$4.13; US$1=R$3.75 (Mar 2016). The unit of currency is the **real**, R$ (plural **reais**). Any amount of foreign currency and 'a reasonable sum' in reais can be taken in, but sums over US$10,000 must be declared. Residents may only take out the equivalent of US$4000. Notes in circulation are: 100, 50, 10, 5 and 1 real; coins: 1 real, 50, 25, 10, 5 and 1 centavo. **Note** The exchange rate fluctuates – check regularly.

Costs of travelling

Brazil is cheaper than most countries in South America though prices vary greatly. Rural areas can be 50% cheaper than heavily visited tourist areas in the big city. As a very rough guide, prices are about half those of Western Europe and a third cheaper than rural USA.

Hostel beds are usually around US$8. Budget hotels with few frills have rooms for as little as US$15, and you should have no difficulty finding a double room costing US$30 wherever you are. Rooms are often pretty much the same price whether 1 or 2 people are staying and aside from hostels prices invariably include a large breakfast.

Eating is generally inexpensive, especially in *padarias* (bakeries) or *comida por kilo* (pay by weight) restaurants, which offer a wide range of food (salads, meat, pasta and vegetarian). Expect to pay around US$4 to eat your fill in a good-value restaurant. Although bus travel is cheap by US or European standards, because of the long distances, costs can soon mount up. Internal flights prices have come down dramatically in the last couple of years and some routes work out cheaper than taking a bus, especially if booking online.

ATMs

ATMs, or cash machines, are easy to come by. As well as being the most convenient way of withdrawing money, they frequently offer the best available rates of exchange. They are usually closed after 2130. There are 2 international ATM acceptance systems, **Plus** and **Cirrus**. Many issuers of debit and credit cards are linked to one, or both (eg Visa is Plus, MasterCard is Cirrus). **Bradesco** and **HSBC** are the 2 main banks offering this service. **Red Banco 24 Horas** kiosks advertise that they take a long list of credit cards in their ATMs, including MasterCard and Amex, but international cards cannot always be used; the same is true of **Banco do Brasil**.

Advise your bank before leaving, as cards are usually stopped in Brazil without prior warning. Find out before you leave what international functionality your card has. Check if your bank or credit card company imposes handling charges. Internet banking is useful for monitoring your account or transferring funds. Do not rely on one card, in case of loss. If you do lose a card, immediately contact the 24-hr helpline of the issuer in your home country (keep this number in a safe place).

Exchange

Banks in major cities will change cash and, for those who still use them, traveller's cheques (TCs). If you keep the official exchange slips, you may convert back into foreign currency up to 50% of the amount you exchanged. The parallel market, found in travel agencies, exchange houses and among hotel staff, often offers marginally better rates than the banks but commissions can be very high. Many banks may only change US$300 minimum in cash, US$500 in TCs. Rates for TCs are usually far lower than for cash, they are harder to change and a very heavy commission may be charged.

Credit cards

Credit cards are widely used. Visa and Mastercard are the most widely used, with **Diners Club** and **Amex** a close second. Cash advances on credit cards will only be paid in reais at the tourist rate, incurring at least a 1.5% commission. Banks in remote places may refuse to give a cash advance: try asking for the *gerente* (manager).

Currency cards

If you don't want to carry lots of cash, prepaid currency cards allow you to preload money from your bank account, fixed at the day's exchange rate. They look like a credit or debit card and are issued by specialist money changing companies, such as **Travelex** and **Caxton FX**, as well as the **Post Office**. You can top up and check your balance by phone, online and sometimes by text.

Money transfers

Money sent to Brazil is normally paid out in Brazilian currency, so do not have more sent out than you need for your stay. Funds can ostensibly be received within 48 banking hours, but it can take at least a month to arrive, allowing banks to capitalize on your transfer. The documentation required to receive it varies according to the whim of the bank staff, making the whole procedure often far more trouble than it is worth.

Opening hours

Generally Mon-Fri 0900-1800; closed for lunch sometime between 1130 and 1400. **Banks** Mon-Fri 1000-1600 or 1630; closed at weekends. **Government offices** Mon-Fri 1100-1800. **Shops** Also open on Sat until 1230 or 1300.

Post

To send a standard letter or postcard to the USA costs US$0.65, to Europe US$0.90, to Australia or South Africa US0.65. Air mail should take about 7 days to or from Britain or the USA. Franked and registered (insured) letters are normally secure, but check that the amount franked is what you have paid, or the item will not arrive. Aerogrammes are most reliable. To avoid queues and obtain higher denomination stamps go to the stamp desk at the main post office.

The post office sells cardboard boxes for sending packages internally and abroad. Rates and rules for sending literally vary from post office to post office even within the same town and the quickest service is **SEDEX**. The most widespread courier service is **Federal Express**, www.fedex.com/br. They are often cheaper than parcel post.

Postes restantes usually only hold letters for 30 days. Identification is required and it's a good idea to write your name on a piece of paper to help the attendant find your letters. Charges are minimal but often involve queuing at another counter to buy stamps, which are attached to your letter and franked before it is given to you.

Safety *See also pages 29 and 88.*

Although you are unlikely to encounter any trouble in Brazil, mugging does take place and can happen almost anywhere. Travel light after dark with few valuables (avoid wearing jewellery and use a cheap, plastic, digital watch). Ask hotel staff where is and isn't safe; crime is patchy in Brazilian cities.

If the worst does happen and you are threatened, don't panic, and hand over your valuables. Do not resist, and report the crime to the local tourist police later. It is extremely rare for a tourist to be hurt during a robbery in Brazil. Being aware of the dangers, acting confidently and using your common sense will reduce many of the risks.

Photocopy your passport, air ticket and other documents, make a record of traveller's cheque and credit card numbers. Keep them separately from the originals and leave another set of records at home. Keep all documents secure; hide your main cash supply in different places or under your clothes. Extra pockets sewn inside shirts and trousers, money belts (best worn below the waist), neck or leg pouches and elasticated support bandages for keeping money above the elbow or below the knee have been repeatedly recommended.

Violence over land ownership in parts of the interior have resulted in a 'Wild West' atmosphere in some towns, which should therefore be passed through quickly. Red-light districts should also be given a wide berth as there are reports of drinks being drugged with a substance popularly known as 'good night Cinderella'. This leaves the victim easily amenable to having their possessions stolen, or worse.

Avoiding cons
Never trust anyone telling sob stories or offering 'safe rooms', and when looking for a hotel, always choose the room yourself.

Be wary of 'plain-clothes policemen'; insist on seeing identification and on going to the police station by main roads. Do not hand over your identification (or money) until you are at the station. On no account take them directly back to your hotel. Be even more suspicious if they seek confirmation of their status from a passer-by.

Hotel security
Hotel safe deposits are generally, but not always, secure. If you cannot get a receipt for valuables in a hotel safe, you can seal the contents in a plastic bag and sign across the seal. Always keep an inventory of what you have deposited. If you don't trust the hotel, lock everything in your pack and secure it in your room when you go out. If you lose valuables, report to the police and note details of the report for insurance purposes. Be sure to be present whenever your credit card is used.

Police
There are several types of police: **Polícia Federal**, civilian dressed, who handle all federal law duties, including immigration. A subdivision is the **Polícia Federal Rodoviária**, uniformed, who are the traffic police on federal highways. **Polícia Militar** are the uniformed, street police force, under the control of the state governor, handling all state laws. They are not the same as the Armed Forces' internal police. **Polícia Civil**, also state controlled, handle local laws and investigations. They are usually in civilian dress, unless in the traffic division. In cities, the *prefeitura* controls the **Guarda Municipal**, who handles security. **Tourist police** operate in places with a strong tourist presence. In case of difficulty, visitors should seek out tourist police in the first instance.

Public transport
When you have all your luggage with you at a bus or railway station, be especially careful and carry any shoulder bags in front of you. To be extra safe, take a taxi between the

airport/bus station/railway station and hotel, keep your bags with you and pay only when you and your luggage are outside; avoid night buses and arriving at your destination at night.

Sexual assault

If you are the victim of a sexual assault, you are advised firstly to contact a doctor (this can be your home doctor). You will need tests to determine whether you have contracted any STDs; you may also need advice on emergency contraception. You should contact your embassy, where consular staff will be very willing to help.

Women travellers

Most of these tips apply to any single traveller. When you set out, err on the side of caution until your instincts have adjusted to the customs of a new culture. Be prepared for the exceptional curiosity extended to visitors, especially women, and try not to overreact. If, as a single woman, you can befriend a local woman, you will learn much more about the country you are visiting. There is a definite 'gringo trail' you can follow, which can be helpful when looking for safe accommodation, especially if arriving after dark (best avoided). Remember that for a single woman a taxi at night can be as dangerous as walking alone. It is easier for men to take the friendliness of locals at face value; women may be subject to unwanted attention. Do not disclose to strangers where you are staying. By wearing a wedding ring and saying that your 'husband' is close at hand, you may dissuade an aspiring suitor. If politeness fails, do not feel bad about showing offence and departing. A good rule is always to act with confidence, as though you know where you are going, even if you do not. Someone who looks lost is more likely to attract unwanted attention.

Student travellers

If you are in full-time education you will be entitled to an **ISIC** (International Student Identity Card), which is valid in more than 77 countries. The ISIC card gives you special prices on transport and access to a variety of other concessions and services. For the location of your nearest ISIC office see www.isic.org. ISIC cards can be obtained in Brazil from **STB** agencies throughout the country; also try www.carteiradoestudante. com.br, which is in Portuguese but easy to follow (click 'pontos de Venda' for details of agencies). Remember to take photographs when having a card issued.

In practice, the ISIC card is rarely recognized or accepted for discounts outside of the south and southeast of Brazil, but is nonetheless useful for obtaining half-price entry to the cinema. Youth hostels will often accept it in lieu of a **HI** card or at least give a discount, and some university accommodation (and subsidized canteens) will allow very cheap short-term stays to holders.

Tax

Airport departure tax The amount of tax depends on the class and size of the airport, but the cost is usually incorporated into the ticket.
VAT Rates vary from 7-25% at state and federal level; the average is 17-20%. The tax is generally included in the international or domestic ticket price.

Telephone *Country code: +55.*

Ringing: equal tones with long pauses. Engaged: equal tones, equal pauses.

Making a phone call in Brazil can be confusing. It is necessary to dial a 2-digit telephone company code prior to the area code for all calls. Phone numbers are now printed in this way: 0XX21 (0 for a national call, XX for the code of the phone company chosen (eg 31 for Telemar) followed by, 21 for Rio de Janeiro, for example, and the

8 or 9-digit number of the subscriber. The same is true for international calls where 00 is followed by the operator code and then the country code and number.

Telephone operators and their codes are: **Embratel**, 21 (nationwide); **Telefônica**, 15 (state of São Paulo); **Telemar**, 31 (Alagoas, Amazonas, Amapá, Bahia, Ceará, Espírito Santo, Maranhão, most of Minas Gerais, Pará, Paraíba, Pernambuco, Piauí, Rio de Janeiro, Rio Grande do Norte, Roraima, Sergipe); **Tele Centro-Sul**, 14 (Acre, Goiás, Mato Grosso, Mato Grosso do Sul, Paraná, Rondônia, Santa Catarina, Tocantins and the cities of Brasília and Pelotas); **CTBC-Telecom**, 12 (some parts of Minas Gerais, Goiás, Mato Grosso do Sul and São Paulo state); **Intelig**, 23.

National calls

Telephone booths or *orelhões* (literally 'big ears' as they are usually ear-shaped, fibreglass shells) are easy to come by in towns and cities. Local phone calls and telegrams are cheap.

Cartões telefônicos (phone cards) are available from newsstands, post offices and some chemists. They cost US$3 for 30 units and up to US$5 for 90 units. Local calls from a private phone are often free. *Cartões telefônicos internacionais* (international phone cards) are increasingly available in tourist areas and are often sold at hostels.

Mobile phones and apps

Cellular phones are widespread and coverage excellent even in remote areas, but prices are extraordinarily high and users still pay to receive calls outside the metropolitan area where their phone is registered. SIM cards are hard to buy as users require a CPF (a Brazilian social security number) to buy one, but phones can be hired. When using a cellular telephone you do not drop the zero from the area code as you have to when dialling from a fixed line.

Some networks, eg **O2**, provide an app so you can use the time on your contract in your home country if you access the app via Wi-Fi.

Internet calls (eg via **Skype**, **Whatsapp** and **Viber**) are also possible if you have access to Wi-Fi.

There are many Brazilian travel guide apps available only a fraction of which are thoroughly researched. Fewer still are updated regularly. You are far better off using Google Maps and asking in the hotel or from local people.

Time

Brazil has 4 time zones: Brazilian standard time is GMT-3 – most of the Northeast lies within this time zone, though the Fernando de Noronha archipelago is GMT-2; the Amazon time zone (Pará west of the Rio Xingu, Amazonas, Roraima, Rondônia, Mato Grosso and Mato Grosso do Sul) is GMT-4, the State of Acre is GMT-5.

There is no daylight saving in the Northeast, but the Southern, Southeast and Central Western Brazil observe daylight saving time (*horário de verão*) from the 3rd Sun in Oct and the 3rd Sun in Feb.

Tipping

Tipping is not usual, but always appreciated as staff are often paid a pittance. In restaurants, add 10% of the bill if no service charge is included; cloakroom attendants deserve a small tip; porters have fixed charges but often receive tips as well; unofficial car parkers on city streets should be tipped R$2.

Tourist information

The **Ministério do Turismo**, www.braziltour.com, is in charge of tourism in Brazil. Local tourist information bureaux are not usually helpful for information on cheap hotels, they generally just dish out pamphlets. Expensive hotels provide tourist magazines for their guests.

Other good sources of information are: **LATA**, www.lata.org. The Latin American Travel Association, with useful country

information and listings of all UK operators specializing in Latin America. Also has up-to-date information on public safety, health, weather, travel costs, economics and politics highlighted for each nation. Wide selection of Latin American maps available, as well as individual travel planning assistance.
South American Explorers, T607-277 0488, www.saexplorers.org. A non-profit educational organization functioning primarily as an information network for South America. Useful for travellers to Brazil and the rest of the continent.

National parks
National parks are run by the Brazilian institute of environmental protection, **Ibama**, T061-3316 1212, www.ibama.gov.br (in Portuguese only). For information, contact **Linha Verde**, T0800-618080, linhaverde.sede@ibama.gov.br. National parks are open to visitors, usually with a permit from Ibama. See also the **Ministério do Meio Ambiente** website, www.mma.gov.br (in Portuguese only).

Useful websites
www.brazil.org.uk Provides a broad range of info on Brazilian history and culture from the UK Brazilian embassy.
www.brazilmax.com Excellent information on culture and lifestyle, the best available in English.
www.visitbrazil.com The official tourism website of Brazil, and the best.

www.gringos.com.br An excellent source of information on all things Brazilian for visitors and expats.
www.ipanema.com A quirky, informative site on all things Rio de Janeiro.
www.maria-brazil.org A wonderfully personal introduction to Brazil, specifically Rio, featuring Maria's cookbook and little black book, features and reviews.
www.socioambiental.org Invaluable for up-to-the-minute, accurate information on environmental and indigenous issues. In Portuguese only.
www.survival-international.org The world's leading campaign organization for indigenous peoples with excellent information on various Brazilian indigenous groups.
www.worldtwitch.com Birding information and comprehensive listings of rainforest lodges.

Tour operators

UK
Brazil specialists
Bespoke Brazil, T01603-340680, www.bespokebrazil.com. Tailor-made trips and private tours throughout the country, even to the lesser-known areas.
Brazil Revealed, T01932-424252, www.brazilrevealed.co.uk. A specialist, boutique and bespoke operator with excellent in-country contacts.
Journey Latin America, T020-8600 1881, www.journeylatinamerica.co.uk.

An enormous range of Brazil trips, including bespoke options.
Sunvil Latin America, T020-8758 4774, www.sunvil.co.uk. Quality packages and tailor-made trips throughout the country.
Veloso Tours, T020-8762 0616, www.veloso.com. Imaginative tours throughout Brazil; bespoke options on request.

Villas
Hidden Pousadas Brazil, www.hidden pousadasbrazil.com. A choice of tasteful small hotels and homestays hand-picked from all over the country and ranging from chic but simple to luxe and languorous.

Wildlife and birding specialists
Naturetrek, T01962-733051, www.nature trek.co.uk. Wildlife tours throughout Brazil with bespoke options and specialist birding tours of the Atlantic coastal rainforests.
Ornitholidays, T01794-519445, www.ornitholidays.co.uk. Annual or biannual birding trips throughout Brazil, including the Atlantic coast rainforest.
Reef and Rainforest Tours Ltd, T01803-866965, www.reefandrainforest.co.uk. Specialists in tailor-made and group wildlife tours.

North America
Brazil For Less, T1-877-565 8119 (US toll free) or T+44-203-006 2507 (UK), www.brazilforless.com. US-based travel firm with a focus solely on South America, with local offices and operations, and a price guarantee. Good-value tours, run by travellers for travellers. Will meet or beat any internet rates from outside Brazil.

Wildlife and birding specialists
Field Guides, T1-800-7284953, www.fieldguides.com. Interesting birdwatching tours to all parts of Brazil.
Focus Tours, T(505)216 7780, www.focus tours.com. Environmentally responsible travel throughout Brazil.

Brazil
Dehouche, T021-2512 3895, www.dehouche.com. Upmarket, carefully tailored trips throughout Brazil.
Matueté, T011-3071 4515, www.matuete.com. Bespoke luxury options around Brazil with a range of private house rentals.
whl.travel, T031-3889 8596, www.whl.travel. Online network of tour operators for booking accommodation and tours throughout Brazil.

Wildlife and birding specialists
Andy and Nadime Whittaker's Birding Brazil Tours, www.birdingbraziltours.com. A good company, based in Manaus. The couple worked with the BBC Natural History Unit on David Attenborough's *The Life of Birds* and are ground agents for a number of the major birding tour companies from the US and Europe.
Birding Brazil Tours, www.birdingbrazil tours.com. First-class bespoke options throughout the country.
Edson Endrigo, www.avesfoto.com.br. Bespoke options only.

Visas and immigration

Visas are not required for stays of up to 90 days by tourists from Andorra, Argentina, Austria, Bahamas, Barbados, Belgium, Bolivia, Chile, Colombia, Costa Rica, Denmark, Ecuador, Finland, France, Germany, Greece, Iceland, Ireland, Italy, Liechtenstein, Luxembourg, Malaysia, Monaco, Morocco, Namibia, the Netherlands, Norway, Paraguay, Peru, Philippines, Portugal, San Marino, South Africa, Spain, Suriname, Sweden, Switzerland, Thailand, Trinidad and Tobago, United Kingdom, Uruguay, the Vatican and Venezuela. For them, only the following documents are required at the port of disembarkation: a passport valid for at least 6 months (or *cédula de identidad* for nationals of Argentina, Chile, Paraguay and Uruguay); and a return or onward ticket, or adequate proof that you can purchase your return fare, subject to no remuneration being received in Brazil and no legally binding or contractual documents being signed. Venezuelan passport holders can stay for 60 days on filling in a form at the border.

Citizens of the USA, Canada, Australia, New Zealand and other countries not mentioned above, and anyone wanting to stay longer than 180 days, *must* get a visa before arrival, which may, if you ask, be granted for multiple entry. US citizens must be fingerprinted on entry to Brazil. Visa fees vary from country to country, so apply to the Brazilian consulate in your home country. The consular fee in the USA is US$50. Students planning to study in Brazil or employees of foreign companies can apply for a 1- or 2-year visa. 2 copies of the application form, 2 photos, a letter from the sponsoring company or educational institution in Brazil, a police form showing no criminal convictions and a fee of around US$70 is required.

Extensions

Foreign tourists may stay a maximum of 180 days in any 1 year. 90-day renewals are easily obtainable, but only at least 15 days before the expiry of your 90-day permit, from the Polícia Federal. The procedure varies, but generally you have to: fill out 3 copies of the tax form at the Polícia Federal, take them to a branch of **Banco do Brasil,** pay US$15 and bring 2 copies back. You will then be given the extension form to fill in and be asked for your passport to stamp in the extension. According to regulations (which should be on display) you need to show a return ticket, cash, cheques or a credit card, a personal reference and proof of an address of a person living in the same city as the office (in practice you simply write this in the space on the form). Some offices will only give you an extension within 10 days of the expiry of your permit.

Some points of entry, such as the Colombian border, refuse entry for longer than 30 days, renewals are then for the same period, insist if you want 90 days. For longer stays you must leave the country and return (not the same day) to get a new 90-day permit. If your visa has expired, getting a new visa can be costly (US$35 for a consultation, US$30 for the visa itself) and may take anything up to 45 days, depending on where you apply. If you overstay your visa, or extension, you will be fined US$7 per day, with no upper limit. After paying the fine to Polícia Federal, you will be issued with an exit visa and must leave within 8 days.

Officially, if you leave Brazil within the 90-day permission to stay and then re-enter the country, you should only be allowed to stay until the 90-day permit expires. If, however, you are given another 90-day permit, this may lead to charges of overstaying if you apply for an extension.

Identification

You must always carry identification when in Brazil. Take a photocopy of the personal details in your passport, plus your Brazilian immigration stamp, and leave your passport in the hotel safe deposit. This photocopy, when authorized in a *cartório*, US$1, is a legitimate copy of your documents. Be prepared, however, to present the originals when travelling in sensitive border areas. Always keep an independent record of your passport details. Also register with your consulate to expedite document replacement if yours gets lost or stolen.

Warning Do not lose the entry/exit permit they give you when you enter Brazil. Leaving the country without it, you may have to pay up to US$100 per person. It is suggested that you photocopy this form and have it authenticated at a *cartório*, US$1, in case of loss or theft.

Weights and measures

Metric.

Footnotes

Basic Portuguese for travellers

Learning Portuguese is a useful part of the preparation for a trip to Brazil and no volume of dictionaries, phrase books or word lists will provide the same enjoyment as being able to communicate directly with the people of the country you are visiting. It is a good idea to make an effort to grasp the basics before you go. As you travel you will pick up more of the language and the more you know, the more you will benefit from your stay.

General pronunciation
Within Brazil itself, there are variations in pronunciation, intonation, phraseology and slang. This makes for great richness and for the possibility of great enjoyment in the language. A couple of points which the newcomer to the language will spot immediately are the use of the tilde (~) over 'a' and 'o'. This makes the vowel nasal, as does a word ending in 'm' or 'ns', or a vowel followed by 'm' + consonant, or by 'n' + consonant. Another important point of spelling is that for words ending in 'i' and 'u' the emphasis is on the last syllable, though (unlike Spanish) no accent is used. This is especially relevant in place names like Buriti, Guarapari, Caxambu, Iguaçu. Note also the use of 'ç', which changes the pronunciation of c from hard [k] to soft [s].

Personal pronouns
In conversation, most people refer to 'you' as *você*, although in the south and in Pará *tu* is more common. To be more polite, use *O Senhor/A Senhora*. For 'us', *gente* (people, folks) is very common when it includes you too.

Portuguese words and phrases

Greetings and courtesies

hello	*oi/olá*
good morning	*bom dia*
good afternoon	*boa tarde*
good evening/night	*boa noite*
goodbye	*adeus/tchau*
see you later	*até logo*
please	*por favor/faz favor*
thank you	*obrigado* (if a man is speaking)/ *obrigada* (if a woman is speaking)
thank you very much	*muito obrigado/muito obrigada*
how are you?	*como vai você tudo bem?/tudo bom?*
I am fine	*vou bem/tudo bem*
pleased to meet you	*um prazer*
no	*não*
yes	*sim*
excuse me	*com licença*
I don't understand	*não entendo*
please speak slowly	*fale devagar por favor*
what is your name?	*qual é seu nome?*
my name is…	*o meu nome é…*
go away!	*vai embora!*

Basic questions

where is?	*onde está/onde fica?*
why?	*por que?*
how much does it cost?	*quanto custa?*
what for?	*para que?*
how much is it?	*quanto é?*
how do I get to…?	*para chegar a…?*
when?	*quando?*
I want to go to…	*quero ir para…*
when does the bus leave?/arrive?	*a que hor sai/chega o ônibus?*
is this the way to the church?	*aquí é o caminho para a igreja?*

Basics

bathroom/toilet	*banheiro*
police (policeman)	*a polícia (o polícia)*
hotel	*o (a pensão, a hospedaria)*
restaurant	*o restaurante (o lanchonete)*
post office	*o correio*
telephone office (central)	*telefônica*
supermarket	*o supermercado*
market	*o mercado*
bank	*o banco*
bureau de change	*a casa de câmbio*
exchange rate	*a taxa de câmbio*
notes/coins	*notas/moedas*
traveller's cheques	*os travelers/os cheques de viagem*
cash	*dinheiro*
breakfast	*o caféde manh*
lunch	*o almoço*
dinner/supper	*o jantar*
Meal	*a refeição*
drink	*a bebida*
mineral water	*a água mineral*
soft fizzy drink	*o refrigerante*
beer	*a cerveja*
without sugar	*sem açúcar*
without meat	*sem carne*

Getting around

on the left/right	*à esquerda/à direita*
straight on	*direto*
to walk	*caminhar*
bus station	*a rodoviária*
bus	*o ônibus*
bus stop	*a parada*
train	*a trem*
airport	*o aeroporto*
aeroplane/airplane	*o avião*

flight	*o vôa*
first/second class	*primeira/segunda clase*
train station	*a ferroviária*
combined bus and train station	*a rodoferroviária*
ticket	*o passagem/o bilhete*
ticket office	*a bilheteria*

Accommodation

room	*quarto*
noisy	*barulhento*
single/double room	*(quarto de) solteiro/(quarto para) casal*
room with two beds	*quarto com duas camas*
with private bathroom	*quarto com banheiro*
hot/cold water	*água quente/fria*
to make up/clean	*limpar*
sheet(s)	*o lençol (os lençóis)*
blankets	*as mantas*
pillow	*o travesseiro*
clean/dirty towels	*as toalhas limpas/sujas*
toilet paper	*o papel higiêico*

Health

chemist	*a farmacia*
doctor	*o coutor/a doutora*
(for) pain	*(para) dor*
stomach	*o esômago (a barriga)*
head	*a cabeça*
fever/sweat	*a febre/o suor higiênicas*
diarrhoea	*a diarréia*
blood	*o sangue*
condoms	*as camisinhas/os preservativos*
contraceptive (pill)	*anticonceptional (a pílula)*
period	*a menstruação/a regra*
sanitary towels/tampons	*toalhas absorventes/absorventes internos*
contact lenses	*lentes de contacto*
aspirin	*a aspirina*

Time

at one o'clock (am/pm)	*a uma hota (da manhã/da tarde)*
at half past two/two thirty	*as dois e meia*
at a quarter to three	*quinze para as três*
it's one o'clock	*é uma*
it's seven o'clock	*são sete horas*
it's twenty past six/six twenty	*são seis e vinte*
it's five to nine	*são cinco para as nove*
in ten minutes	*em dez minutos*
five hours	*cinco horas*
does it take long?	*sura muito?*

Days

Monday	*segunda feiro*	Friday	*sexta feira*
Tuesday	*terça feira*	Saturday	*sábado*
Wednesday	*quarta feira*	Sunday	*domingo*
Thursday	*quinta feira*		

Months

January	*janeiro*	July	*julho*
February	*fevereiro*	August	*agosto*
March	*março*	September	*setembro*
April	*abril*	October	*outubro*
May	*maio*	November	*novembro*
June	*junho*	December	*dezembro*

Numbers

one	*um/uma*	fifteen	*quinze*
two	*dois/duas*	sixteen	*dezesseis*
three	*três*	seventeen	*dezessete*
four	*quatro*	eighteen	*dezoito*
five	*cinco*	nineteen	dezenove
six	*seis* ('*meia*' half, is frequently used for number 6 ie half-dozen)	twenty	*vinte*
		twenty-one	*vente e um*
		thirty	*trinta*
		forty	*cuarenta*
seven	*sete*	fifty	*cinqüe*
eight	*oito*	sixty	*sessenta*
nine	*nove*	seventy	*setenta*
ten	*dez*	eighty	*oitenta*
eleven	*onze*	ninety	*noventa*
twelve	*doze*	hundred	*cem, cento*
thirteen	*treze*	thousand	*mil*
fourteen	*catorze*		

Useful slang

that's great/cool	*que legal*
bloke/guy/geezer	*cara* (literally 'face'), *mano*
cheesy/tacky	*brega*
in fashion/cool	*descolado*

Glossary

azulejo	tile	*forró*	music and dance style from Northeast Brazil
baía	bay		
bairro	area or suburb	*frevo*	frenetic musical style from Recife
bandas	marching bands that compete during Carnaval		
		gaúcho	cowboy, especially from Rio Grande do Sul
bandeirantes	early Brazilian conquistadors who went on missions to open up the interior		
		garimpeiro	miner or prospector
		igreja	church
barraca	beach hut or stall	*ilha*	island
berimbau	stringed instrument that accompanies *capoeira*	*jangada*	small fishing boats, peculiar to the Northeast
		jardim	garden
biblioteca	library	*lanchonete*	café/deli
bilhete	ticket	*largo*	small square
botequim	small bar, open-air	*leito*	executive bus
caboclo	rural workers of mixed descent	*litoral*	coast/coastal area
cachaça	cane liquor	*mata*	jungle
cachoeira	waterfall	*mercado*	market
caipirinha	Brazilian cocktail, made from cachaça, lime, sugar and ice	*Mineiro*	person from Minas Gerais
		mirante	viewpoint
câmbio	bureau de change	*mosteiro*	monastery
candomblé	African-Brazilian religion	*Paulista*	person from São Paulo
capela	chapel	*ponte*	bridge
capoeira	African-Brazilian martial art	*praça*	square/plaza
Carioca	person from Rio de Janeiro	*praia*	beach
carnaval	carnival	*prancha*	surfboard
cerrado	scrubland	*prefeitura*	town hall
cerveja	beer	*rio*	river
churrascaria	barbecue restaurant, often all-you-can-eat	*rodoviária*	bus station
		rua	street
empadas	mini pasties	*sambaquis*	archaeological shell mounds
estrada	road	*sertão*	arid interior of the Northeast
favela	slum/shanty town	*Sertanejo*	person who lives in the *sertão*
fazenda	country estate or ranch	*vaqueiro*	cowboy in the north
feijoada	black-bean stew		
ferroviária	train station		

Acronyms and official names

FUNAI	Fundação Nacional do Índio (National Foundation for Indigenous People)
IBAMA	Instituto Brasileiro do Meio Ambiente E Dos Recursos Naturais Renováveis (Brazilian Institute of Environment and Renewable Natural Resources)
MPB	Música Popular Brasileira
RAMSAR	Wetlands Convention

Index

Entries in bold refer to maps

FOOTPRINT

Features

Credits

Footprint credits
Editor: Jo Williams
Production and layout: Emma Bryers
Maps: Kevin Feeney
Colour section: Angus Dawson

Publisher: Felicity Laughton
            Patrick Dawson
Marketing: Kirsty Holmes
Sales: Diane McEntee
Advertising and content partnerships:
Debbie Wylde

Photography credits
Front cover: The Visual Explorer/
Shutterstock.com
Back cover: Alex Robinson Photography
Inside front cover: Alex Robinson
Photography

Colour section
Alex Robinson Photography

Duotones
Page 26: Alex Robinson Photography
Page 84: Alex Robinson Photography

Printed in Spain by GraphyCems

Publishing information
Footprint Recife & Northeast Brazil
3rd edition
© Footprint Handbooks Ltd
May 2016

ISBN: 978 1 910120 69 9
CIP DATA: A catalogue record for this book
is available from the British Library

® Footprint Handbooks and the
Footprint mark are a registered
trademark of Footprint Handbooks Ltd

Published by Footprint
6 Riverside Court
Lower Bristol Road
Bath BA2 3DZ, UK
T +44 (0)1225 469141
F +44 (0)1225 469461
footprinttravelguides.com

Distributed in the USA by
National Book Network, Inc.

Every effort has been made to ensure that
the facts in this guidebook are accurate.
However, travellers should still obtain advice
from consulates, airlines, etc about travel
and visa requirements before travelling.
The authors and publishers cannot
accept responsibility for any loss, injury
or inconvenience however caused.